Lincoln County, Montana

CELEBRATING 100 YEARS

Edited by

Melody Condron

with historical contributions by

Rich Aarstad

Jim Calvi

Darris Flanagan

& Mark White

A joint project of

Lincoln County Public Libraries Foundation,

Lincoln County Public Libraries & Lincoln County

ISBN 10: 1-59152-059-2
ISBN 13: 978-1-59152-059-7

Cover design by Melody Condron & Alchemy DTP. Cover photo by Melody Condron with coin art design by Patty Rambo. Back cover photo by Kootenai Aviation.

For more information about our books, contact the Lincoln County Public Libraries, 220 W. 6th St., Libby, MT 59923 (406) 293-2778.

Created, produced, and designed in the United States.
Printed in Canada.

15 14 13 12 11 10 09 1 2 3 4 5 6 7

All of this — the wonderful tomorrow, the busy, happy today, and the glorious yesterday — will furnish the themes of these pages.

The fond dream of the publishers is that future generations of Lincoln County children will find some measure of interest and inspiration in what is set forth here.

— C.A. Griffin, Lincoln County History

Tobacco Valley High Country Horsemen. Photo by Katherine Hoagan.

Gold Panning Opening Day at Heritage Museum in Libby. Photo courtesy of Heritage Museum.

Community ❧ Natural Beauty ❧ Heritage
Lincoln County, Montana

Cabinet Mountain Wilderness. Photo courtesy of Kootenai Aviation.

Introduction

Bordering Canada to the north and Idaho to the west, Lincoln County is the most northwest county in Montana. Census Bureau estimates put the 2009 county population at 18,971, just 100 more than it was 10 years ago. With a heritage heavily dependent on natural resources, Lincoln County still enjoys frontier status according to the Federal Government. Nestled in the Purcell and Cabinet Ranges of the Rocky Mountains, the county has been carved from the rocky landscape by the Kootenai, Tobacco, Yaak, and Fisher Rivers. Three distinct regions exist in the county. Libby is the County Seat and largest area of population, sitting on the shores of the Kootenai River. Eureka, the hub of activity in the northern section of the county, is located on the Tobacco River within 10 miles of the Canadian border. Finally, Troy, the smallest of the three regions, is located on the Kootenai River less than 20 miles from Idaho. Many other smaller communities can also be found in Lincoln County, including Rexford, Yaak, Savage Lake, Trego, Fortine, Happy's Inn, and West Kootenai.

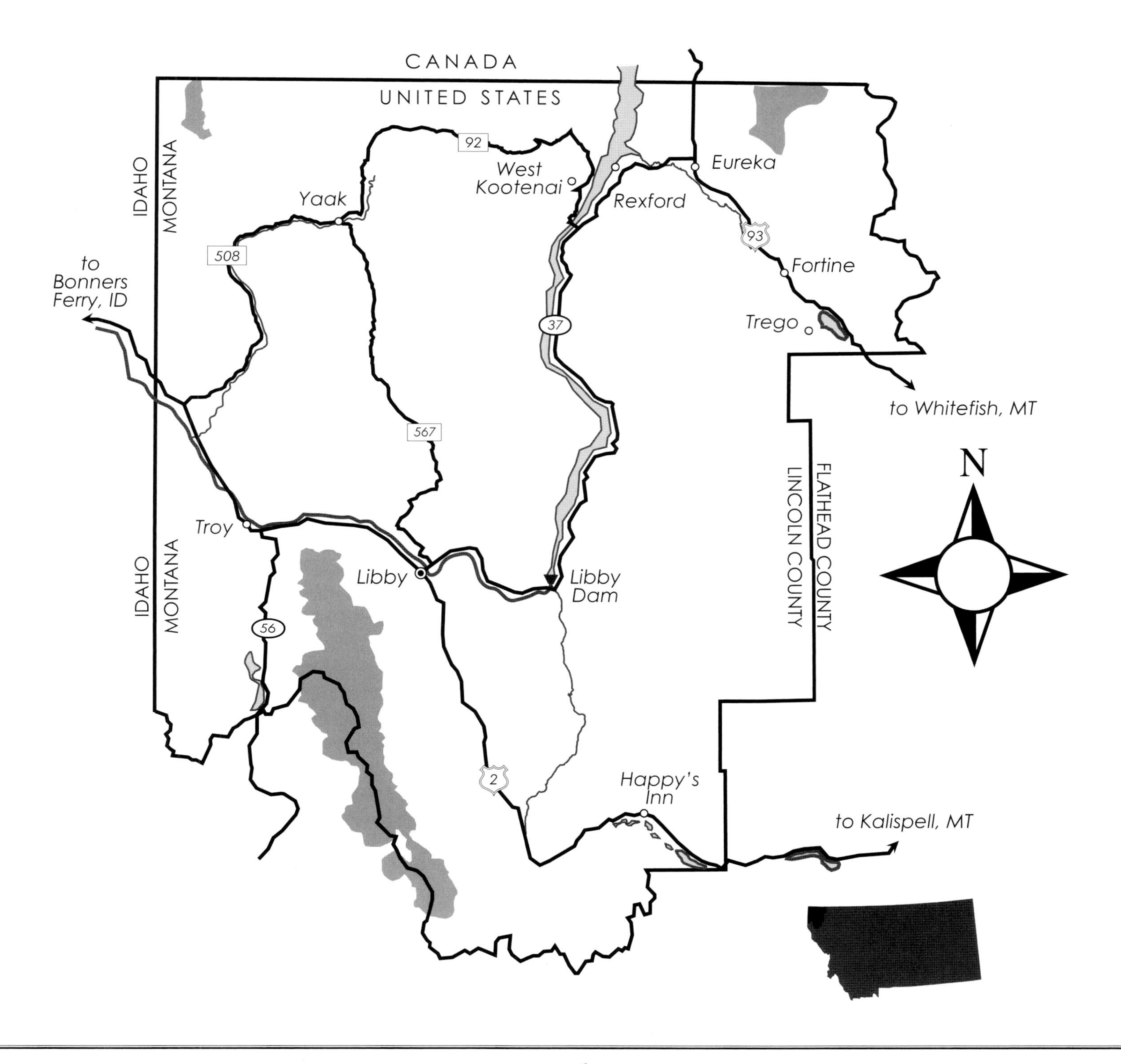

Timeline of Lincoln County History

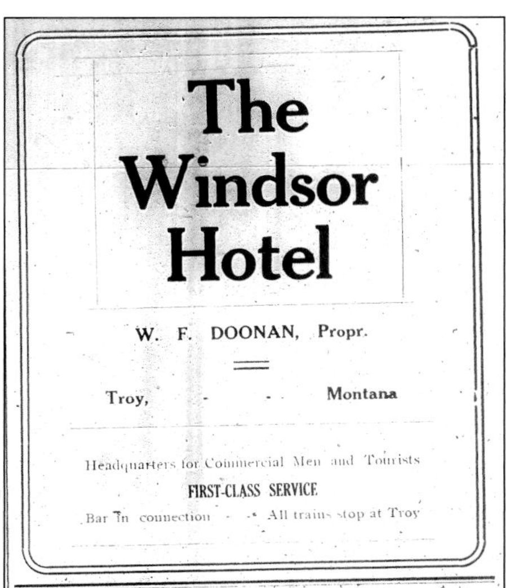

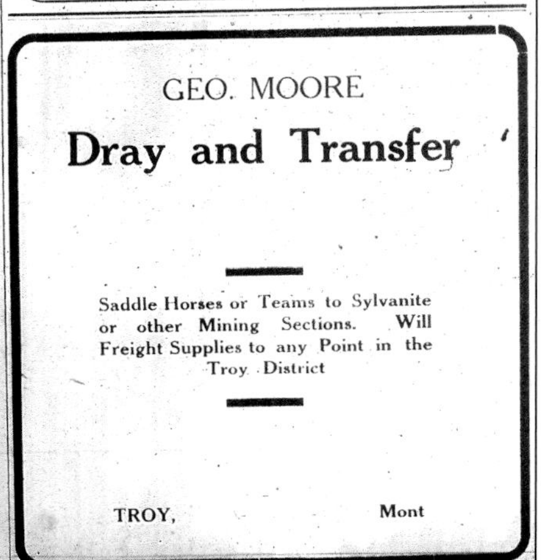

1720-1760 - Montana first peoples acquire horses and guns

1805-1806 - Lewis and Clark Expedition journeys through Montana
1807 - Manuel Lisa establishes first fur trading post in Montana at confluence of Yellowstone and Big Horn Rivers – Fort Ramón
1808 - North West Company explorer/fur trader David Thompson descends Kootenai River
1808 - NWC Finan MacDonald establishes trading house near present day Canoe Gulch Ranger Station

1846 - 49th Parallel established as boundary between Canada and the United States

1853 - Western Montana becomes part of Washington Territory
1855 - Washington Territorial Governor Isaac I. Stevens signs treaty with Kootenai sending them to the Jocko Reservation south of Flathead Lake

1861 - American Civil War begins
1862 - Grasshopper Creek gold strike results in creation of Bannack
1862 - Homestead Act passed
1863 - Western Montana becomes part of Idaho Territory
1864 - Montana Territory created
1865 - Kootenai country becomes part of Missoula County Montana Territory
1865 - American Civil War ends
1866 - Montana's first constitutional convention
1867 - Libbysville mining camp established

1872 - Federal government establishes Yellowstone National Park
1878 - Timber and Stone Act passed

1883 - Northern Pacific Railroad completed through Montana
1884 - Montana's second constitutional convention
1889 - Montana becomes a state & ratifies state constitution

1891 - Great Northern Railway completes railroad line through northwest Montana
1892 - Town of Troy established
1892 - Steamboat traffic begins on the Kootenai River between Jennings, MT and Fort Steele, B.C.
1892 - *Libby Miner* first newspaper published in Libby
1893 - Flathead County created encompassing Kootenai country
1893 - Great Northern Railway Company completes transcontinental through Montana
1896 - On June 18, Great Northern No. 15 wrecks in a washout above Kootenai Falls. Sixteen railroad cars and at least six people go over Kootenai Falls.

1902 - Great Northern Railway branch line completed between Jennings, MT and Fernie, B.C.
1903 - First log drive on the Kootenai River by the Bonners Ferry Lumber Company
1903 - Great Northern Railway re-routes mainline through Tobacco Plains (Eureka)
1904 - Eureka newspaper *Tobacco Plains Journal* begins publication
1905 - Sanders County created
1905 - Department of Forestry transferred from Department of Interior to Department of Agriculture, becoming United States Forest Service (USFS)
1906 - Kootenai Forest Reserve created
1906 - Congress passes the Forest Homestead Act June 11
1906 - The initiative and referendum adopted in Montana
1909 - Governor Edwin L. Norris signs legislation creating Lincoln County
1909 - Eureka holds first Lincoln County Fair
1909 - Congress passes the Enlarged Homestead Act

1910 - Eureka wins election for county seat
1910 - Fires of 1910 scorch NW, burning Sylvanite & part of Troy
1910 - *Troy Echo* publishes first newspaper

1910 - Lincoln County population 3,638—Montana's foreign born population exceeds 25%
1910 - Federal government creates Glacier National Park
1911 - Montana State Supreme Court awards contested Lincoln County seat to Libby
1914 - Montana women receive the right to vote
1915 - City of Troy incorporates
1916 - Montana goes dry with passage of state prohibition
1917 - MT Congresswoman Jeanette Rankin votes against U.S. entry into World War I
1917 - U.S. enters World War I
1917 - Industrial Workers of the World strike Eureka Lumber Company
1918 - Influenza Pandemic kills 5,000 Montanans (50 million people world wide)
1918 - World War I ends
1918 - Montana's economy begins to fail
1919 - 18th Amendment to the U.S. Constitution makes Prohibition the law of the land

1920 - Lincoln County Commissioners authorize county library
1920 - *Western News* editor C.W. Griffen publishes Lincoln County's Contributions During the Great War
1920 - Lincoln County population 7,797
1920 - 19th Amendment to the U.S. Constitution gives women the right to vote
1921 - Montana banks begin to fail
1924 - U.S. Congress passes the Indian Citizenship Act
1925 - The last county created in Montana (Petroleum County)
1929 - U.S. stock market crashes
1929 - Great Depression begins

1930 - Lincoln County population 7,089
1933 - Prohibition ends with the repeal of the 18th Amendment

1940 - Lincoln County population 7,882
1941 - Montana Congresswoman Jeanette Rankin votes against U.S. entry into World War II
1941 - United States enters World War II
1943 - Italian detainees assigned to USFS work camp at Warland, MT
1943 - J. Neils Lumber Company purchases tracts of timber land along Fisher River and Wolf Creek drainages
1945 - World War II ends

1950 - Lincoln County population 8,693
1950 - Congress authorizes Libby Dam Project
1950 - Korean War begins
1952 - U.S. Air Force establishes the Yaak Air Force Station manned by elements of the 680th Aircraft Control and Warning Squadron; housing for Air Force personnel established near Dirty Shame
1953 - Butte television state begins first TV broadcasts in Montana
1953 - Korean War ends
1958 - Nation's Christmas Tree cut on the Kootenai National Forest
1959 - Vietnam War begins

1960 - Lincoln County population 12,537
1960 - U.S. Air Force re-designates the unit at Yaak Air Force Station as the 680th Radar Squadron and the Yaak station becomes an unmanned radar site
1964 - Congress passes the Wilderness Act
1964 - Cabinet Mountain Wilderness Area created
1966 - Construction begins on Libby Dam
1966 - City of Rexford incorporates

1970 - Lincoln County population 18,063
1971 - President Richard M. Nixon visits Libby Dam
1975 - President Gerald Ford dedicates Libby Dam
1975 - Vietnam War ends
1979 - Confederated Salish and Kootenai Tribes create the Mission Mountains Tribal Wilderness

1980 - Lincoln County population 17,752
1989 - Capitol Christmas Tree cut on the Kootenai National Forest

1990 - Lincoln County population 17,481
1997 - In January, Marianne Roose is appointed County Commissioner to District 3
1998 - In November, John Konzen elected County Commissioner to District 2
1999 - EPA is sent to Lincoln County to assess asbestos clean-up in Libby & Troy

2000 - Lincoln County population 18,837
2008 - In November, Tony Berget elected County Commissioner to District 1
2009 - Lincoln County becomes part of the "Top Ten Scenic Drives of the Northern Rockies"

Post offices with operation dates according to Lutz, Dennis J. MD and Montana Chapter No. 1 National Association of Post Masters of the United States. Montana Post Offices & Postmasters (Johnson Printing Company Rochester, MN 1989).

Post Office	Dates of Operation
Eureka	1904-
Fortine	1905-
Gateway	1902-1919
	1919-1950
Jennings	1908-1952
Libby	1891-
Manicke	1915-1935
Rexford	1903-
Ripley	1908-1909
Snowshoe	1896-1912
Stryker	1902-
Sylvanite	1910-1913
Taylor	1912-1913
Trego	1911-1919
	1919-
Troy	1893-
Ural	1909-1959
Warland	1907-1957
Yaak	1914-1917
	1920-1953

A House Divided against Itself Cannot Stand

The Creation of Lincoln County and the Battle for County Seat 1909-1911

by Rich Aarstad

During the first two decades of the Twentieth century, Montana experienced a population explosion that changed the face of the state. Local newspapers promoted their communities and promised opportunity for those willing to take a chance. Homesteaders arrived in droves, to stake out the plains of eastern Montana as small communities sprouted like winter wheat along the Northern Pacific, Great Northern, and Milwaukee railroad lines. This growth spurt produced a restless population eager to prove itself; community boosters eagerly promoted their towns as the next great agricultural center of the state. One way to ensure economic prosperity and growth was to become a county seat.

County division invariably resulted in bruised feelings between those residents advocating the division and their opposition. Acrimonious to say the least, local newspapers spewed venom at their rivals while hailing their own community as the only logical choice for the honor. Although not apparent at the time, these battles in several cases determined the life or death of a community. Abraham Lincoln's comment that "a house divided against itself cannot stand" rang true during the height of Montana's county splitting frenzy.[1] Many disgruntled communities, denied the permanence offered by the county seat designation, flooded the Montana state legislature (1911-1920) with petitions for county splitting.

The creation of Lincoln County in 1909 and the bitter rivalry between Libby and Eureka for the permanent county seat proved no exception. While the legislative body created counties sparingly, senators and representatives submitted bills for the creation of twenty-two counties during the state's first twenty years. The Montana legislature did not take county division lightly and pushing a bill through required persistence.

Undaunted, several legislators and lobbyists arrived in Helena for the 1909 legislative session ready to submit, defend, cajole, and shepherd their county division bills through both legislative houses to the desk of Governor Edwin L. Norris. Two such bills called for the division of Flathead County: one sponsored by residents of Libby who hoped to create Cabinet County with Libby as the temporary county seat; another with the aim of creating Kootenai County with Eureka as the county seat. Libby struck some observers as a more logical location. Helena's *Montana Daily Record* reported on the division of Flathead County, "in the opinion of some [...] Libby is much better situated geographically than is Eureka, which is only six miles from the international boundary line."[2]

WHY CABINET COUNTY SHOULD BE CREATED

Area of proposed county	3,595 sq. miles
Assessed valuation Flathead county 1908	$13,500,000
Assessed valuation of proposed county	4,023,000
Total valuation railroads in proposed county	1,026,000
Valuation all other property in proposed county	2,710,000
Valuation school districts tributary to Libby and including Libby district	2,710,000
Valuation school districts tributary to Eureka and including Eureka district	1,313,000
Railroad assessment in Libby	1,290,000
Railroad assessment in Eureka area	705,000
Property other than railroad in and around Libby	1,416,000
Property other than railroad in and around Eureka	611,000
Assessed valuation Libby school district	656,000
Assessed valuation Eureka school district	294,000

VOTE OF 1908 IN PROPOSED COUNTY

Eureka	262	Libby	177
Fortine	53	Cabinet	17
Gateway	35	Yahk	8
Rexford	36	Warland	23
Total	386	Troy	102
		Snowshoe	6
		Jennings	17
		Total	350

Total vote cast in proposed county - 736

DISTANCES TO KALISPELL (Present County Seat)		DISTANCES TO LIBBY (Seat of Proposed County)	
Libby to Kalispell	140	Troy to Libby	18
Troy to Kalispell	158	Yahk to Libby	35
Jennings to Kalispell	*127*	*Jennings to Libby*	*13*
Cabinet to Kalispell	160	Warland to Libby	25
Snowshoe to Kalispell	160	Snowshoe to Libby	20
Yahk to Kalispell	175	Cabinet to Libby	20
Warland to Kalispell	115	Rexford to Libby	50
Rexford to Kalispell	90	Gateway to Libby	56
Gateway to Kalispell	96	Eureka to Libby	64
Fortine to Kalispell	64	Fortine to Libby	76
Eureka to Kalispell	*76*		

Six old counties in the state by the vote of 1908 show less than one thousand voters, as follows:

Broadwater	861
Granite	912
Meagher	831
Rosebud	780
Sanders	860
Sweetgrass	826

Assessed valuation of seven old coun- ties for the year 1908:

Broadwater	$2,677,423
Granite	2,408,233
Meagher	4,869,376
Powell	4,153,030
Sanders	3,888,283
Sweetgrass	4,704,182
Ravalli	4,760,242

Western News (Libby) article, February 4, 1909.

Perly N. Bernard, publisher of Eureka's *Tobacco Valley Journal*, defended his community's bid for county seat: "If the new county materializes, whether under the name of 'Cabinet' as the Libbyites desire, or 'Kootenai' as the Eurekans prefer, as the matter stands today Eureka is the proper place for county seat, and there is no getting away from it if merit is to decide the question."[3] Bernard claimed that fully three-fifths of the population for the new county resided within twenty miles of Eureka. While Eureka boldly cast its bid for county seat, the Libby faction seemed more concerned with the politics of promoting their bill in the legislature.

Striking early in the session, State Senator Thomas D. Long of Flathead County introduced Senate Bill 65 titled, "An Act to create the county of Cabinet, designate its boundaries, and to provide for its organization and government."[4] Referred to the committee on Counties, Towns, and Municipal Corporations, deliberations began on the merit of the bill. Meanwhile, residents of Kalispell stayed abreast of the situation concerning their county through the *Daily Inter Lake*. The paper indicated that Libby and Eureka were working together on county division and would each present their case before the senate committee, with the only disagreements being a slight boundary change and, of course, the home of the temporary county seat.[5]

As the editorial back-and-forth on county division continued, the committee passed the Libby bill to the floor of the senate with a few amendments. Chief among them was the name for the new county. The legislature had recently designated Abraham Lincoln's birthday a legal holiday. While no minutes from the Senate Committee on Counties, Towns, and Municipal Incorporations remain, it seems that in recognition of this new law, the committee members proposed the new county should take Lincoln's name. As such, the name Cabinet was struck from the text and amended to Lincoln. Libby's *Western News* reported, "The name of the proposed new county has been settled upon by both Libby and Eureka. In honor to America's greatest president, Abraham Lincoln, the name was changed to Lincoln county [sic]."[6]

After SB 65 passed unanimously in the Senate, Representative Pomeroy attempted to introduce a bill in the house for the division of Flathead County with Eureka as the temporary county seat.[7] At this late juncture, the bill received little notice and quickly died. As Eureka's bill died, so did their enthusiasm for county division. This prompted the *Kalispell Journal* to publish the editorial "Eurekaites Changed Their Minds." The editorial suggested that the Eureka forces began applying the brakes to county division when the Libby bill sailed through the Senate and reached the House. The newspaper claimed that "enthusiastic Eureka boomers" conceived the idea for county division the previous fall (1908) when they got their man, Pomeroy, elected for the purpose of splitting Flathead County.

"Their calculations were rudely upset, however, for some of the old war horses at Libby began to prick up their ears and wondered why it would not be a good thing for Libby to land

Ads like this one led every front page of Eureka newspapers during the battle.

the seat of government [...] When it came down to a matter of wire pulling it seems that Libby had the better of the argument, and things took on a bad look for the Eureka crowd."[8]

Eureka businesses and area residents urged Governor Norris to hold off signing the bill into law until they could successfully demonstrate through petition that the majority of the residents in the proposed county opposed the bill.[9] They flooded the governor's office with telegrams to that effect. Governor Norris acknowledged receipt of a telegram asking him to "defer action" on the bill until petitions from Fortine, Troy, Eureka, Rexford, and Gateway could reach him, "I shall be pleased to consider the petition if it reaches me before it becomes necessary for me to pass upon the bill."[10]

Opposition arose from other interested individuals outside Eureka. The governor received a letter from the Rustler Mining and Milling Co., owners of the Snowshoe Mine near Libby, urging him to veto the bill:

SENATE PASSES CO. DIVISION BILL

It is Confidently Thought the Bill Will Also Get Through the House— Every One of the Officers Named on the Ticket are Good Reliable Men

Special to the Western News:

HELENA, Mont., Feb. 16—The senate today passed, unanimously, the bill creating Lincoln county. The bill names Libby as the county seat.

The following are named as officers for the new county:

Commissioners—Edwards of Eureka, Walter Wilder of Warland, and P. D. Pratt of Libby.

Treasurer—M. Brandenberg of Eureka.

Sheriff—M. A. Shannahan of Libby.

Assessor—James Stonechest of Troy.

Clerk of District Court—P. R. Long of Kalispell.

Clerk and Recorder—R. T. Fleck of Eureka.

Superintendent of Schools—F. D. Head of Troy.

Surveyor—Samuel Ratekin of Snowshoe.

Public Administrator—M. J. Brown of Libby.

Coronor—Dr. F. B. Bogardus of Eureka.

The bill provides that the new county shall be organized on the first day of July this year.

Western News reprint of the February 16, 1909 Helena release.

"The country is sparsely settled and, from the fact that the area embraced within the proposed new county is practically all mountainous, it is quite likely to remain so, at least for many years.

A glance at the map will show that fully 90% or more is embraced in National Forests. There are neither the people nor the industries to support a county government and its maintenance will result only in excessive and unnecessary burden on the taxpayers.

The movement was started by the owners of the Libby townsite and it will be an imposition on the people if they [are] taxed to provide benefits for this company alone."[11]

John E. Lewis of Whitefish agreed with this assessment and claimed, "the creation of Lincoln County is nothing more than the Boom of the Libby Townsite Co."[12]

On the heels of these telegrams and letters, petitions began arriving opposing the bill: from Fortine eighty-three signatures, forty-five signatures from Warland, forty-six signatures from Rexford, and fifty-two signatures from Troy. Three petitions came from Eureka for a total of three hundred and thirty-five signatures.[13] In an affidavit, several Troy businessmen stated that a petition circulated in 1908 contained a number of signatures from Libby residents who also opposed county division.[14] Nelson J. Wyckoff of Troy confirmed that a petition opposing county division circulated in 1908. He claimed that the Libby Townsite Co. circulated the petition and then held it back in case their bid for county division with Libby as the temporary county seat failed.

On March 9, Governor Norris wrote L.J.B. Chapman, cashier for the Farmers and Merchants State Bank in Eureka, to inform him that "the creation of new counties is a matter purely within the discretion of the Legislative Assembly, and that discretion having been exercised by the creation of Lincoln county, I do not feel it proper for me to interfere therewith." This became Governor Norris' standard response to those correspondents writing in opposition to the new county.[15] Despite a spirited resistance, Governor Norris signed the bill creating Lincoln County. The *Western News* announced the news:

"Montana had a new county created within her borders by the last session of her legislature.

The name of the new county is Lincoln, in honor to the memory of President Lincoln, Libby was named as the county seat and the new county will open its doors for business on Thursday, July 1st, 1909 [...] If the citizens of this section are jubilant over the winning of the fight, why shouldn't they rejoice? It was a fair and a clean fight. They not only showed that the new county had the resources but that Libby easily outclassed her contestant for county seat honors."[16]

The *Western News* also heaped praise on Senator Long, John. H. Geiger and L.H. Faust for spearheading the effort and seeing the bill through to the end.

The *Tobacco Plains Journal* was less positive about the situation. The newspaper chided Governor Norris for his apparent haste in signing the bill. They questioned his ability to ignore petitions from Troy, Warland, Ural, Rexford, Gateway, Fortine, Trego, and Eureka: "fully six-sevenths of those directly interested in the formation of the new county were ignored and the handful of people who favored it were endorsed." The *Journal* lamented, "It goes to show how little weight the expressed desires of a people are when they run counter to the wishes of politicians, and we presume that, under the circumstances, we ought to look pleasant and say we like it whether we do or not."[17]

The act creating Lincoln County designated the boundaries of the new county and placed it under the jurisdiction of the 11th Judicial District. It also stipulated that Libby would serve as the temporary county seat until the permanent county seat was established by a vote of the people in November 1910. In the interim, the following appointees held office until the general election: County Commissioners Elzeor Demers, Walter Wilder, and Paul Pratt; Treasurer M. Brandenburg; Sheriff M.A. Shannahan; Assessor James Stonechest; Clerk of Court Philip R. Long; Clerk and Recorder R.T. Fleek; Superintendent of Schools F.D. Head; County Surveyor Sam Ratekin; Public Administrator M.J. Brown; and Coroner Dr. A.D. Bogardus. Construction of the courthouse could not take place until the voters determined the site of the county seat.[18]

Eureka questioned the validity of the act on two points: "(1) the enrolled bill contains certain amendments, whereas the amendments were in fact, not adopted, and (2) the enrolled bill differs materially from the bill which passed the two houses." Despite the argument, the Montana State Supreme Court rendered its decision and declared the Lincoln County bill constitutional. The *Helena Daily Independent* announced, "Lincoln county has passed the Rubicon and its constitutionality has received the sanction of the supreme court." A *Western News* editorial declared:

"Until the next election Libby will be the seat of government of the new county. At that time the people of Lincoln county will assemble at the various voting places and by their ballots at that time say at which place within the county the permanent county seat shall be. The wish of the majority at that time will become the law and whether the successful aspirant be Libby, Eureka, Troy, Rexford, Jennings, Warland or some other place, the decision will be final and binding upon all."[1]

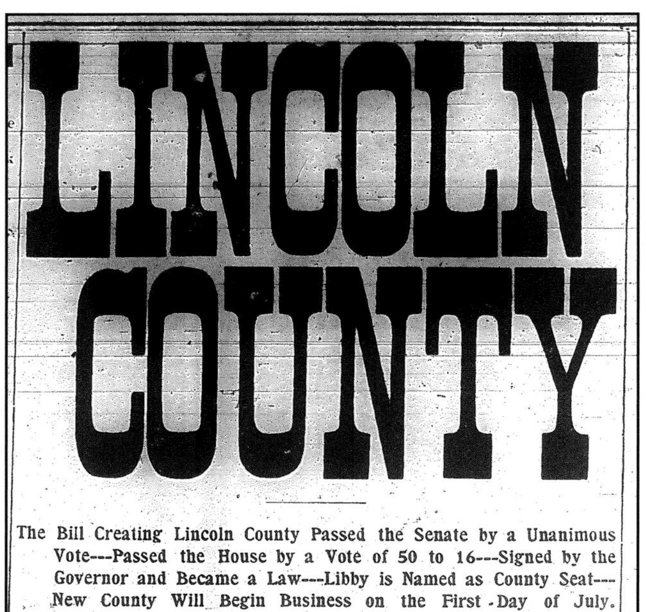
LINCOLN COUNTY

The Bill Creating Lincoln County Passed the Senate by a Unanimous Vote---Passed the House by a Vote of 50 to 16---Signed by the Governor and Became a Law---Libby is Named as County Seat---New County Will Begin Business on the First Day of July.

The *Tobacco Plains Journal* seemed amenable to the decision, indicating that now no one could question the validity of the act.[20] Lincoln County officially became Montana's twenty-eighth county on July 1, 1909.

With over a year until the election, both Libby and Eureka had plenty of time to lobby for votes throughout the county. Although Eureka had mustered serious opposition to the Libby bill, they tossed their hat enthusiastically into the ring for county seat. The war of words that ensued in October 1910 turned into a slugfest between Eureka and Libby. The *Eureka Journal* struck first with a front-page article promising voters that if they elected Eureka, area businessmen would guarantee "a free new Courthouse to Lincoln County and no charge for moving records and furniture." This would alleviate the need to increase the tax burden county-wide. The *Journal* asked "Is this county seat to be located somewhere to build up a town? [...] If the temporary county seat remains where it is, will there be a town?" The article questioned Libby's qualifications for permanent county seat, claiming that in terms of economic growth, population, and opportunity, Eureka far outstripped its neighbor.[21]

Libby hit back a week later, when the following headline appeared in the *Western News*: "IT WILL COST LINCOLN COUNTY TAXPAYERS $50,000 TO CHANGE THE COUNTY SEAT FROM LIBBY TO EUREKA." The *Western News* concluded that the only beneficiary of a move to Eureka would be to those individuals in Eureka who had city lots for sale. As the election drew near, both the *Eureka Journal* and the *Western News* kept hammering their readers repeatedly with the same arguments. On November 8, 1910 Lincoln County voters went to the polls to decide the question.

Due to the size of the county and lack of connecting roads, election results were slow to arrive. On November 11, the *Eureka Journal* rejoiced, "EUREKA WINS PERMANENT COUNTY SEAT." According to their unofficial tally, Eureka received 656 votes to Libby's 606. The *Journal* urged residents of the county to set aside their differences and "join in pushing Lincoln County to the front. It was a square, honest fight from start to finish on the part of Eureka and the workers are to be congratulated."[22] But the *Western News* had its own version of the outcome and informed its readers that Libby had been victorious. Though the *News'* unofficial tally indicated 658 votes for Eureka and 634 for Libby, due to the close vote and some "small errors" the newspaper speculated that "the question will not be settled until it is passed upon by the courts."[23] As an interested observer, the *Troy Herald* conceded a close race with a slight edge of fifteen votes for Eureka but indicated that Libby would surely contest the election. "This contest has overshadowed everything else and the situation today is more tense than ever [...] And the end is not yet."[24] Over the next week, Eureka held onto a slim fifteen vote lead. However, commissioners still had not received all of the election returns for their official canvass.[25]

WESTERN NEWS.

OL. VII. LIBBY, MONTANA, THURSDAY JULY 1, 1909. NO. 52.

LINCOLN COUNTY GOES INTO EXISTENCE TODAY

New County Starts Housekeeping with Practically no Indebtedness and with a Tax Roll of Over $4,200,000---Libby Is Named as County Seat and the County Is Annexed to the Eleventh Judicial District- -Contains an Area of About 3600 Square Miles---There Are in the New County 20,000,000,000 Feet of Standing Timber, Immense Areas of Fine Fruit and Farming Lands and a Mining District at Libby which will Become Another Coeur d'Alenes.

On November 24, the *Western News* finally reported on the commissioners' results:

"County Clerk and Recorder R.T. Fleek had refused to officially accept the election returns from Rexford precinct, on the grounds that they had been sent in by express instead of registered mail, as the law provides, and further that the returns had been broken open in a manner to indicate that they might have been tampered with."

According to the newspaper, irregularities also appeared in the official canvass of the Eureka precinct.

"The tally books showed four tally marks for Libby for the county seat, and in the total column the figure '4' appeared. There were no other tally marks shown but in the total column were also the figures '390,' indicating the vote in that precinct for Eureka as the county seat. It looked as though the four Libby votes had been counted and the others credited up to Eureka without counting in the usual manner.

Commissioner Pratt objected to canvassing a vote sent in with such an apparent irregularity, but was outvoted and the work proceeded.

The final count showed that Eureka had won by the narrow margin of 15 votes, not taking any of the alleged incongruities into consideration. The members of the board were then served with an injunction restraining them from taking any action towards moving the county seat for the time being, and the matter will now be threshed out in the courts."[26]

Both newspapers informed their readers that committees from Libby and Eureka comprised of J.M. Kennedy, John H. Geiger, L.H. Faust, Wave Brown, L.J.B. Chapman and F.P. Garey would meet to discuss their differences and seek an amicable resolution. If they could not reach an agreement, both parties would attend the upcoming Montana Legislative Assembly in 1911 and seek to divide the county.[27] Neither side was willing to capitulate. The injunction ensured that the contested election would only be resolved in the courts.

As both sides considered their next move, the *Troy Herald* made known their opinion:

"In view of this wide margin of difference and inability to agree, and the prospects of a long-drawn-out contest, we would suggest that both Eureka and Libby step aside and let Troy have it. We intend to have it anyway some day, for Troy will be the largest town in the county, and if it is handed over now it will save a lot of worry and trouble and expense, not to speak of premature gray hairs and probable candidates for Warm Springs."[28]

Whether by agreement or the necessity of just taking a breather, the question of the contested election drew little attention in the courts over the next few months. In the interim, the 1911 Montana Legislature began deliberations in Helena. Perhaps a new strategy was in order for both camps.
As the legislators met, county splitting was in the air. Both the *Western News* and the *Eureka Journal* reported on efforts to ease the process of county splitting, and standing in the forefront of this battle was Representative P.N. Bernard of Lincoln County. Bernard arrived in Helena with a bill for the division of Lincoln County. The primary reason for the division, of course, rested with the bitter county seat fight being waged between Libby and Eureka. Resurrecting the old Libby bill, the new act sought to create Cabinet County by dividing Lincoln County along an east/west line and naming Libby the county seat; Eureka would remain in Lincoln County and become that county's seat of government.[29] However, the proposed bill died in the legislature and both communities had little recourse but to continue their legal battle.

As the gavel signaled the end of the 12th Legislative Assembly, John H. Geiger submitted a writ that launched the court case out of the lower courts and directly to the Montana State Supreme Court.[30] For the second time in two years, the question of the validity and constitutionality of the act creating Lincoln County was heard before Montana's highest court. This time, curiously enough, the Libby faction contested part of its own bill. On April 28, the court rendered its decision ruling in favor of Eureka. Associate Justice Henry C. Smith stated that a county is not "fully created until its county seat has been definitely fixed and located," which is exactly what the November election accomplished. However, the opinion of Associate Justice W.L. Holloway gave Libby a little wiggle room: "A provisional county seat is the purest creation of the imagination. Our constitution speaks only of a county seat, and if prior to the last election Libby was the county seat of Lincoln county, it was as much a county seat as Helena, Butte, or any other seat of county government."[31]

The *Eureka Journal* gushed about what the decision meant to the community, but Libby did not give up so easily. Geiger had another ace up his sleeve that he now played. He submitted an "application of the people of Libby for a re-hearing in the case of the county seat fight with Eureka."[32] Libby's attorneys outlined the reasons for a re-hearing on the following grounds:

"Because the court has failed to give any force or effect to the provision of section 26 of article V of the constitution prohibiting local and special legislation 'locating county seats.'

Because the court has apparently overlooked section 29 article III of the constitution which provides that 'the provisions of this constitution are mandatory and prohibitory, unless by express words they are declared to be otherwise.' Because the court has recognized and given effect to the argument ab inconvenient while admitting that the law in question is a local and special law and that there is no doubt as to the meaning of the provision of section 26 of article V of the constitution prohibiting local and special legislation 'locating county seats.'

Because the court has overlooked sections 2 and 3 of article X of the constitution, which recognizes that a state may be created and organized without providing for a permanent seat of government. If this is true of a state, it must be true of a political subdivision of a state."[33]

The Court granted the re-hearing and hoped to adjudicate the decision in June. When it did, the Montana State Supreme Court, in a stunning reversal, overruled its previous decision and awarded the county seat to Libby. In a two-to-one decision, Associate Justice Holloway, with the concurrence of Chief Justice Theodore Brantley, ruled in favor of Libby: "The act creating Lincoln county, insofar as it attempts to make provision for the permanent location of the county seat is unconstitutional, and void, being a local and special act, directly prohibited by section 26, Article V of the constitution."[34] Associate Justice Smith refused to be swayed from his earlier judgment. The *Helena Daily Independent* declared, "The contest between Eureka and Libby for the honor of being the seat [has] been one of the most bitterly fought struggles in the history of the state."[35]

The court's decision meant that while the bill creating Lincoln County was valid, that same bill could not dictate an election for a permanent county seat. Instead, the decision for permanent county seat election had to come from the people. Since this had not occurred, the vote for county seat was declared null and void. As far as the Montana State Supreme Court and the state were concerned, the matter was settled.

It was now the *Western News*' turn to extend an olive branch in peace. The News acknowledged the "stubborn contest," but claimed both sides retained the "best of good feeling" during the fight. The editorial assumed that with the issue settled both communities could work towards the common goal of developing the county.[36] Apparently still not ready to work for that goal, the *Eureka Journal* fired back that "County division is in the air."[37] Given the rancor of the recent battle and the inability of either party to graciously withdraw, the *Western News* finally admitted that perhaps county division was the only way to end the "ill feeling between the two sections." If they did not divide the county, the editorial claimed that the "differences will deter many from settling in Lincoln county, [and] relations will be strained between the two communities that should work in harmony rather than at cross purposes."[38]

Less than two weeks after the Supreme Court decision, the *Troy Herald* reported the circulation of a petition calling for special election to determine the county seat. This prompted the *Herald* to suggest that if Eureka and Libby wanted to continue the battle then their backers should be willing to foot the bill and leave the rest of the county out of it: "If Libby and Eureka want to scrap further on this much-frazzled question of locating or re-locating or changing or moving a temporary county seat, or a permanent county seat, or just a plain county seat, let them have their way about it by all means, but make them 'pay the fiddler'."[39]

Splitting the county remained on Eureka's agenda at least through the 16th Legislative Assembly (1919). That year, Representative Charles Weil of Lincoln County informed Oscar Wolf, editor of the *Eureka Journal*, of the many reasons for not introducing such a bill. Chief among them was the legislature's refusal to consider any county splitting bill "where there is any objection to the division by the people affected." In this instance, Libby, Warland, and Fortine had already registered their objections to county division.[40] This ended Eureka's bid for its own county.

After a decade Lincoln County seemed justified in touting the potential of the area, and bad feelings from the county-splitting controversy abated. The 1920 federal census revealed that Eureka and Libby had both doubled in population, as had the entire county.[41] In time of crisis, the people of Lincoln County had set aside the bitter feelings associated with the hotly contested county seat battle and pulled together for the greater good. They had lost twelve of their own serving in the military during World War I, survived the ravages of the 1918 Influenza Pandemic, and purchased over $800,000 in war securities while donating more than $50,000 to charitable organizations in support of the war effort.[42]

The citizens of Lincoln County had been through the crucible. If they could survive the maelstrom of their first ten years then they could certainly survive whatever came next. Nothing represents the sense of prosperity and hope more than the publication of *Lincoln County, Montana: History, Resources, Industrial Development and Record in the Great War*. Published by the *Western News*, this publication promoted the enterprise of the county and its various communities:

"Newcomers to Lincoln county will find a population small in number but great in honest industry, enthusiasm, progressiveness and intelligence. During the single decade since the county was organized its people have written a record of achievement of which they have every right to be proud. [...] Beautiful homes, prosperous industries, productive farms, in all parts of the county, bear witness to their energy and diligence."[43]

The resilience of Lincoln County's residents had been tested as they learned to bend and accept change without breaking. As the county prepares to celebrate the centennial of its birth, it seems appropriate to once again pause and take stock of what makes Lincoln County a special place to live.

Notes

1 *"House Divided" speech delivered by Abraham Lincoln on July 16, 1858.*

2 *Montana (Helena) Daily Record 9 January 1909; see also Western News (Libby, MT), 14 January 1909.*

3 *Tobacco Plains Journal (Eureka, MT), 15 January 1909.*

4 *Senate Journal of the Eleventh Session of the Legislative Assembly of the State of Montana, Published by Authority (Helena, MT.: Indepen-*

dent Publishing Co.) pp. 104, 221, 410. Hereafter Senate Journal 1909.
5 *Daily Inter Lake (Kalispell, MT), 3 February 1909.*
6 *Western News (Libby, MT) 18 February 1909.*
7 *Tobacco Plains Journal (Eureka, MT) 19 February 1909.*
8 *Kalispell (MT) Journal, 1 March 1909; see also Western News (Libby, MT) 4 March 1909.*
9 *Tobacco Plains Journal (Eureka, MT) 5 March 1909.*
10 *Governor Norris to L.J.B. Chapman 5 March 1909, MT Governors Records MHS, MC 35 box 4 folder 4.*
11 *Rustler Mining and Milling Co. to Governor Edwin L. Norris, 6 March 1909. MC 35, MT. Governor's Records MHS, box 4 folder 4.*
12 *John E. Lewis to Governor Edwin L. Norris, 6 March 1909. MC 35, MT. Governor's Records MHS, box 4 folder 4.*
13 *Petitions to the office of Governor Edwin L. Norris, n.d. MC 35, MT. Governor's Records MHS, box 4 folder 4.*
14 *To Edwin L. Norris Governor of Montana State of Montana Flathead County Affidavit 8 March 1909. MC 35, MT. Governor's Records MHS, box 4 folder 4.*
15 *Governor Norris to L.J.B. Chapman 9 March 1909. Box 4 folder 4 MC 35, MT. Governor's Records MHS.*
16 *Western News (Libby, MT) 11 March 1909.*
17 *Daily Inter Lake (Kalispell) 13 March 1909. See also The Tobacco Plains Journal (Eureka, MT), 12 March 1909.*
18 *Laws of Montana 1909, p. 193-198.*
19 *Western News (Libby, MT) 24 June 1909.*
20 *Tobacco Plains Journal (Eureka, MT) 25 June 1909.*
21 *Eureka (MT) Journal 7 October 1910.*
22 *Eureka (MT) Journal, 11 November 1910.*
23 *Western News (Libby, MT), 10 November 1910.*
24 *Troy (MT) Herald, 11 November 1910.*
25 *Western News (Libby, MT), 17 November 1910; Eureka Journal (Eureka, MT), 18 November 1910; Troy (MT) Herald, 25 November 1910.*
26 *Western News (Libby, MT), 24 November 1910.*
27 *Ibid. See also, Eureka (MT) Journal, 25 November 1910.*
28 *Troy (MT) Herald, 20 January 1911.*
29 *Western News (Libby, MT), 23 February 1911.*
30 *Troy (MT) Herald, 24 March 1911.*
31 *Troy (MT) Herald, 28 April 1911.*
32 *Troy (MT) Herald, 2 June 1911.*
33 *Western News (Libby, MT), 11 May 1911.*
34 *Helena Daily Independent (Helena, MT), 2 July 1911.*
35 *Ibid.*
36 *Western News (Libby, MT), 6 July 1911.*
37 *Eureka (MT) Journal, 21 July 1911.*
38 *Western News (Libby, MT), 20 July 1911.*
39 *"Petition for Special Election on County Seat;" "Let Them that Profit Pay the Fiddler," Troy (MT) Herald, 21 July 1911.*
40 *C.A. Weil to Oscar Wolf, 27 January 1919, Oscar Wolf Papers, Small Collection 1999, folder 1. Montana Historical Society Research Center, Archives, Helena.*
41 *1920 census figures.*
42 *C.A. Griffin, ed., Lincoln County Montana: History, Resources, Industrial Development, and Record in the Great War (Libby, MT: Western Montana Publishing Co., 1920).*
43 *Ibid.*

Lincoln County Roll of Honor

2009

In late 2008 / early 2009 the residents of Lincoln County were asked to nominate individuals in the county for the roll of honor in this volume. The criteria asked that nominees be current residents of the county who had contributed to their communities in a memorable way, either through volunteer work, leadership, or similar.

Nominations were reviewed by a committee of individuals from all three regions of the county (Eureka, Libby, and Troy). The resulting list, the Lincoln County roll of honor, is presented here with biographical information where available.

The 178 men and women of the 2009 roll of honor have been nominated by their peers and loved ones as deserving thanks and honor in our communities. They are the leaders, organizers, and behind-the-scenes workers that make our communities great. It is with great excitement that they are honored here for future generations to remember.

EYLER & KAREN ADAMS

Karen Adams was born in Kalispell, MT in 1958 to LaVerne Kenneth and Doris Bernice (Vachal) Seney, both of ND. She graduated from Flathead County High School and later from the University of Montana in Missoula with a degree in Wildlife Biology. Eyler was born in Kalispell in 1956 to Hugh Adams of the Flathead Valley (born at Fort Peck) and Marlene (McKinley) Adams of Columbia Heights (born in Oregon). Eyler attended various Montana schools and graduated from Flathead County High School. Together Eyler and Karen have three children: Havehn Benjamin of Trego; Thane Eyler of Guam; and Erin LaVerae of Phoenix, AZ. The latter two currently serve in the United States Air Force. Karen is currently department head for the general merchandise department for Super One Foods in Columbia Falls. Eyler is employed by Johnson Brothers pellet mills and Montana Renewable Resources in Columbia Falls and Superior. Both have been involved in a number of community efforts. In 2004, they both received the Tobacco Valley Improvement Association Award for outstanding achievements over the previous two years in the Tobacco Valley. Karen was a 4-H leader for many years, is a former member of the Mt. View Homemakers Club, and was active in the Caring and Loving All Special Persons organization. In her free time, she quilts, sews, travels, gardens, and reads. Eyler has been a member of the Eureka Volunteer Fire Department since their family arrived in the area in 1989. He is formerly active in the Boy Scouts and was a scout leader for many years. His hobbies include professional logging sports, outdoor living, and studying alternative energy.

TAMMY ANDERSON

Tammy was nominated for her service as former President of the Troy Chamber of Commerce and for volunteer work and leadership, including many years organizing Troy's Old Fashioned 4th of July celebration.

RYAN ANDREESEN

Ryan is an avid outdoorsman and dedicated fireman. Born August 31, 1976 in Salmon, ID, Ryan moved to Libby with his family in 1984. Ryan grew up in his father's business, Timberline Auto, and is still there today as general manager. He and his wife Katie have two daughters: Alex and Ellie. Ryan's favorite hobbies include outdoor activities, being with his family, and being a member of the Libby Volunteer Fire Department. He says, "The most rewarding part of Libby for me is being a member of the Fire Department and spending time with my kids. I want them to grow up here, as I did."

DON AUGER

As the Commander of the Austin Reedy Post #97 American Legion in Libby, Don Auger has taken the lead on many community projects. His leadership helped send Libby high school students to learn about Montana government and contributed to American Legion Baseball in the area. Don and the American Legion Post also contribute to the white cross program, maintaining and repainting highway crosses each spring to encourage road safety and awareness. The white cross program posts crosses on county roads where highway fatalities have occurred. Don is also a member of the American Legion Honor Guard and Firing Squad that serves at military funerals throughout Lincoln County. They are also called upon over 40 times a year to lead parades, banquets, and other functions.

KEN BAETH

But for his service in World War II, Ken B. Baeth has lived in Libby all of his life. He was born to George Henry and Myrtle (Parks) Baeth who moved to Lincoln County when he was one. Ken married Kitty in 1945 and together they had three children: Roger, Randy, and Janet. He worked with J. Neils Lumber Company and was superintendent of construction for the new stud mill and for a Libby sewage treatment plant. Working for Libby Public Schools, Ken oversaw the construction of the school shop and supervised twenty-four bus routes, maintenance at six schools, and the summer work program. As a volunteer, he oversaw construction of the log building behind the Libby Heritage Museum, the outdoor shelter at the Libby Care Center, and the Nordicfest Viking ship float. Ken is a charter member of the Libby Ambulance Service (an EMT for five years) and of Lincoln County Parks and Recreation. He is also a long-standing member of Christ Lutheran Church where he formerly served as congregational president.

LARRY BAKER

Larry was nominated for his service on Troy's City Council.

DON BANNING

Don was nominated for his work as City Council President in Troy. He is devoted to the improvement of Troy. He and his wife Patty are both active in the Troy Church of Latter Day Saints. Don also served on the Troy Area Community Association before its dissolution in 2008.

American Legion Honor Guard (Don Auger, Post Commander). Photo courtesy of Kootenai Valley Record.

GAYLA BENEFIELD

Gayla made a significant impact in the Lincoln County community as the whistle-blower in the asbestos contamination case against W.R. Grace. Gayla brought the truth about W.R. Grace and the asbestos in south Lincoln County to the media and was both honored and ostracized in the years that followed. The International Asbestos Organization, the Asbestos Disease Awareness Organization, the Montana Trial Lawyers Association, the Workers' Industry and Law Advocate Group, and the City of Libby have all honored Gayla. Her involvement was instrumental in bringing the Center for Asbestos Related Disease (CARD) to the Libby community and her documentation of contamination secured a new, safe running track and other sports equipment for Libby High School, Little League Baseball, and others. She courageously faced down a large company, championing for the general population of the region and, in doing so, made the community a safer place to live. She still considers herself an advocate for asbestos victims in Libby and across the country.

AMY BENNETT

A lifetime resident of Libby, Amy Bennett can't see herself living anywhere else. She enjoys Libby's sense of community. Born to parents Jerry and Malia Bennett in 1980, Amy's immediate family also includes brother Coby. She currently works at Lincoln County Credit Union and enjoys scrapbooking, photography, and horseback riding in her spare time. Amy has volunteered for Logger Days, St. John's Lutheran Hospital Foundation, Libby Area Chamber of Commerce, and Libby Baptist Church. For her, the most rewarding part of living in Lincoln County is watching the community come together for different events.

JERRY BENNETT

Jerry Bennett was born in Fairbanks, AK in 1956 to Jerry and Shirley Bennett. He was raised in Libby by his mother and step-father, Bill Taylor, and has lived here most of his life. Jerry and his wife Malia have two children, Coby and Amy, who also live in Libby. Professionally, Jerry has worked as a logger, at W. R. Grace, and in retail and wholesale business. He currently owns and operates JMF Services. His hobbies include working with horses and any activities that positively affect the Libby area. Formerly, Jerry has served as a board member and chairman of the Pregnancy Care Center, Libby Area Chamber of Commerce, and Libby Parks District. He is a former member of the Libby Saddle Club and former member and Chief of the Fisher River Volunteer Fire Department. Currently, Jerry sits on the board at St. John's Lutheran Hospital Foundation and has worked for many years organizing Logger Days. Jerry also represents House District 1 as a Republican in the Montana Legislature. "Getting involved to help maintain the quality of life we have in Libby" is the primary motivation for Jerry's contributions. He believes Lincoln County is "the last, best place to live."

TODD BERGET

Born in Turtle Lake, ND to Charles and Janice Berget, Todd has been a resident of Libby since 1965. Todd and his wife Donna have three children: Trista, Kody, and Kacie. Todd has worked at the Libby High School for half of his career and at the Central Alternative School for the other half. He coached eight years of high school football and wrestling and has served on the board for the Wrestling Club since 1988. Todd is responsible for many sculptures and beautification projects in Libby, including

Todd Berget builds one of the many eagle sculptures seen around Libby. Photo courtesy of Kootenai Valley Record.

the large metal eagles stationed at the Chamber of Commerce and many area businesses. His hobbies include anything to do with art/painting/sculpting, kayaking, Native American Studies, and just being in the outdoors. He has chosen to make Libby his home because of the logging heritage and his personal history growing up in the area.

TONY BERGET

Tony was nominated for his many years of service and volunteer work, including his position as Mayor of Libby for many years, his current position at County Commissioner for District 1, and Rotary.

BILL BISCHOFF

Bill was nominated for his work on the Libby City Council. He is the head of the Lincoln County Personnel Department and Executive Assistant to the Lincoln County Commissioners.

LEE BOTHMAN

Lee was nominated for his work on the Libby City Council. He is also the owner/operator of the Printing Press and Kootenai Valley Record newspaper.

STEVE BOWEN

Steve was born in Libby on January 24, 1960 to parents Clyde and Sandy Bowen. His parents, who were from Philipsburg, MT and Broomfield, CO, respectively, moved to the area in 1955. Steve has been in the hardware business for his entire life and owns Gambles Hardware in Troy. He has been involved in many organizations over the years, most notably the Troy Area Community Association, City Planning and Zoning, the Community Gardens, and the Troy Chamber of Commerce, where he is currently Treasurer/Secretary. Steve enjoys fishing and skiing. He finds that the most rewarding part of his volunteer work is the recognition and appreciation from people for the things he gets involved in (for example, the planning on the 4th of July celebration in Troy). Steve lives in Lincoln County because he has lived here his entire life and he loves the country. He says that he would not want to live anywhere else.

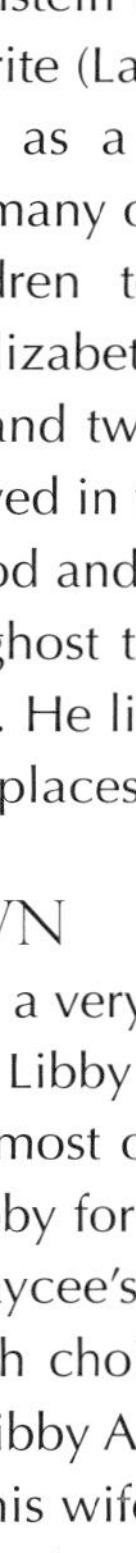

Steve Bowen. Photo by Melody Condron.

KENNY BREITENSTEIN

Kenneth Breitenstein was born in the Yaak Valley in 1934 to Margurite (Lander) and Albert Breitenstein. Kenny worked as a logger for J. Niels Lumber Company and many others. He and his wife, Edith, had two children together: Kenneth (now deceased); and Elizabeth of Libby. He also has two grandchildren and two great-grandchildren. Kenny has been involved in the National Rifle Association and the Yaak Rod and Gun Club. He enjoys hiking, exploring old ghost towns, and repairing old cars and equipment. He lives in the Yaak because, "it is one of the best places around."

FRED BROWN

Fred has played a very active role in the Libby community. Born in Libby to Ellwood and Grace Brown, Fred has lived most of his life in Libby. He served as Mayor of Libby for 24 years. In addition, he was active in the Jaycee's and sang in the St. Joseph's Catholic Church choir. Fred earned Citizen of the Year from the Libby Area Chamber of Commerce in 1985. He and his wife Marilee have eight children: Michael, Barb, Julie, Paul, Peggy, Andrea, Jennifer, and Frank. Fred enjoys woodworking projects and gardening. He is retired from teaching science at Libby High School after 32 years. Fred has chosen to make Lincoln County his home because of his love of teaching Libby's youth, his family, and an overall respect for the community and surrounding beauty.

DAWAIN BURGESS

Dawain was nominated for his work as Fire Chief on the Trego-Fortine-Stryker Volunteer Fire Department.

JUNE BURNS

June was nominated for her volunteer work with the Troy Friends of the Library and her church.

JIM CALVI

Jim was nominated for his work as local historian. He has written numerous books about the Troy and Yaak regions of Lincoln County.

BASIL & WINNIE CANAVAN

Both Basil and Winnie have been involved in the Yaak community for over 50 years. Basil was born in Troy, but has been a lifetime resident of the Yaak River Valley. His father homesteaded on the land off Vinal Lake Road where Basil and his wife Winnie still live. Basil is 83 years old and currently holds the position of Yaak Fire Chief. He oversees everything that goes on at the Volunteer Fire Department. Basil made his living primarily as a logger and continues to fill his time with trapping and hunting. Winnie is active in the Yaak Women's Group and organizes events at the Yaak Community Center. Basil and Winnie have three daughters who were born, raised, and educated in the Yaak, graduating from the Yaak School.

EILEEN CARNEY

Eileen Carney

Eileen Carney has held many leadership roles in the Libby community. She was born in Billings, MT in 1942 and moved to Libby in 1975 to become a foreign language teacher at Libby High School. Recently retired, she found a reason to make Lincoln County her home: beautiful mountains, her affection of the outdoors, and her hobbies. Eileen served in the Montana House of Representatives as a Democratic legislator from 2001 until 2005. She has served in many roles in the community, including: President of Kootenai Pets for Life; volunteer at the Heritage Museum, where she also holds the position of President; volunteer member of the Hospital Board; and formerly as part of the Woman's CAG Board and Resource Advisory Council. The most rewarding part of her life in Libby is her work for Kootenai Pets for Life.

MANUEL "BOB" CASTANEDA

Bob was nominated for his work on the Libby Chamber of Commerce Board of Directors and Libby Area Chamber of Commerce, and as Forest Supervisor of the Kootenai National Forest.

GENE CHAPPELL

Gene Chappell, native of Lead Hill, AR, has called Libby home since 1986. He and his wife, Carol, have four children. Gene is a career wood products employee. He began working for Stimson Lumber Company in Washington, then worked for Champion International before finishing his career with Stimson Lumber Company. Gene is now retired from his position as the manager of the Libby plywood and fingerjoint plants. He has been involved with St. John's Lutheran Hospital Foundation and the Cabinet View Country Club, serving on their respective boards. Gene has lived all over the west coast and decided to stay in Libby following retirement. He enjoys the people, the beauty of the valley, golf, and fishing the Libby waters.

Frank Chiaverini. Photo courtesy of Kootenai Valley Record

FRANK CHIAVERINI

Frank is a professional guitarist and mandolin player who has spent his entire adult life in the music industry. He has worked at major venues across the country and performed on stage with many prominent talents including the late Vassar Clements, Delbert McClinton, and the late Clarence "Gatemouth" Brown. Frank's band, Live Wire Choir, was featured in an article in 1978 in *Esquire* magazine. He worked for some time in Reno, Nevada, where he performed at various big-name casinos. Frank's band once performed at a private birthday party for the late Sammy Davis, Jr. Frank is responsible for operating the sound system at many area festivals including Nordicfest, Libby's Irish Fair, and Troy's Old Fashioned 4th of July. July 4, 2008, marked Frank's 32nd year at the Troy sound board. Since 1991, Frank has provided professional music services at his Troy recording studio, making it possible for local musicians to record professional quality tapes and CDs without leaving the area. Since 1996, Frank has provided a weekly music venue for local and regional musicians at his store, Northwest Music and the Hot Club Coffee House. These "Friday Night Concerts" offer low-cost entertainment for all ages.

JOAN CLOUGH

Joan was born in Texas but was raised in Libby. Her parents, Elmer and Betty Heisel, were from Missoula, MT and Pennsylvania, respectively. They came to Libby in the late 1940s. Joan left Libby for a time but returned with her husband of 16 years, George, because "it always felt like home." Joan has two children: Michael and Corinna. She attended Montana State University for Liberal Arts and Chemistry. Professionally, she worked in various employment and government agencies over the years. As a volunteer, she has been involved in the Libby Economic Development Council, Literacy Volunteers of America, the Lincoln County Public Libraries, Friends of the Library, WINGS, and Community Thrift, where she currently serves as a board member. In her free time, she enjoys fishing, camping, quilting, gardening, reading, hiking, snowshoeing, boating, camping, and horseback riding.

LES COFFMAN OF TROY

MIKE & BEEGEE COLE

Mike and BeeGee were both born in Whitefish, MT. Mike's parents, Ray and Ruth Cole, originally lived in Old Rexford. BeeGee's father, Kenneth Gwynn, was from Ohio and her mother, Donna (Sabin), was a Eureka native. Mike and BeeGee have three children: Chance, Dannee Rodriguez, and Sara Rodriguez Sherwood. They also have five grandchildren. Mike attended school in Polson and Columbia Falls, MT, while BeeGee attended and graduated from all Eureka schools. Both are organizers for the Tobacco Valley Rodeo Association, as well as "The Bull Thing" during the Lincoln County Fair in August. In addition, Mike is chairman of the Lincoln County Fair Board. In 1998, they both received the Tobacco Valley Improvement Association Award for outstanding achievements in the Tobacco Valley over the previous two years. They are half-owners and managers of Montana Market and enjoy horses and gardening. When asked why they have chosen to make Lincoln County their home, BeeGee responded, "It has been my home for all of my life and I wouldn't have it any other way."

CLAY COKER

One of the multiple nominations received for Clay reported, "Police Chief Clay Coker is one of the most dedicated leaders in Lincoln County. He is always thinking of the community and how he can serve them better through his law enforcement knowledge and position. He is progressive and proactive, keeping up to times with law enforcement around the country and bringing it to our community. He is very approachable and is an honorable man." Clay started the police department in 1996 with just two officers, no office, very little money, and used Highway Patrol cars. Through grants, determination, and a lot of volunteer time, he built the department into what it is today. Clay has saved the City of Libby hundreds of thousands of dollars by pursuing grant funding whenever possible. In 2002, his office received the Certification of Integrity from the National Institute of Ethics. Libby's department was the first in the state of Montana to receive this award and the 11th in the nation. Clay is also involved in law enforcement on a state level, which in turn brings support to Libby when needed. He is an instructor at the Montana Law Enforcement Academy, volunteering his time to teach each session. He is also the State Chapter Director of the International Association of Ethics Trainers and is an executive board member for the Montana Chiefs of Police. Recently, Clay was asked to be on the Professional Standards and Integrity Committee for POST. Clay has received commendations for saving several lives in Libby and was a member of David Thompson Search and Rescue on the dive team. He helped write a grant that brought Libby's first Resource Officer to the schools. Last year, Clay was asked by the director of the underage drinking task force to help and spent many extra hours driving to Eureka and meeting with others working on the same project. Chief Coker is currently working on a centennial project for the Libby Police Department, which includes a history of the department as well as a department time capsule. His efforts and commitment to the community have made it a better, safer place to live.

RITA COLLINS

Rita was born in Baltimore, MD on July 27, 1951. Her mother, Margaret (Strobel), was born in Wilmington, DE and her father, William Chalmers, was born in Baltimore, MD. Rita has one son, Steven Collins. She graduated from Woodlawn High School in Baltimore and did undergraduate work at St. John's College in Annapolis, MD. She also earned a Master's Degree in Special Education from Lewis and Clark College in Portland, OR and a Doctorate in Education from Portland State University. Rita is temporarily abroad teaching as a professor of English Language and Literature in the Czech Republic. Her favorite activity is sitting in a cafe talking to people. Other hobbies include reading, creating art, playing music, and traveling (which she considers more of a lifestyle than a hobby). In 2005, Rita received the Tobacco Valley Improvement Association Award for outstanding achievements over the previous two years in the Tobacco Valley. She says of the Tobacco Valley, "[It] has my heart. When I am there, it feels like home. The independent thinking that is evident everywhere and the sense that people support each other in countless ways, considering the size, it is one of the most creative places I've ever come across. I am continually amazed by the talented people in the valley."

LARRY CORYELL

Larry was nominated for his work on Troy's City Council.

HERB COUP

Herb was nominated for his service as a former member of the American Legion and the American Legion Honor Guard and Firing Squad that serves at military funerals throughout Lincoln County.

DAVE COX

Dave was nominated for his efforts on the St. John's Lutheran Hospital Foundation board and for community leadership throughout south Lincoln County.

BILL CRISMORE

Bill Crismore was born in Camas, MT in 1933 to parents Herman and Sarah Crismore. He is a self-described "Old Logger." Now retired, Bill is still involved in the family business, Crismore Logging, now owned by his son Stuart. Bill and his wife Carol have seven children and many grandchildren. Bill has been involved in road building and the logging industry nearly his entire life. He enjoys hunting, fishing, spending time with his family, and the annual Father's Day Fishing Derby hosted by his family. Bill has been involved with the Lions Club, has been a very dedicated 4-H supporter, and has volunteered at Logger Days. Crismore Logging and Bill's family organized Logger Days logging competitions for many years. Bill is most proud to be a part of the highly successful Sally Sauer Heart Fund fundraiser he organized with Jerry Okonski. This fundraiser, which took place in 1991, was led by logging contractors who donated time and equipment to raise money for Sally Sauer, who was in desperate need of a heart transplant. Bill says Libby has always been home to him. He enjoys the quiet and the clean air and feels blessed to have been able to raise his kids here.

CHARLIE CROUCHER

Charlie Croucher was born in Libby in 1948 to parents Frank and Joan Croucher. Charlie grew up in the Warland and Rexford areas while his father worked as a contract logger for J. Neils and St. Regis Lumber Companies. His childhood home was located along Parsnip Creek between Libby and Eureka on a place now under Lake Koocanusa. Charlie graduated from Lincoln County High School in 1966 and began sawing logs for his father until he turned 18. He then hired on with the St. Regis Company logging department. He worked in the woods until Champion International closed the woods operations in 1986. He went on to work in the sawmill and in 1988 he transferred to the fingerjoint plant. He remained there until retiring in 2009 as plant manager. Charlie and his wife, Lois (Butts) of West Kootenai, raised their family in Libby and built two homes at Sheldon Flats. When Libby became the first town in Montana to train EMTs for the Libby Volunteer Ambulance Service, Charlie was in the first class to become certified. He served for many years as an ambulance volunteer. Charlie is also well known as a Little League and Babe Ruth baseball and softball coach. He has also served as a ski patrolman at Turner Mountain. Charlie has chosen to live in Libby because he can't think of anywhere else to live that has the natural advantages of Lincoln County.

MIKE & JOAN CUFFE

Mike and JoAn were nominated for their many years of service in the Eureka community.

AUBYNN ANN CURTISS

Aubynn Ann Curtiss was born in Park City, MT to Perry David Armstrong and Rose Ina (Guthrie) Armstrong. Perry Armstrong was born in Grundy County, MT, while Rose was born in Milford, IA and came to Montana to visit her sister in Molt. She attended school at Dillon, MT, where she met Perry. The couple came to Deep Creek at Fortine in 1931. Aubynn attended the University of California at Los Angeles and married David Curtiss in 1945 in Great Falls after he returned from World War II. They lived in Spokane where he worked at Seiger Field. In 1946, they moved to Deep Creek, where David's family homesteaded. The couple had three children: Sue, who owns the Curtiss family homestead settled by David's father; Mark, of Fortine; and Gareth, of Olympia, WA. David passed away in 2005. Aubynn has five grandchildren. Aubynn has been a senator in the state legislature for seven years after spending sixteen years in the Montana State House of Representatives. She served as a political consultant, was chairman of the Montana State Republican Party from 1979 to 1984, was appointed by President Ronald Reagan to serve as Montana Commissioner of the White House Presidential Scholars Commission, and served under both President Reagan and President Bush. She calls herself a grassroots activist and a strong supporter of states' rights. She served of her own initiative as liaison between legislators and Western States Coalition to defend them from public mandates regarding regulation on land use. Aubynn has also served as a member of the Western Conference of the Council of State governments nationwide, represented Montana on the legislative conference on river governance for the Columbia River Basin, and served several terms on the Pacific Northwest Economic Region as one of four members from Montana. Her hobbies are fishing, photography, and water skiing.

CHARLIE DECKER

Charlie was nominated for his work in the Rocky Mountain Elk Foundation. He is a former logger and has been involved with organizing Logger Days and Nordicfest in Libby.

RAY DEDIC

Ray was nominated for his service as a former member of the American Legion and the American Legion Honor Guard and Firing Squad that serves at military funerals throughout Lincoln County.

BARB & JOHN DESCH

Barb and John were nominated for their volunteer work at Libby's annual Nordicfest. John has also been active in the community as a representative of Flathead Electric and as a former Rotary President.

MARGE DIERMAN

Marge was nominated for her community service over many years in Eureka. In 2003, she received the Tobacco Valley Improvement Association Hall of Fame Award for marked contributions to the development of the area.

LELAND & FAYE DRIGGS

Leland and Faye were nominated for maintaining the 101 Ranch, the oldest family-owned cattle ranch in the county.

CRAIG EATON

Craig was born in Forsyth, MT in 1956. His mother, Frances Eaton, was born in Anaconda, MT, while his father, Garrett, was born in the Terry area of eastern Montana. The family moved to Eureka in 1967. Craig married Wendy Peltier in 1975. They have one grandchild and two children: Rebecca "Becky" Catherine Stillo of Kalispell; and Christopher Chance of Honolulu, Hawaii. Craig attended elementary schools in Chester and Whitefish and graduated from Lincoln County High School. He is currently a communications technician for Flathead Electric Cooperative in Kalispell and previously worked as a manager for the Gwynn Company reload station in Eureka. He served as Mayor of Eureka for 12 years and at that time was a member of the League of Cities and Towns of Montana. He has been on the Eureka Airport Board since 1993. He helped to organize and was the first president of the Amateur Radio Club. He is a member of the Eureka Volunteer Fire Department since 1976. Craig spent over 20 years with the Eureka Volunteer Ambulance service. Additionally, he has been a member of Interbel Telephone Coop Board of Directors for over three years. He and Wendy enjoy the quality of life in Lincoln County. They enjoy the beauty of the area and think it was a great place to raise a family. Craig's hobbies include amateur radio, snowmobiling, fishing, and camping.

CHARLES EVANS

Charles is currently the City Attorney for Libby. He worked two years serving the civil side of the City Attorney's office and the last two serving the office in full capacity, civil and criminal. Charles began his law practice in Libby in October, 1984. During the past 25 years, he has served on the Boards of Recovery Northwest, the Lincoln County Library, and the L.A.M.P. programs. He has served on a pro bono basis, helping many organizations in the community to set up Articles of Incorporation and Bylaws.

RAY FINLEY

Ray was nominated for his volunteer work as a member of the American Legion Honor Guard and Firing Squad that serves at military funerals throughout Lincoln County.

DARRIS FLANAGAN

Darris Flanagan is very active locally. He is a member of the Lincoln Conservation District Board, the Tobacco Valley Improvement Association Board of History, and Kootenai River Network. He has written several books over the last ten years detailing the history of the Tobacco Valley area and some of the individuals who have been important or interesting in its development. He is well respected as an historical researcher and writer and also as an advocate in natural resource issues.

BOBBI FLETCHER

Bobbi was nominated for more than a decade of service as a veteran driver for the VFW in Libby, transporting veterans to Washington for medical care.

TED GARDENER

Ted was nominated for more than a decade of service as a veteran driver for the VFW in Libby, transporting veterans to Washington for medical care.

IDA GEHRING

Born in Kalispell on May 14, 1924 to Henry and Mabel Fisher, Ida Gehring has lived in Libby most of her life. She and husband Lee had five children: Jack, Edward, Phyllis, Rodney, and Christie. They stayed in Libby because of Lee's employment with the sawmill and also because of his attachment to the various baseball programs in town. Ida was a homemaker and enjoys flower arrangements, quilting, golf, and bowling. She is the former President of the Libby Women's Club, has been part of the American Legion Ladies Auxiliary for 52 years, and has volunteered for the American Red Cross. The best part of her life in Libby is witnessing the growth the area has experienced and the change is has endured to make it a growing development.

GEORGE GERARD

George first came to Lincoln County in 1956 to work in the woods during his summer vacation from Gonzaga University in Washington. After teaching in Ewan, WA he interviewed for a position in Libby and in 1968 moved his family there. He first taught 5th grade at Lincoln Elementary, later teaching at Asa Wood and McGrade Elementary before becoming principal at Lincoln. In addition to his day job, George became Libby School District's Adult Education Supervisor/Director and Federal Programs Coordinator. George was the principal of Plummer Elementary School from 1975-1990. He was a cofounding member and the first president of Libby's Economic Development Council, served a term on the Chamber of Commerce Board, and was on the St. John's Lutheran Hospital Board of Directors from 1981-1989. After retiring in 1990, George earned a Master's Degree in Marriage and Family Counseling and works pro bono for couples who would not otherwise be able to afford counseling. He served as Interim Director of the Lincoln County Campus of Flathead Valley Community College and raised funds to complete the new campus on Highway 2 in Libby. Most recently, George served as president of the Libby Rotary Club (2007-2008) and continues to serve on the board as Past President. In that role he also spearheaded the fundraising effort for a Rotary International water project in Pasin, Guatemala.

CAROL GIBBONS

Carol Gibbons was born in Helena, MT in 1927 to parents Frederic Scherrer, who was born in Helena but homesteaded at Augusta, MT, and Pearl (Mayer), born in Augusta. Carol is married to Walter S. "Joe" Gibbons and their children are: Joanne Rachele of Carlsbad, NM; Walter of Eureka; Lois Benedict of Lonetree, CO and Katy, TX; and Larell Reese of Columbia Falls, MT. They also have seven grandchildren and one great-grandchild. Carol attended school in Augusta and graduated with a degree in Home Economics in 1949 at Bozeman. She worked as an assistant home demonstration agent in Yellowstone County when she and Joe married. They moved to Eureka in 1954 when he joined his father, Walter, in the family business, Chevrolet Garage (formed in 1923). Carol did office work in the business until 2005 when Joe died and the business passed on to their son, Walter. Carol's hobbies have been art, music, and reading. She has been a member of the Sundowners Club for over 50 years, St. Michael's and All Angels Episcopal Church, and the American Legion Auxiliary. In 2003, she received the President Award from the Tobacco Valley Improvement Association, awarded to the most outstanding individual in the Valley. She was also a member of the Art Club during its tenure in the 60s and 70s. She served as a Fair judge for many years. Carol loves her home in the Tobacco Valley and was happy to raise her children here.

JOHN GIBBONS OF EUREKA

HAROLD GILDON

Harold was nominated for his volunteer efforts in Libby's Volunteer Ambulance Service.

GLEN GILL

Glen was nominated for his volunteer work with the Troy Movers 'n Shakers Beautification Committee, City Planning and Zoning, Troy Area Community Association, and the Troy Chamber of Commerce.

BILL & EDNA GWYNN

Bill and Edna Gwynn are both active members of St. Michaels and All Angels Church in Eureka. Bill Gwynn was born March 5, 1927 in Logan County, OH to Thurman Gwynn and Edna Oder (both of OH). Bill's parents came to Lincoln County in 1929 headed for Washington (they stayed in Eureka instead). Bill spent his early school years at the Cuffe school near the Shea Ranch before entering the Eureka Public Schools until age 17. He joined the Navy and served for the duration of World War II, returning for school and graduation in 1947. Edna Gwynn was born in Eureka on June 9, 1932 to John R. McKenzie (originally of Leeds, SD) and Grace Pomeroy (originally of Kalispell, MT). Edna's parents lived in the Meadow Creek area of Fortine before homesteading on Black Lake near Eureka. Together Bill and Edna have four children: Cindy, Susie,

Shelley, and Kelley—as well as twelve grandchildren, and eleven great-grandchildren. Edna spent her early school years at Fortine, finishing school in Eureka. Bill grew up working with his father in the Christmas tree and timber industry and eventually worked in his own year-round Christmas tree business. Edna worked with the family tree and wreath business, too, while also being a stay-at-home mom to their four daughters. Both have served as leaders and volunteers in a number of area organizations: Edna in the Eastern Star, Sundowners Club, treasurer for St. Michaels and All Angels Episcopal Church, school board, and country Foster Review Care Board; Bill served on the state timber task force and school board and was instrumental in establishing American Legion Baseball in Eureka. Bill was also the mayor of Eureka during the 1970s and served a 3-year term in the Montana House of Representatives in the 1970s. In his free time Bill has enjoyed woodworking and antique cars. He even has a Glacier Park dignitary car in his possession. He has enjoyed living in Lincoln County, with woods and other outdoor places to walk in. He also notes that there are fewer people here than in other places, something he enjoys. Edna enjoys spending time with her kids and grandchildren and gardening. She stays in Lincoln County because she loves the open space and beauty.

MIKE GWYNN

Mike was nominated for his many years of service as a "behind the scenes" volunteer at many events in Eureka.

BILL & TERESA HAFEN

Teresa was born in Las Vegas, NV on December 22, 1961 to parents James Henry Roso of Covington, KY and Eva Jewl Skidmore (Marts) of Cincinnati, OH. Bill was born on March 31, 1959 in Provo, UT to parents Brooksley Ernest Hafen of Southern Utah and Alice Tenney (Boyce) of the Phillipine Islands. Bill and Teresa have four children: Joshua David of Whitefish, MT; Jesse Brooke of Bozeman; Daniel James of Eureka; and Sarah Renae of Whitefish, MT. They also have two grandchildren. Both Bill and Teresa attended Las Vegas schools and Bill went on to the University of Nevada. In Eureka, Teresa owns a book store, while Bill is a cell phone equipment technician. He is also a student of Biblical Studies and the ancient languages of Hebrew and Greek and has taught classes on the subject. Both Bill and Teresa are dedicated to relief and missionary service, both locally and overseas. Bill's hobbies include gardening, hiking, canoeing, and studying. Teresa enjoys reading, canoeing, and hiking. They both enjoy traveling. Though they have no formal membership in any organization, they have been involved in many service projects. In 2004, they both received the Tobacco Valley Improvement Association Award for outstanding achievements over the previous two years in the Tobacco Valley. Twenty years ago, Bill and Teresa moved to Lincoln County after seeking out a place to live a simple life and pursue their interests. A home in Edna Creek at Trego won out over St. Joe, Idaho and the Black Hills of South Dakota. When their children got involved in high school activities they moved to Eureka and have stayed there ever since.

JUDY HALZER

Judy was nominated for more than a decade of service as a volunteer veteran driver for the VFW in Libby, transporting veterans to Washington for medical care.

JIM HAMMONS

Jim was nominated for his many years of service to Troy, including his current position as Mayor.

CAROL HANSON

Carol Hanson was born in Whitefish, MT on August 31, 1951. Her parents, Donald and Emogene Boslaugh were from Iowa and Colstrip, MT, respectively. They moved to Eureka in 1946, where Donald served as Lincoln County High School principal and Emogene was an elementary school teacher. Carol attended Eureka schools for twelve years before moving on to Eastern Montana College at Billings until 1973. She married Ron Hanson and they together have children Amy and Andy, as well as six grandchildren. Like her mother, she was an elementary teacher and worked from 1978 until her retirement in 2003. Since then she has worked at Off-the-Wall Frame Shop and Hansons's Hothouse. In addition, she is on the Steering Committee for the Eureka Montana Annual Quilt Show and is deaconess at First Baptist Church. She enjoys photography and has been a photo judge at the Lincoln County Fair. She also volunteers as a reader for library story time at the local library. While they moved away for a time, Carol says that her family returned for family reasons since both she and Ron were from the Eureka area. She commented, "It's a good place to be a kid, and to raise a family."

RAE LYNN HAYS

Rae Lynn, presently the Montana State University Lincoln County Extension agent, has held her position for several years. She has been very instrumental in reviving and invigorating a successful 4-H program in Lincoln County. She has also been actively involved in many efforts to create and support community development projects in the county, leads an after school group periodically in Eureka and Troy, is called upon to facilitate many and varied public meetings, and has presented many workshops throughout the county designed to help residents in many different aspects of their lives. She is an active rodeo participant, excelling in barrel racing. She is the mother of two daughters and stepmother to one son.

Larry Hebenstreit. Photo courtesy of Kootenai Valley Record.

LARRY & MARY HEBENSTREIT

Larry was born in Decatur, IL on January 25, 1938 to Monna and Lawrence Hebenstreit. Larry was a sales associate and an Installed Home Improvement Specialist at Sears Roebuck before he retired. Mary was born in Chicago, IL on September 1, 1942. Mary's parents Joseph and Alice Lamono were also from Chicago. Mary has been a therapist for most of her life. She has worked in an agency for therapy and in private practice. Larry and Mary have three children: Susan, Larry, and Sharon. Larry likes to read, golf, play cards, and socialize. He is a member of Heritage Museum, Cabinet View Country Club, Libby Spinning Squares, Libby Senior Center, and he serves as treasurer of the Libby Food Pantry. He moved here because he thought it was a really nice place to live. Mary's favorite hobby is reading. She also loves to garden and plant flowers. Mary has been a volunteer at the Libby Heritage Museum since 1993. She has also been on the Memorial Center Council and has worked in Kiwanis Service Club for Family Children. She received Kiwanis of the year in 2002 and 2007. Mary has chosen Libby for her home because she loves the people and the atmosphere of Libby. The most rewarding part of her life here is the friends she has made and the contribution she has been able to make here.

TYANN HERMES

Tyann was nominated for her volunteer activities in many organizations, including: Troy Fine Arts Council, Troy Chamber of Commerce, PTA, and Kootenai ROCKS climbing wall club. She and her husband, Chris, have two children and own Kootenai Drug in Troy.

Tyann and Chris Hermes. Photo courtesy of Troy Chamber of Commerce.

HUGH HOLLYDAY OF YAAK

ANGELA HUCHALA HOLIDAY

Angela was born in Floweree, MT on May 31, 1915. She is the daughter of Peter and Theresa Huchala. Angela received her nursing degree from Sacred Heart School of Nursing in Spokane, WA. She was a nurse for Libby Public Schools for many years. Angela was married to Edward Holiday. Her hobbies include gardening, crocheting, fishing, and hunting.

DALE HUDSON

Dale Hudson was born January 22, 1931 in Billings, MT to parents Horace B. Hudson (originally of Missouri) and Bina E. Blackburn Hudson (originally of North Carolina). Horace and Bina moved to Lincoln County from Hardin, MT in 1938 and moved to Flathead County for some years before returning to the Eureka area until their deaths in 1980 (Bina) and 1983 (Horace). Dale arrived with his parents in 1938 and attended most of his primary schooling in Eureka, graduating from Lincoln County High School. He also spent four year in Texas in the Air Force during the Korean War. Dale married Edith (Butts), born in Eureka, and they had two children: Esther Brandt of Eureka; and Howard of Kalispell. They now have three grandchildren and ten great-grandchildren. Dale was a self-employed trucker most of his life and operated Kootenai Motor Freight between Kalispell and Eureka through the 1960s. He also operated Hudson Heavy Hauling, where he hauled logs with a self-loader, and Valley Machine Shop. Dale served on two school boards for a total of twelve years, was on the Tobacco Valley Improvement Association board, and the Lincoln Electric Board of Directors. He supervised the construction of Holy Cross Lutheran Church, built with volunteer labor, and is still active there. Dale owns a small plane and enjoys piloting as a hobby along with hunting, fishing, gardening, woodworking, fabricating in his shop, and inventing things. He lives in Lincoln County because he has found no better place.

JOYCE HUDSON

Joyce Hudson was born on November 15, 1928 in Ogden, UT to parents Elmer S. and Thelma Davies Saunders. The family moved to Missoula, MT when Joyce was 10 years old. Joyce attended schools in Ogden, Utah, Preston, Idaho, and then Missoula. Before marriage, she was a waitress at original 4 B's Restaurant in Missoula. Later she worked with local dispatch (and served on the Dispatch Board), as Eureka town clerk (18 years), and as an EMT with Eureka Volunteer Ambulance with Clarabelle Dierman and Barbara Morgan (36 years) until retirement. She helped to establish volunteer ambulance services in the Eureka area. She was also the local Justice of the Peace for four years during the late 1960s. Joyce married Omer Hudson who passed away in 1971. They had three children: Alan, Peggy, and Patty. Joyce now has eight grandchildren and seven great-grandchildren. She enjoys needlework like embroidery and is a long-time member of the Church of Latter Day Saints. Many summers have been spent with Joyce taking her children, their cousins, and friends to Sophie Lake to swim. Joyce says that she married a local boy and they made their home here. "Family and friends made it home," she says.

RUSS HUDSON

Russ was nominated for years of service as a forester involved in effective reforestation.

GARY HUNTSBERGER

Gary Huntsberger was born in Great Falls, MT on November 12, 1944 to Ray and Eleanor Huntsberger. Gary attended Great Falls High School. After high school, he attended college in Bozeman for two years, entered the Army, and then returned to school and graduated with a business degree from Eastern Montana College. He received a Master's Degree in Special Education, also from Eastern Montana College. Gary is married to Kate. Their children are: Heidi, Andy, Vince, Jolene, and Ronnie. Gary came to Libby in 1976 to be the director of the Shelter Workshop. He then became a Schrader Stove dealer and installer along with a chimney sweep. Gary likes the outdoors especially skiing and fishing. He also likes to read and socialize. He is currently the President-elect of Rotary, and a member of the Libby Tree Board, Healthy Communities Committee, and Heritage Museum. He is a past member of Libby Chamber of Commerce, Libby Volunteer Ambulance, Northwest Human Resources, Resource Advisory Committee, Libby City Council, and Libby School Board. Gary originally moved to Libby for a job but stayed because he liked it. Gary says that for a person who likes the outdoors, it is the largest playground left.

BARB HVIZDAK

Barb Hvizdak was born in 1959 Manitowoc, WI to Frank and Catherine Abendroth of Appleton, WI. Barb graduated from Appleton High School West in 1977 before earning degrees from Montana State University in 1983 and University of Montana in 1988. She is married to Ron Hvizdak and enjoys the many outdoor opportunities that can be found in Lincoln County, including the proximity to water and the mountains. However, she says, "you can find those things all over the west. What makes Eureka special is the people. Despite the growth and change in our community over the past decade, Eureka is still a small town where you're greeted by name on the street and in the stores. I originally came to Eureka to work a summer job in order to pay for college, I never expected to be here 30 years later! If you stay long enough, you become part of the community and the community becomes part of you." Barb works in Customs and Border Protection at the Port of Roosville as a Mission Support Assistant. Prior to that she taught and coached in the Eureka Public Schools. When not working, Barb enjoys running, fishing, camping, skiing, quilting, and spending time with her two dogs. Since 2004 she has also served on the committee for the Eureka Montana Quilt Show.

JUDY HYSLOP

Judy Hyslop was born in 1947 in Pinehurst, NC to Winnifred and Harris Rush. She made her way to Evergreen State College, earning her B.A. in Communications. She worked as Communications Director for the United Way and also for the Corell Corporation in Camden, NJ. She came to Libby in 1991 to work in the home health care area and has since become involved in many activities. She loves the mountain vistas surrounding the Libby community and says she fell in love with Libby as she was driving down Whiskey Hill for the first time. Judy currently works for Libby Public Schools as a custodian and is also the owner/operator of Judy's Helping Hands Services. Her volunteer activities include serving on the Christ Lutheran Church Council and Kootenai Pets For Life. She is past President of Kootenai Pets for Life and is currently Vice President and shelter director.

DAVID JAMES

David was nominated for his volunteer work in the Eureka Community. In 2003, David received the Tobacco Valley Improvement Association Award for outstanding achievements over the previous two years in the Tobacco Valley.

CURT JONES

Curt Jones has been a member of the Libby Volunteer Fire Department for 25 years. He has loved Libby since he moved here with parents Arlene and General Jones in 1959. Curt has raised two children: Ryan and Travis. Curt is the owner of long-time Libby business Johnnie's Auto Parts. The business was established by his grandfather, John Hustuft, in 1947 and Curt learned the parts business by working alongside his grandfather as a child. Supporting their family by being a working member of Johnnie's Auto Parts for years, he has chosen this town as his home so his kids are blessed to live here as well. In his spare time, Curt loves hiking and fishing.

LEROY "JERRY" JORGENSON

Jerry Jorgenson was born to LeRoy and Evelyn Jorgenson in Williston, ND in 1942 He enjoys the quality of life and climate in Libby compared to where he grew up and is proud to have been able to raise his children there. Jerry has three children: Dawn, Karie, and Mike. Professionally, he has worked for the Internal Revenue Service and United States Forest Service. Jerry was also the Kootenai National Forest Budget Officer, Administrative Officer, and worked with the Forest Service law enforcement. Now retired, he works two days a week at the Montana Athletic Club and enjoys gardening, hiking, hunting, and fishing during his free time. Jerry served the Methodist Church as its treasurer, served two terms on the Lincoln County Credit Union Board of Directors, was president of the Lincoln County Combined Campaign, and was active in Crime Stoppers since its inception. He is currently on the Board of Directors of the Lincoln County Community Health Center. Jerry has stayed in Libby because he does not like big cities and thinks Libby is a "nice spot." He also thinks it is a great place to raise children and retire.

CHARLIE JUDKINS

Charlie was nominated for his service as a member of the American Legion Honor Guard and Firing Squad that serves at military funerals throughout Lincoln County.

JOE KELLY

Joe was nominated for his service as a member of the American Legion Honor Guard and Firing Squad that serves at military funerals throughout Lincoln County.

JERRY KENSLER OF TROY

ROGER KENSLER

Roger was nominated for his many years of service to Troy, including formerly holding the position of Mayor.

FRED KING

Frederick "Fred" Oliver King was born December 25, 1920 in Liverpool, England. His parents Percy Edward King and Alice Forman King were also from Liverpool, relocating to a ranch on the Tobacco Valley in 1924 (they never left). Fred attended all Eureka schools and graduated from Lincoln County High School. He married Beulah (Byers) and they have been married 60 years; they now have two children, two grandchildren, and two great-grandchildren together. Professionally, Fred started out with a chainsaw working for J. Neils Lumber Company in 1942. After a logging-sawmill partnership from 1946-1950, he spent most of his career as an independent logger in all phases of logging and related road construction (King Construction; King-Paola during Libby Dam days). Fred pioneered the use of rubber-tired skidders in the Tobacco Valley in 1967, and in 1970 he introduced the first "feller-buncher" to the area for small timber. He was named the Big Sky Championship Logger of the Year in 1981. He also started and for many years owned Pinkham Mountain Radio system. Fred previously served on the board of directors for First National Bank of Eureka, Lincoln Electric Co-op, and Mountain View Manor Nursing Home. He has been a member of Lion's Club, and earned Tobacco Valley Improvement Association awards for local benevolent projects. Fred was a pilot with his own plane for most of his life. He participated in cross-cut saw events at Libby Logger Days and Lincoln County Fairs until retired from competition in 1978. He now enjoys gardening and spending time with his two dogs. He staying in Lincoln County because his family is here and there was plenty of work ("in those days").

LARRY KING

Larry was nominated for his service as a member of the American Legion Honor Guard and Firing Squad that serves at military funerals throughout Lincoln County.

PETER VIGO KLINKE

Peter Klinke was born in Fortine on July 17, 1920 to parents Peter V. Klinke, Sr., originally of Minnesota, and Petronella (Zeller) Klinke, originally of Wisconsin. His parents met in Kalispell, MT and moved to Lincoln County in 1909 where Peter Klinke Sr. and his brother owned the Fortine Store. Peter Klinke Jr. stayed in the county, attending grade school in Fortine and high school at Lincoln County High School. He married June (Scouten) and together they had two children: Janice Neuman of Eureka; and Craig Klinke, who died in an automobile accident in 1973. He also has two grandchildren and two great-grandchildren. When asked about his profession, Peter jokes that he has worked all over, but his major profession was for the U.S. Forest Service where he was in charge variously of thinning, planting, and fire crews. He was also self-employed in the Christmas tree business, both raising and selling trees. Seasonally he would take truckloads of trees as far as California to sell. In World War II, Peter served in the Army Air Corps in North Africa as an engineer and turret gunner. He has served as post commander at the local Veterans of Foreign Wars (VFW) for five years and as district commander for one year. He is also an active member of both Montana and national Christmas Tree Associations. As might be imagined, he enjoys gardening and raising and selling Christmas trees. He has chosen to stay in Lincoln County because he was born here, has roots here, and has many family and friends. In addition, he has been all around the world and has found no better place to be than Lincoln County.

REUBEN KNELLER

Reuben was born in Saskatchewan, Canada. His father, Gottlieb, was from Poland and his mother, Nettie, was from Russia. Reuben attended school in Saskatchewan and British Columbia before moving to the Yaak in 1973. Reuben worked for many different companies during his logging career in the Yaak. He and his wife Delma (now deceased) had five children: Dan, Linda, Susan, John, and David. He currently has twelve grandchildren and seven great-grandchildren as well. Reuben has been involved in many things over the years, most notably the cemetery committee and the volunteer fire department, which he resigned from in 2009 after many years service. His hobbies are gardening, greenhouse work, woodworking, and sawmilling. He likes living in the Yaak River Valley for its simple lifestyle.

JOHN KONZEN

John was nominated for his many years of service promoting Troy and serving as County Commissioner in District 2.

KARIN LAMB

Karin Lamb was born in Annapolis, MD to parents Charlie Lamb of Annapolis and Marilyn Asplin, born in Minneapolis, MN. Karin is married to Jeff Witbrod, owner of Sherman Creek Log Works Inc in Eureka. They have two children: Laffrey Witbrod of Denver, CO; and Reed Witbrod of Bozeman, MT. Karin attended Key School in Annapolis and graduated from Baltimore Experimental High School and the Maryland Institute College of Art. She is a professional artist with a home studio in Eureka and her pottery is marketed locally and in other western states. Karin's hobbies include gardening and music. She is a member of the Tobacco Valley Improvement Association Board of Arts and the Folk Music Society, and is very active with the Creative Arts Center in Eureka. In 2003, she received the Tobacco Valley Improvement Association Award for outstanding achievements over the previous two years in the Tobacco Valley. The family moved here 28 years ago and sons were born in Lincoln County. They love this area for the clean air, clean water, and the friendly people. "I have made more friends here than anywhere else I have ever been," said Karin.

PAUL LAMMERS

Paul was nominated for his volunteer work and leadership in the Libby Rotary Club.

FLORENCE LARSON OF TROY

GREG LARSON

Greg was nominated for his work on the Troy Area Community Association and in county planning.

OVE LARSON

Former owner of what is now Larson Lumber, Ove is nominated for his many years of community leadership.

ROGER LARSON

Roger was born in San Francisco, CA on January 1, 1945. His parents were Milton Larson and Meryle (Bartow). His mother lived in Troy from 1980 to 1999. Roger has a bachelor's degree in business administration and was a Technical Manager - Quality Assurance for AT&T before retirement. His hobbies include reading and hiking. Roger has been involved with: the Troy Area Community Association, as the Vice Chairperson; Troy Chamber of Commerce; Troy City Planning and Zoning, as Chairperson; Troy Beautification Committee, as Chairperson; Troy Community Garden, as Chairperson; Troy Historical Preservation Society, as Chairperson; and Troy Friends of the Library where he is a past president and currently treasurer. Roger moved to Troy after his mother told him what a beautiful place it was.

STEVE LAUER OF LIBBY

Steve was nominated for his work at the Libby Volunteer Fire Department where he currently serves as Treasurer and assistant Fire Marshall.

JON LEONARD

Jon is a fifth generation Eureka resident. His parents are Jim Leonard and Caroline "Pat" (Doble). Jon graduated from Lincoln County High School in 1983 and received a degree in business from Montana State University in 1987. He is married to Karyn and has two children: Austin and Michelle. Jon enjoys fishing, camping, skiing, and other outdoor activities. Together with Randy Wilson, Jon is a cochair of the annual "Eureka Rendezvous" event. Together they have taken this event an upgraded it to a regional destination through long and hard hours planning and coordinating it. Jon is also a member of the Tobacco Valley Community Development Council, Tobacco Valley Toastmasters, and the Eureka School Board, and helps other organizations when they need an auctioneer for their activities. Jon left Eureka for fifteen years and was able to return to raise his children. He strongly believes that everyone needs to help and care for each other to make a community successful.

DANIEL LEWIS OF LIBBY

BEVERLY & JOHN LIVINGSTON

John was born in Pueblo, Colorado and Beverly was born in Great Falls, Montana. They came to Lincoln County in 1972. John was working for United States Customs and was transferred from Idaho. They chose to stay because they liked the area. John had attended college in Bozeman and Great Falls before entering the Air Force during the Korean War. Beverly received her nursing degree from Columbus School of Nursing in Great Falls and worked part-time for many years at Mountain View Manor in Eureka. They have two children, Mark Livingston and Mary Hinkle. They also have five grandchildren. Beverly likes to quilt, garden, travel and read. She is a member of the Eureka Friends of the Library, Weedettes Garden Club, and Tobacco Valley Improvement Association. John has been a member of the Eureka Volunteer Fire Department for thirty-three years and is also a member of the Veterans of Foreign Wars. In 2005, he earned the Tobacco Valley Improvement Association Hall of Fame Award for marked contributions to the development of the area and in 2001 he received the Tobacco Valley Improvement Association Award for outstanding achievements over the previous two years in the Tobacco Valley.

CONRAD MALECHA

Conrad Malecha of Eureka was born in Fairboult, MN to John and Elizabeth Malecha. He went to school in Fairboult and moved to Lincoln County in 1988. "It reminded me of home without the high humidity and large population, more laid back with lots of opportunity for recreation and friendly people," he says. Conrad has children Malissia Malecha Levy and Bailey Malecha, as well as four grandchildren. He has worked as a self-employed handyman, as a farm and ranch hand, and for the U.S. Forest Service. In 2004, he received the President Award from the Tobacco Valley Improvement Association, awarded to the most outstanding individual in the Valley. He enjoys camping, woodworking and refinishing old furniture.

St. John's Lutheran Hospital chief executive officer Bill Pattern, Florence Larson, Bonnie Larson, Ove Larson, and hospital foundation director KC Hoyer raise money for digital mammography. Photo courtesy of Kootenai Valley Record.

LAURIE MARI

Laurie was born in Alameda, CANovember 4, 1955. Her father is Tanjore E. Splan who lives in Sault Ste. Marie, MI and her mother is Beverly J. Splan of Alameda, CA. Laurie's most recent career was as a Fire and Police Dispatcher in Piedmont, CA. The last school she attended was St. Joseph's Notre Dame High School in Alameda, CA. Her current hobbies include quilting and other sewing. Her husband is Jim. Laurie has one daughter, Donna, and six step-children: Debi, Angelina, John, Damon, Nicole, and Christopher. She is involved in U Serve Libby, Inc. and is currently the treasurer. Other organizations Laurie is involved with are: Heritage Museum, where she is the past secretary and past treasurer and currently chair of exhibits; American Legion Auxiliary; and

Laurie Mari receiving a check for Libby Community Tennis Courts from Gary Spencer of Glacier Bank. Photo courtesy of Kootenai Valley Record.

Cabinet Back Country Horsemen. Laurie moved to Lincoln County because she and her husband wanted a small town atmosphere that was a safe, affordable place for their daughter to go to high school. They had vacationed here in the past and knew it would be a good fit. Laurie knew from the first moment that this was the place to live.

BECCA MARTIN

Becca was nominated for her volunteer work on the Troy Movers 'n Shakers Beautification Committee, Troy Friends of the Library, the Community Garden, Troy Schools, and at her church.

Becca Martin. Photo by Melody Condron.

WALT MASON

A former member of the American Legion Honor Guard and Firing Squad that serves at military funerals throughout Lincoln County.

CAROL MCALISTER

Carol is the chief fund-raiser for Kootenai Pets for Life (KPFL). She spends countless hours on the rummage sale, duck races, Bow-Wow Bash and other activities to ensure that animals in Lincoln County are taken care of and that KPFL work continues. She is also involved in the new shelter construction, seeing the new building in Libby to its completion.

JOHN K. MCBRIDE

John was born on January 30, 1928 in Ft. Totten Long Island, NY. His parents were John McBride and Dorothy Kenly McBride. John has a degree in forestry from University of Maine. He had spent the summers of 1949 and 1950 in Lincoln County working for the US Forest Service. He moved to Libby permanently in June of 1952 to work for J. Neils. John worked in many forestry related positions such as a Manager of Government Affairs for St. Regis and Kootenai Area Manager for Champion. John's wife is Carolyn Simpson McBride and their children are: Dorothy McBride, Karen Larsen, John S. McBride, and Janet Kvernvik. John enjoys collecting firearms, especially U.S. military weapons. He has also done a great deal of target shooting and horseback riding. John also enjoyed teaching hunter's safety for forty years and volunteering in the schools by teaching special classes on the Civil War. He is a member of the Cabinet Back Country Horsemen, National Rifle Association, Montana Arms Collectors Association, and the Society of American Foresters.

HEATHER MCDOUGALL

Heather was nominated for her volunteer work for Troy's Old Fashioned 4th of July parade, Troy School Board, and All-School Reunion in Troy.

MARC MCGILL

Marc was nominated for his volunteer service as a fireman and assistant fire chief in Libby, 1972-1995. Marc recently retired as director of Lincoln County Emergency Management.

RANDY MCINTYRE

Randy was born in Gillette, WY. He and his wife since 1972, Sandy, have three children: Amber of Wisconsin, and Tracy and Kelly of Eureka. He also has 5 grandchildren. Randy is the Executive Director of the Eureka Chamber of Commerce, Chairperson of the Rendezvous Committee, and President of Lincoln County Tourism Board. He sits on the Glacier Country Tourism Board of Directors as a representative of Lincoln County. Randy is also a western wildlife artist and was recently named the first Treasured Montana Artist by the Montana Secretary of State's office. His art was featured in the Secretary of State's lobby in the Capitol Building in Helena in early 2009. In 2008, Randy received the Montana Small Business Association Home Based Business Champion of the Year and the Region VIII Home Based Business Champion of the Year for the Home Business Expo in Eureka. When he is not working or painting, Randy is a rockhound and likes to hike. When asked, Randy said that the greatest part about living in Lincoln County was freedom.

KEITH MEYERS

Keith is originally from Kennewick, WA. He moved to the Libby area in 1996 because it looked like a great place to raise kids. Keith has been an auto mechanic most of his adult life and is the owner of the Magic Wrench in Libby. He and his wife Sue have three daughters: Traci, Jennifer, and Heather. They also have one grandson. Keith is an organizer for Libby's annual Relay for Life event and is very involved in the theater. He has organized and participated in a number of theater events, including children's events for the Troy New Horizons after school program and the Heron Players. Many people also recognize Keith's voice as a radio personality (again, volunteer) for Libby radio station KJRZ. When he is not busy with him many activities, Keith can be found enjoying time with his family and fishing. He says that meeting and learning from people is one of the best parts of volunteering and living in Lincoln County.

JASON MOBLEY

Jason Mobley is seen throughout Libby with his friend Ron Sagen. Jason, born in Yakima, Washington lives in Libby with his parents Bill and Laura. He graduated from Libby High School in 1997. Jason has a business, Jason's Lawn and Snow Removal, and can be seen throughout Libby tending to his business. When not working, Jason enjoys riding his bicycle and playing basketball. He enjoys volunteering at the Montana Avenue group home. He "just helps with stuff that needs to be done." Whenever there is an event going on, Jason can be seen pushing his friend Ron, around in a wheel chair, something they've been doing for 15 years. Jason is most proud of the five gold medals he and his teammates have earned playing in the Montana Special Olympics. His team, the Lincoln County Wolfpack, is one of the strongest teams in Montana. Jason's hobbies are hunting, fishing, and getting to know the people in Libby.

LEN & TODDY MOSSEY

Len and Toddy were nominated for their home and garden decorations, which change during the different seasons and beautify Troy.

KATHERYN MOUNTEER

Katheryn was nominated for her volunteer work in organizing the annual Eureka quilt show.

DAVID NEWBURN OR EUREKA

GAYLE NEWMAN

Gayle was nominated for her volunteer work with the Tobacco Valley Improvement Association Board of History.

TRENT OELBERG

Trent Oelberg was born in Kirby, OH in 1941 to Cyril and Elizabeth Oelberg. He and his wife Peggy currently live in Libby and are parents to four children. Trent served as an electronic engineer civilian for the Naval Ocean Systems Command. He also worked as a builder in Whitefish, MT, before finally attending Bethel Theological Seminary in San Diego. He was most recently Associate Pastor at the Nazarene Church and since retiring, has been involved in several volunteer efforts around Libby. In his spare time, Trent likes to golf and fish the Kootenai River. When not recreating, he is involved in church activities, and is heavily involved in the Libby Revitalization Main Street Project. Trent and Peggy chose to retire in Libby because they fell in love with the "genuine people" of the area. "The people, river, and mountains make Libby a wonderful place to live."

BOB PARKER

Bob was nominated for his volunteer work with Libby Volunteer Ambulance, Troy Volunteer Ambulance, and the David Thompson Search and Rescue. His nomination reports that he even left his family on Christmas day to do a patient transfer to Kalispell.

DAVE PETERSON OF EUREKA

MARY LOU PETERSON

Mary Lou was nominated for her volunteer work throughout the Eureka community.

BOB PETRUSKA

Bob was born in Ironwood, MI on June 13, 1925 and came to Libby with his parents (Mac and Betty) and sister Jena in 1927. He was employed by several companies, primarily W.R. Grace and the sawmill (J. Neil's, St. Regis, and Champion). He was involved in Knights of Columbus, VFW, American Legion, Elks, Lions, and Kootenai Winter Sports. His main involvement was in the American Legion Libby Austin Reedy Post 97, where he served as the local Post Commander several times and the Montana State Commander for three terms. While in the Legion, he was instrumental in the Cross Painting program, often making the crosses in his own garage on several occasions. He is still an active member of the Legion Honor Guard and has honored nearly 200 military veterans at burial services. He spent time on many community projects, including the first electric score board at the city ball park and building the original lifts at Turner Mountain. He served as a catechism teacher at St. Joseph's Catholic Church. Bob is possibly best known for his personable nature and sense of humor, and as a man who is mechanically inclined. In his multiple nominations for the Roll of Honor, every one mentioned Bob using his abilities to fix things for others, whether it was a well pump, a church boiler, or some other machinery. He is an avid outdoorsman who loves the land and respects it as well. Bob has enjoyed hunting, camping, boating, and fishing his entire life. Previously, Bob was the proprietor of the Snell Creek Cabin in the Fisher River country where he and several other guided hunters from California in the 1950s and early 60s. He later built a cabin on Thompson Lake on ACM property before the fall of the big Larch trees. As a young man, Bob enjoyed building and racing stock cars in the original track on the north side of Highway 37 and flying a private plane for many years in the Libby area. Bob married Lorainne O'Brien in 1949 and raised 4 children in Libby: Marilyn, Jeanette, Tony, and Frank. He will be 84 in 2009.

PAT PEZZELLE

Pat was born to Karl and Betty Pezzelle on April 10, 1950 in Rochester, PA. He is married to Beverly Pezzelle and has a daughter, Jennifer Stidham and a son, Ryan Pezzelle. He received his bachelor's degree in secondary education from Illinois State University and a Master's degree in adult education from the University of Phoenix. Pat retired from the Phoenix Police Department as a Detective Sergeant after twenty years of service. He then was a high school teacher, owned a custom golf club company, and was a consultant to the United States Department of Justice. He is currently the Director of Extended Learning for Lincoln County Campus – Flathead Valley Community College. Pat's hobbies include golfing, fishing, being a grandfather, cooking, and whatever his wife wants to do. In the past, Pat has belonged to the Fraternal Order of Police, Phoenix Law Enforcement Organization, and Libby Area Development Corporation. He was also a board member of the Kootenai River Development Corporation. He is currently a member of Libby Rotary, Montana Economic Development Association, St. John's Lutheran Capital Campaign Committee, Bass Anglers Sportsmen Society, and is the former chairperson and current member of the Lincoln County Public Libraries Board of Trustees. Over the course of his careers, Pat has earned over twenty-five service commendations from the Phoenix Police Department, a service award from the Arizona POST, 1995 Teacher of the Year, and the Spark Plug Leadership Award from the Montana Department of Labor and Industry. He is also an honorary member of the NSF in Beirut and received a service award for his duties in Bangladesh.

SAMI PIERSON

Sami Pierson. Photo by Melody Condron.

Sami was born in Livermore, California. Sami holds a B.A. in History and has earned a Master of Art in Public History from Colorado State University and an Master's in Library and Information Sciences from the University of Southern Mississippi. During her studies, she was the recipient of the PEEL Scholar Award from the Montana State Library. She and her husband Eric Wilson (originally of Libby) have two sons, Brody and Aidin. She is the current Director of the Lincoln County Public Libraries and was previously an Archivist for the Libby Heritage Museum. In addition, she frequently teaches classes for the Flathead Valley Community College. She has been involved in Rotary, KIWANIS, and the Lincoln County Literacy Coalition and loves reading and gardening.

JASON PLACE

Jason was nominated for his service as Fire Investigator on Libby's Volunteer Fire Service and for his dedication in law enforcement.

MIKE POWERS

Mike Powers, following a long a distinguished career in the United States Navy, has become as active in a community as a person can. Born in Centerville, IA to parents Duane and Helen in 1937 (stepfather Ed Hildebrand), Mike worked construction jobs following graduation from high school. He is married to wife Georgine and they have three children: Michael, Mitch, and Maria. Mike then served in the United States Navy for 24 years retiring as a Lt. Commander in the Medical Services Corp. While in the Navy, Mike served three tours in Vietnam, was a pharmacist, and worked as a hospital administrator. Following Mike's Navy service, he came to Libby and was administrator of St. John's Lutheran Hospital. Mike is probably best known for being the only full-time collector in Libby. While his collections are too numerous to mention, he is especially fond of his collection of half-tones, and owns and operates a fully functional linotype machine. He has served in many capacities, including: Lincoln County Fair Commissioner, Republican Party politics, Libby Saddle Club, and is past chairman of the

Heritage Museum. In 1967, Mike was named Sailor of the Year by the US Navy in San Diego. Mike says he came to Libby for a job, had no intention of staying past 2 or 3 years, and fell in love with the area. The most rewarding part of his time here has been getting to know some of the old timers, most notably, Inez Herrig.

ROBERT PROWSE

Robert was nominated for his service as a former member of the American Legion Honor Guard and Firing Squad that serves at military funerals throughout Lincoln County.

Viola Rambo. Photo courtesy of the Rambo Family.

VIOLA RAMBO

Viola M. Rambo was born in Hingham, MT on January 20, 1916 to Hilda and Alphonse Muller. In June of 1939 she married Howard Rambo and together they had four children: Kathleen Rambo Bache of Libby; Arthur J. Rambo (deceased); Patty Rambo of Libby; and Daniel Rambo of Ottowa, Canada. Viola and her husband moved to the area in 1947, purchasing a ranch on Farm to Market Road. Viola was active in the Farm Women's Club, the Catholic Church Altar Society, Little League, Babe Ruth and American Legion baseball, and the Republican Party, VFW Auxiliary. She is also a co-founder of the Lincoln County Credit Union, sometimes doing the books on her dining room table in the evenings after working full time for the U.S. Forest Service. While wintering in Tucson, AZ, Viola volunteered at a VA Hospital and for the Vietnam Veterans of America. She is a Gold Star Mother; son Arthur was killed in Vietnam on November 26, 1969.

AL RANDALL

Al was born in Naches, WA to Alvin and Iris Randall. Al received his undergraduate degree from Western Washington College in Bellingham, Washington and a Master's in library science from Peabody College in Nashville, TN. Al is married to Marbie Randall and they have two children: Allan and Kayleen. Al came to Libby in 1972 to be the Libby High School librarian and held that position for 28 years. Even though the Randalls originally came for employment, they stayed in Libby because they loved the area and all the outdoor opportunities. Al was involved with David Thompson Search & Rescue for twenty years, specializing in mountain rescues. He also coached cross country running, junior high track, and the cross country skiing club. Al was a member of Libby Rotary and the Lincoln County Library Board of Trustees. Al has many hobbies such as hiking, fishing, climbing, skiing, canoeing, photography, traveling and reading.

RON REUTELER

Ron was nominated for his service as a member of the American Legion Honor Guard and Firing Squad that serves at military funerals throughout Lincoln County.

MARY REYNOLDS

Mary was nominated for her volunteer work as an after school teacher, with the Troy Friends of the Library, and at her church.

GREG & SUSIE RICE

Doug and Susie were nominated for their efforts in organizing the annual STOKR race and their continual commitment to Habitat for Humanity.

JACKIE ROBINSON

Jackie Robinson was born in Norman, OK in 1944 to parents Jack and Betty Robinson of Olathe and Gardner, KS. She attended Iola, Kansas High School and Iola Junior College. In higher education, she went to the University of New York, Albany, the Fashion Institute of Technology in New York City, and Kansas State University. Professionally she has worked as a consultant, pattern designer, fabric designer, and international teacher of quiltmaking. She has two children, Serge Traylor of St.Louis, Missouri, and Bevin Traylor of Denver, Colorado. She and her husband Jerry Wyatt found Eureka while passing through on vacation and found it to be full of gracious, friendly people. Jackie is very involved with the Eureka Montana Quilt Show and considers Eureka the best place she has ever lived.

DOUG ROLL

Doug was nominated for his service on City Council, as Libby's current Mayor, and for his place on Libby's Volunteer Fire Service.

ERNIE & JEANIE ROO

Ernie and Jeanie were nominated for their efforts in organizing Eureka's Rendezvous celebrations.

MARIANNE ROOSE

Marianne Roose was born at Kalispell General Hospital on October 29, 1944. Her mother Marie Louise Schwenke was born in Minnesota and her father Ted Burke was born in Valier. Marie and Ted married in 1935 and moved to the family logging camp at Trego in 1950. On the logging camp, Marianne and her sister Daisy assisted their mother in cooking for their family and 18 employees. Marianne attended Trego Elementary School and graduated from Lincoln County High School in 1962. She married Kent Roose and together they have three children: Jeana Roose King, Brent, and Joshua. They also have nine grandchildren. Marianne and Kent live in Fortine. She serves as County Commissioner for Lincoln County. Her duties as commissioner take her all over the country. In her spare time she enjoys crocheting, gardening, reading, and making greeting cards. Marianne is currently involved in many organizations, including Montana Representatives for Forest Counties and Schools, Flathead Valley Chemical Dependency Board, Board of Directors for the Center for Asbestos Related Disease in Libby, Board of Directors for the Resource Advisory Committee for Forest Service, Board member for Eureka River Walk, Montana County Printing

Libby Mayor Dooug Roll and County Commissioner Tony Berget discuss the state of Libby. Photo courtesy of Kootenai Valley Record.

Board, Area 6 Council on Aging Board, Montana Hard Rock Mining Board, Northwest Montana Disaster and Energy Services Board, Montana Tobacco Prevention Advisory Board, and member of Holy Cross Lutheran Church. She is also the Vice President of the Directors of Lincoln Electric, co-chairman of the annual Louise Burk Breast Cancer annual banquet, and Governor Brian Schweitzer's personal representative to the Pacific Northwest Economic Region. Previously she has served as a 4-H organizational leader for many years, Lincoln County Fair Juvenile Superintendent, Lincoln County Extension Council member, and President of the Homemaker Extension Club. In 2004, she received the Tobacco Valley Improvement Association Hall of Fame Award for marked contributions to the development of the area.

Marianne Roose. Photo courtesy of Lincoln County.

ROXIE RUBIER

Roxie was nominated for her volunteer work in the Troy Movers 'n Shakers Beautification Committee, City Planning and Zoning, the Community Gardens, and the Senior Center Garden in Troy.

JOAN RUNYAN

Joan Runyan is a transplant, moving to the area in 1936 from Havre, MT. Her parents, Leonard and Ida Brown, moved to Libby so Leonard could manage an H. Earl Clack service station. Joan graduated for Libby High School in 1943. She has one daughter, Barbara that was born to her and her husband, Charles. Charles passed away in a car accident in 1968. Joan worked at various office jobs around town. Her first job, at the First State Bank, was right out of high school. She then attended Kinman Business University in Spokane. Following this, she taught school for one year, and came back to Libby to work at the Kootenai Mercantile in the office before working for Zonolite and W.R. Grace in the office for 24 years. She enjoys volunteering at the Heritage Museum, the Community Thrift Store, and also belongs to the Libby Pioneer Society. Joan continues to live in Libby because she likes the people of Libby and love's it's history. "It's home [and] I don't have any plans to leave, " Joan says.

FAYE SCHOKNECHT

Faye Schoknecht was born on February 10, 1928 in Lathum, KS. Her parent's were Ben and Dorothy Mathews. Her husband's name was Mark Schoknecht (now deceased). She has two children: Paula Sandman and Joel Schoknecht. She has been a homemaker, loving wife and mother, with many additional hours doing community volunteer work. Her hobbies include golf and playing bridge with her friends. Her volunteer work consists of Red Cross Volunteer for many years, St. John's Lutheran Hospital Auxiliary, sponsor of Junior Miss candidates, and working with Libby's own Nordicfest. Faye moved to Libby in 1940 and has loved it ever since. She has chosen to make Lincoln County her home because of the many friends she has made, the beautiful landscape, and her church. The most rewarding part of her life in Lincoln County has been her role as a loving and supportive wife and mother.

CATHERINE SCHROEDER

Catherine was nominated for her volunteer work at the Eureka Historical Village.

BETH MANESS SCHWEITZER

Beth was born in Libby, Montana on January 31, 1942. Her parents are Roy and Margaret Maness. Her father was born in Bonners Ferry, ID and moved to Troy later in life. Her mother was born in Roundup, MT and came to Troy for her first teaching job in the mid 1930s. Beth, herself, was a teacher for her entire career, teaching every grade level from kindergarten through eighth at one time or another. Beth attended Eastern Washington University, Northern University in Havre, and University of Montana, Missoula. She met her husband, Marvin, while attending school in Havre. They have one daughter, Suzanne. Beth's hobbies include volunteering, stained glass work, and socializing. She has belonged to several organizations in the past such as Eastern Star, where she held several offices, and Takima Club. Currently she is President of the Troy Museum, a member of the Breast Cancer Club, and a member of the Lincoln County Public Library Board of Trustees. Beth left Troy after high school, wanting to see the world, and then after about 10 years wanted to come back. She loves the friendly people and small town atmosphere found in Troy.

LAURA SEDLER

Laura was nominated for her work as a hospice care provider and her participation in Relay for Life.

JOAN SHIRLEY

Joan Shirley was born July 13, 1931 in Gettysburg, SD to parents Claude E. Knight and Clara Graf Knight, both of Gettysburg. Joan's husband was Richard C. Shirley and children: Stephen, Robert, Kathy, and Keith. Joan currently has nine grandchildren and one great-grandchild. She attended elementary school on Overwhich of the West Fork of the Bitterroot River and in Hamilton, MT and graduated from high school at Hamilton. In addition, she attended Montana State University at Missoula. As a teenager Joan started working as a reporter for the *Ravalli Republican* in Hamilton until she married. She and her husband purchased the *Hot Springs Sentinel* in Hot Springs, MT and in 1960 they moved the plant to Eureka to start the *Tobacco Valley News*. In 1976, they sold that paper and moved to Spokane, Washington. There, Joan was the owner of two retail clothing stores until the death of her husband in 1977. After owning a western store in Mesa, Arizona Joan finally retired to a Dickey Lake home in 1992. A major hobby of Joan's for many years was painting in water color, oils, and acrylics. She has been a quilter at the Tobacco Valley Improvement Association (TVIA) Historic Village since 1972, was active in organizing the Tobacco Valley Art Club, is the choir director at the First Baptist Church in Eureka during the 1970s, and is a volunteer at the Historic Village. She is now secretary-treasurer of the Eureka Friends of the Library and secretary to the TVIA Board of History. She moved back to Lincoln County because she loves the mountains, the lakes, and the wonderful friends here.

LAURA SHRADER

Laura was nominated for her service on Troy's City Council.

JIM SIEFFERT

Jim was nominated for his volunteer work at many Libby and Troy events and in many organizations, including the South Lincoln County Community Foundation.

JEAN SONJU OF LIBBY

FRAN STANTON

Fran has been involved in a number of fundraisers for local residents who need help. She pursues business and individual donations and organizes events to raise money for people who cannot provide for medical or other needs on their own.

LYNETTE STARLING

Lynette was born in Kelso, WA in 1942 during the brief period when her parents lived away from Eureka. Her father, Lynn Workman, was born in Lincoln County and her mother, Peggy (Speyer) was born in Havre, MT. Lynette was raised in Eureka and graduated from Lincoln County High School in 1960. While she has served in a number of positions professionally, Lynette has served in her current position as Manager for the Lincoln County Fair the longest, at 13 years and counting. In addition, she is also administrative support for the county extension office. Lynette and her husband, Robert D. Starling, have three children: Robert L., Karen Suchy, and Karmen McKinney. She has been involved with the Lutheran Women's Missionary League (former Zone President), is a co-chair for the Louise Burke Luncheon, and is a member of the Tobacco Valley Toastmasters. In 2001, she received the Tobacco Valley Improvement Association Award for outstanding achievements in the Tobacco Valley. She enjoys reading, hiking, scrapbooking, camping, and spending time with family. When asked why she has chosen to live in Lincoln County, Lynette responded, "We would not dream of living anywhere else. It is our home, our heritage, our history, and our future. Everything we have invested in is here, both emotionally and financially."

RALPH STEVER

Ralph was nominated for his volunteer work at the Troy after school program and his efforts on the Troy Fine Arts Council, including the organization of the Timberbeast FOLF tournament and the Kootenai River Bluegrass Festival.

LISA STEWART

Lisa was nominated for her work with the Tobacco Valley Improvement Association.

MARIE STOECKLEY

In 2004, Marie received the Tobacco Valley Improvement Association Award for outstanding achievements over the previous two years in the Tobacco Valley.

LARRY STROKLUND

Larry Stroklund was born in Devil's Lake, ND in 1947 to Marjorie and Glenn Stroklund. He has called Libby home since retiring from the United States Army following 21 years of service. He retired as a Major, serving one tour in Vietnam and being a member of the All Army Rifle Marksmanship Team for two years. He was awarded the Silver Star and also served as an Army Ranger and Green Beret. His family includes wife Mary Beth and children: Aunisa, Christopher, and Suzanne. He enjoys spending his free time traveling, fixing things, hunting, and fishing. His volunteer activities include membership in the American Legion, Veterans of Foreign Wars, Elks Lodge, Hunter's Safety instructor, and Boy Scouts assistant scoutmaster. Larry moved to Libby for family reasons and fell in love with the area. He plans on staying because he can think of no place better to live and for the fact there is little wind here.

BEA TALLMADGE OF TROY

TINA TAURMAN

Tina was born in Whitefish, MT on December 4, 1958 to Keith Goldie Colvert. Tina married Ron Taurman and together they have two children: Shannon Kayleen of Missoula, MT; and Shelby Colvert Taurman. She attended elementary school in Trego and graduated from Lincoln County High School in 1977, later attending the University of Montana at Missoula. Currently, Tina works as a medical office manager of North Country Medical Clinic in Eureka. She also served with "Montana Covering Kids" as a children's advocate, as well as holding jobs for the U.S. Postal Service and the U.S. Forest Service. She enjoys quilting, walking, swimming, jeeping on back roads, and gardening. She has been involved in many organizations, including Families in Partnership, Sunburst Foundation Board of Directors, Lincoln Electric Board of Trustees, and the Trego School Board. She was a 4-H member and leader for many years and in 2008 received an "outstanding 4-H Alumni" award. In addition, in 2003 Tina received the Tobacco Valley Improvement Association Award for outstanding achievements over the previous two years in the Tobacco Valley.

LIREVA WALL

Livera was nominated for her volunteer work with the Tobacco Valley Improvement Association.

JERRY WANDLER

Jerry was nominated for his leadership in the Troy community, as President of the Troy Snowmobile Club, and as a teacher. As a motivated local business owner, he sets a high standard and works hard to make Troy a great place to live and work.

JIM WARDENSKY

Jim was nominated for his service as a member of the American Legion Honor Guard and Firing Squad that serves at military funerals throughout Lincoln County.

BILL WATT

Bill was nominated for his work in the Libby Volunteer Fire Department. He is currently the 1st Assistant Chief for the department and also serves as Fire Marshall.

LARRY WATT

Larry was nominated for his volunteer work in the Troy Chamber of Commerce and at the 4th of July celebration, as well as other work promoting Troy as a business owner.

MARK WHITE

Mark White has been the Libby Ranger District Archaeologist and Historian for more than 20 years. He has a unique ability to remember historical names and dates and is the unofficial local history expert in Libby. Mark has made many presentations on local history and has been involved with the Libby Heritage Museum, Libby Pioneer Society, and the Lincoln County Centennial Committee. On many occasions he has worked with local schools to get kids involved in local history. He has located and recorded many hundreds of historic and prehistoric sites as Forest Service Archaeologist. Mark has assisted at least three authors who have written books on David Thompson's travels through Lincoln County. He also re-discovered the remains of a David Thompson Fur Post, ca. 1811. The Canadian Parks Archaeologists have recommend excavation and analysis of this site, as it is one of the earliest and most important historic sites in Montana.

TAMMY WHITE

Tammy is the Kootenai Pets for Life volunteer program coordinator and volunteers at the shelter 3+ times a week herself. She is diligent in organizing teams and people and in making sure that the animals of Kootenai Pets for Life are taken care of.

NICK WHITEMAN OF LIBBY

Nick was nominated for his service as a Libby volunteer fire fighter and for his generosity and willingness to help others in the community.

ISAIAH WILLIAMS

Isaiah was nominated for his service as President of the Trego-Fortine-Stryker Volunteer Fire Service.

PEGGY WILLIAMS OF LIBBY

Peggy was nominated for her service on Libby's City Council and at the Episcopal Church.

RANDY WILSON

Randy Wilson was born in California in 1954 to parents Buck and Colleen Wilson. He is the father of Casey, Kelly, Tyler, Jessica, and Christy. For over 30 years he has worked in telecommunications, with 12 years (and counting) at Interbel Telephone Cooperative. Randy has led the Coop to be proactive in the technology field giving our area high quality service and high speed internet long before many other areas of our state. His hobbies include spending time with his children and horses. He also makes time for Eureka Rendezvous. As current cochair of the event, Randy's nomination reported that he and fellow cochair Jon Leonard "have taken this event and upgraded it to a regional destination. They have put in long and hard hours planning and executing it." Randy has made Lincoln County his home because it is a nice place to raise a family. It is also a small town with great schools, a friendly community, good weather, and a lot to do outdoors.

Libby Main Street leaders present an award to Tungsten Holdings for support in revitalizing downtown Libby. From left to right, Libby Main Street Representatives Phillip Erquiaga, Trent Oelberg, and Gary Njrich, Tungsten's John Vignali, and Main Street board member Tom Wood.

BETTY JO WOOD

Born in Kalispell in 1974 to Tom and Melanie Wood, Betty Jo enjoys raising her family in the same town she grew up in. Allowing her children to live near their grandparents and develop close relationships with them is a very rewarding part of her life. She is married to Scott Beagle and they have two sons: Jay and Ryan. Betty Jo has worked in the non-profit sector since returning to Libby after college. She has worked for Families in Partnership, Libby Revitalization, and currently works at the CARD Clinic as Development Officer. She enjoys singing, exercising, playing tennis, and interior design. Volunteering takes up much of Betty Jo's time, as she is involved with Libby's Main Street Program, the St. John's Lutheran Hospital Foundation, WINGS, Families in Partnership, St. Joseph Catholic Church, Asa Wood School, and the Make a Wish Foundation.

TOM WOOD

Tom Wood was born in Libby on July 6, 1950. Tom's parents were Ernest and Trudy Wood, both born and raised in Libby. Tom and his wife Melanie have one daughter, Betty Jo Wood. He has hosted several foster children in hopes of a better life for them. He always felt like he had a calling for the sales of insurance and has been working in it for the past 40 years. He serves as Fire Chief at the Libby Volunteer Fire Department and has been Chief for 15 years. He has been in the department for 37 years. Tom is a very social person in the community of Libby. He was on the City Council for 12 years, Libby Revitalization for 5 years, a member of the Elks Club, Knights of Columbus, and has served as President of the Libby Chamber of Commerce. Throughout his life he has received many awards for service. In 1972 he received the Young Man of the Year award and in 1989 he received the Outstanding Young Man of America award. In addition, Tom has been awarded the Certificate of Service from the Libby mayor for his 35 years service with the Libby Volunteer Fire Department. He has chosen to make Lincoln County his home because the community has been always so friendly and helpful and because all of his family was born and raised here He also feels a strong historical connection to Libby; his grandfather, Frank Pival, is responsible for the building of many of the early schools, the sawmill, and many early Libby homes. The most rewarding part of his life here has been making a successful living as an insurance salesman and raising his family and foster children. He also loves to be outdoors and enjoy the beautiful Lincoln County landscape.

Tom Wood. Photo courtesy of Kootenai Valley Record.

WALT WREST

Walt was nominated for his service as a former member of the American Legion Honor Guard and Firing Squad that serves at military funerals throughout Lincoln County. As part of the Honor Guard, he was often called upon 40-50 times a year (with no compensation) to lead parades, banquets, and other functions.

KATHERINE WRIGHT-HANDY

Kay moved to Eureka from Craig, CO in 1987. She moved to Eureka to be close to her children and stayed because it was a great spot with friendly people. She is married to Daryle Handy and they have seven children: Christine Brunner, David Wright, Shaylene Wright, Dwight Handy, Deborah Bates, James Handy, and Jacob Handy. Kay is active with the Scraps and Threads Quilt Guild quilt show as a member of the Steering Committee. She is also a member of the VFW and the Northwest Artist Society. Her hobbies include quilting, painting, fishing, hunting, and target shooting.

LEWIS & LYNDA YOUNG

Lynda has been chairman of the Historical Village for many years. Both she and Lewis have spent many hours improving and maintaining the buildings in the village, including painting and repair. Both are active in the Audubon Society and help with annual bird counts in the Eureka area. In addition, Lewis is an authority on bats. As such, he travels for bat and habitat research and has facilitated many programs. Lewis is also a volunteer with the ski races at Big Mountain.

BRUCE ZWANG

Bruce was born in Libby and has lived here his whole life except during his college years. His parents were Willard and Florence Zwang. Bruce is married to Mary Jo and they have two children: Jeff and Kelly. After graduating from Libby High School, Bruce attended University of Montana and graduated with a degree in accounting. Bruce likes to ski and hike. He is currently president of Kootenai Winter Sports that operated Turner Mountain Ski Area. Bruce has chosen to continue to be a resident of Lincoln County because he likes the area and the small town feel, and because it is a great place to raise a family.

Lincoln County, Montana

ABOUT THE COUNTY

Lincoln County was created in 1909 and has thrived through the industries of logging and mining. The county experienced dramatic growth in the 1950s, 60s, and 70s during the building of the Libby Dam. Population county-wide decreased after the dam-building era into the 1980s. From 1990 to 2000, however, the county saw growth again at a rate of 7.8%. Ranching and agriculture have also historically played a part in shaping the county's economy, primarily in the Tobacco Valley; the southern part of the county is not as suitable for agricultural pursuits due to the mountainous terrain and narrow river valleys.

Recently, outlook for the tourism and service industries have improved where others have downsized. Ample fishing, hunting, hiking, and camping opportunities and rural lifestyle have attracted new people to the area, both as visitors and new residents. Only 9% of Lincoln County is privately owned, making it attractive to those who enjoy outdoor activities. Today, the primary industries employing the residents of Lincoln County are educational, health and social service, retail, and manufacturing. In 2000 (the most current census year), Lincoln County was home to 18,837 residents. Of those, 76.6% of families owned their own homes, 12.3% owned their own businesses, and 20.1% had served in the military at some time in their lives.

The County Seat of Lincoln County is located in Libby with most departmental offices in the county building at 512 California Avenue. The County government provides oversight and leadership for County parks, transportation through Lincoln County Transportation Services, Clerk and Recorder's office, County Nurse, Clerk of Court, County Attorney, Emergency Management, environmental health and sanitation, County Planning, schools, Lincoln County Public Libraries, County Treasurer, road, weed, and land maintenance, and many other areas of management and cooperation throughout the region.

Notable County Parks include the 101-acre J. Neils Park in Libby an the 135-acre Kootenai Falls area between Libby and Troy.

Lincoln County building from California Avenue. Photo by Melody Condron.

COUNTY COMMISSIONERS

Tony Berget, District 1 (Libby)
John Konzen, District 2 (Troy)
Marianne Roose, District 3 (Eureka)

Lincoln County building from 6th Street. Photo by Melody Condron.

2008 ELECTION RESULTS

In the last general election, Lincoln County residents voted for both Democrat and Republican candidates. The top two candidates garnering votes from Lincoln County Voters in the 2008 election are as follows:

President: (R) John McCain/Sarah Palin (5,699); (D) Barack Obama/Joe Biden (3,018)

U.S. Senator: (D) Max Baucus (5,615); (R) Bob Kelleher (3,447)

U.S. Representative: (R) Denny Rehberg (6,326); (D) John Driscoll (2,318)

Governor/Lt. Governor: (D) Brian Schweitzer/John Bohlinger (5,108); (R) Roy Brown/Steven Daines (3,706)

Secretary of State: (R) Brad Johnson (3,706); (D) Linda McCulloch (3,492)

Attorney General: (R) Tim Fox (5,016); (D) Steve Bullock (3,656)

State Auditor: (R) Duane Grimes (4,891); (D) Monica J. Lindeen (3,705)

State Superintendent of Public Instruction: (R) Elaine Sollie Herman (4,631); (D) Denise Juneau (3,342)

Public Service Commission District 4: (R) Doug Mood (5,080); (D) Gail Gutsche (3,287)

Supreme Court Chief Justice: Mike McGrath (5,307); Ron Waterman (2,113)

State Representative District 2: (R) Chas Vincent (3,240); (D) Timothy P. Linehan (1,653)

State Representative District 1: (R) Gerald A. Bennett (2,413); (D) Eileen J. Carney (1,491)

County Commissioner District 1: (R) Anthony Berget (5,433); (write-in) Jerry Okonski (2,422)

LINCOLN COUNTY PUBLIC LIBRARIES

In response to a petition signed by three hundred taxpaying residents of Lincoln County, the Board of County Commissioners established the Lincoln County Public Library on July 9, 1920. Charged with a mission of providing library services to the entire county, the new library was to given a small budget with which to hire a full-time librarian and to "[buy] books and [keep] up to date in every particular." Prior to the creation of a county library, the Libby Woman's Club had sponsored a small private library to serve the citizens of Libby. Members of the Woman's Club voted to donate their collection of two thousand volumes to the new library to serve as a basis with which to begin the circulating collection.

Libby Library. Photo by Melody Condron.

Library services began in December 1920 under the direction of Miss Antonia Grandjean. The library board leased the former Libby Woman's Club building to serve as the first home of the Lincoln County Public Library. The Woman's Club served as the library until 1923, when services were moved to the former First National Bank building and then, subsequently, to rented rooms in the Hotel Libby from 1929 to 1936. In 1936, the library moved to a wing of the new county courthouse which had been built specifically for library use. The building the Libby Library currently occupies was built in 1964. The building was renamed the Inez R. Herrig building in honor of Lincoln County's long-serving library director.

In accordance with its charged duty, The Lincoln County Public Library's services were expanded to include branch libraries in Troy (1922) and Eureka (1923), which are still in operation. Additional services in Fortine and Rexford were also established, but have since been discontinued. Remote regions of Lincoln County were provided with service through the use of a bookmobile from 1956 through 1976.

As Lincoln County has grown, the services provided by the Lincoln County Public Libraries have been expanded to meet patron needs. Through such timely innovations as hiring the libraries' first pages in 1945, automating circulation services in 1991, and becoming one of the first libraries in the state of Montana to offer free public access to the Internet, the libraries continuously strive to provide county residents with the best service possible.

Various construction projects have helped improve the county's libraries. In 1998 the Libby library was remodeled, a project which nearly doubled the size of usable space in the building through the addition of the Reference Room in the lower level. The renovation of the interior of the Eureka Library in 2002 involved the installation of new shelves, new carpeting, and a new circulation desk and book return.

Most recently, in September 2008, the Lincoln County Public Libraries joined the Montana Shared Catalog, a cooperative project spanning more than ninety libraries throughout Montana. This latest undertaking provides Lincoln County residents with a valuable, collaborative resource which promotes the sharing of information in the form of print, audio, and visual materials.

LINCOLN COUNTY PUBLIC LIBRARIES FOUNDATION

Lincoln County Public Libraries Foundation provides fundraising support for the benefit of all three libraries. The areas of fundraising include endowments, memorials, and tax-deferred gifts. The main goal of the foundation is to establish an endowment fund to ensure the future of the Lincoln County Public Libraries. The foundation also fundraisers for specific projects at each individual library which cannot be covered by the regular library budget. All gifts are invested in the endowment unless otherwise requested, such as for a specific project. Past projects of the Lincoln County Public Libraries Foundation include new shelving and circulation desk at the Eureka Branch Library, new shelving and circulation desk at the Troy Branch Library, and new carpet, shelving, and circulation desk at the Libby Library. All proceeds from *Lincoln County: Celebrating 100 Years* will support the Lincoln County Public Libraries Foundation.

LINCOLN COUNTY TOURISM

Lincoln County Tourism (LCT) is a non-profit organization with the mission of enhancing tourism for Lincoln County through education, promotion, communication, and development. Lincoln County Tourism is the only county tourism board in the state of Montana. Membership is made up of members from all three area chambers of commerce, as well as business owners and others invested in tourism throughout the county. To achieve its mission, LCT has four primary goals: educate businesses, government, and the public about the economic impact of tourism and its advantages to the local economy; develop hospitality training programs for businesses to improve interactions between customers and owner/employees; encourage Kootenai River Country as a "destination location" offering a wide range of attractions; and promote and strengthen tourism and economic development activities in the region. Current LCT officers are: Randy McIntyre, President; Debbie Davidson, Vice President; and Melody Condron, Treasurer/Secretary.

LINCOLN CONSERVATION DISTRICT

Conservation districts in Montana assist their residents in conserving soil, water, and other renewable natural resources. Lincoln Conservation District promotes the education of the public and coordinates with other public agencies such as the Montana Department of Fish Wildlife and Parks and the Department of Natural Resource and Conservation to protect natural resources. Each year the District helps local high schools, participate in the annual Envirothon and Lincoln County Fair, offers the annual tree and shrub sale, and presents educational workshops. Lincoln Conservation District administers the Natural Streambed and Land preservation Act, also known as the "310 Law." Any individual or corporation proposing construction in a perennial stream must apply for a 310 permit is to promote sustainable resource management for all natural resources in the county. Lincoln Conservation District is a subdivision of the State of Montana under the umbrella of the Natural Resource and Conservation Service. The conservation district covers all

Volunteers Jerry Jenks and Paul Roe work on the new Kootenai Pets for Life Shelter. Photo courtesy of Kootenai Valley Record.

of Lincoln County, except within the city limits of Libby and Troy. Funding for the operation and activities of the conservation district comes from a mill levied on real property within the boundaries of the county. Current Board Supervisors are: Mike Justice, Darris Flanagan, and Susan Ennenbach, Eureka; Don Gillard, Rexford; and Wayne Maahs, Don Crawford, and Mark Romey, Libby. Associate supervisors are Sarah Canepa and Steve Johnson.

WOMEN INFANTS AND CHILDREN

Women, Infants, and Children (WIC) was started in Lincoln County in Libby in March of 1975. It was one of the first ten counties in Montana to start a WIC program and is one of 27 local WIC agencies contracting with the state. WIC serves to safeguard he health of low-income women, infants, and children who are at risk by providing nutritious foods, information on healthy eating, and referrals to health care. In Lincoln County, WIC has offices in Libby, Troy, and Eureka. Linda Wagner, Program Director, and Peggy Smith RN, Competent Professional Authority, are the only two staff members for Lincoln County.

KOOTENAI PETS FOR LIFE

Organized in 2001, Kootenai Pets for Life (KPFL) works to eliminate the use of euthanasia as a method to control the abandoned animal population of south Lincoln County. KPFL has rescued and found loving homes for over 1,200 cats, dogs, and rabbits. They also run an aggressive spay and neuter campaign to lessen the number of animals that have to be put to death and help people with veterinary care so they can keep their animals in their homes. Since the organization began the rate of euthanasia at the county shelter has fallen by about 90%. Present officers are President Eileen Carney, Vice-president and Shelter Director Judy Hyslop, Secretary Connie Holthaus, and Treasurer Lynn Hagerty. Board members are Claire Evans, Tammy White, Carole McAlister, Anita Beasley, Linda Newstrom, and Linda Lampton. KPFL is an all volunteer organization and in 2008 had 105 volunteers who contributed 5,208.75 hours of service. Numerous fundraisers keep the organization running, including an annual rummage sale, duck races, Bow Wow Bash, and Meow Mania Dinner and Auction. In 2009, KPFL contracted with the county animal control offices to manage animal housing when their new Libby shelter is finished.

LINCOLN COUNTY COMMUNITY FOUNDATION

The Lincoln County Community Foundation was started in 1997 with $5,000 in seed money from a 1995 grant given by Plum Creek Timber to the counties in which they do business. The foundation is a non-profit organization set up to provide a way to seek donations for a permanent endowment, which is invested to provide only the greatest return. Only the earnings are spent to fund a wide variety of projects for non-profit organizations in the Libby and Troy areas. To date our endowment approaches $200,000 in value and over $25,000 in grants have been disbursed to non-profits in Lincoln County. The Foundation also received $25,000 in Montana Community Foundation Renaissance grants and used funds to provide furnishings and carpet for the City of Libby's Ponderosa Room. Improvement included a dance floor, handicapped door access, commercial dishwasher, table service for 150, a commercial vacuum cleaner, door entry coverings, and large framed photos of the Lincoln County area for the walls. The organization was founded by Carolyn Stamy, who served as chairman until 2003. Of the original 17 member board, four are still with the board. They are: Paula Darko-Hensler (Chairperson), Linda Gerard, Steve Dalby, and Jim Seifert (Secretary-Treasurer). Other board members are Gwenn Hensler, Kerry Munro, Heather McDougall, and Cynthia Kessler. The foundation motto is "Showing we care, today and tomorrow. "The Lincoln County Community Foundation, Inc. is a steward through which private assets entrusted to us by donors are invested to meet the challenges of contemporary life. We are committed to respecting the trust and intent of our donors, while maintaining our integrity and responsiveness as a community foundation."

Lincoln County Community Foundation 2008 grant recipients (left to right): Tyann Hermes for Kootenai ROCKS; Sami Pierson for Lincoln County Public Libraries; Beth Schweitzer for Troy Museum; Vicky Silcox for Kootenai Pets for Life; Maxine Slater for Lincoln County Crisis Solutions; Deb Bond for Lincoln County Youth Soccer Association; Sandy Hauck for U Serve Libby, Inc.; Jim Luscher for Cabinet View Fire Department; Trent Oelberg for Libby Revitalization, Inc.; and Jim Germany for Libby Youth Baseball/Softball Association. Photo courtesy of Kootenai Valley Record.

LINCOLN COUNTY COMBINED CAMPAIGN

Lincoln County Combined Campaign began because of the communities within the county wanted a one-time donation collection for the many groups in the region. As a result, for more than 30 years Combined Campaign has allowed groups to save resources and volunteer time through cooperation in fund-raising. Many groups have participated over the years. Member agencies in 2009 were Lincoln County Foster Parents, Lincoln County Literacy Coalition, Diabetes Support Group, Boy Scouts of America, Girl Scouts, Lincoln County Crime Stoppers, Flathead Valley Chemical Dependency Clinic, Pregnancy Care Center, and Families in Partnership, Inc. Combined Campaign is volunteer staffed and allows residents to support one, some, or all of the member agencies through individual or payroll deductions. Current officers are Lynn Zimmerman, Chairperson; Donna Parrish, Secretary; and Lois Osteen, Treasurer.

CABINET BACKCOUNTRY HORSEMEN

Cabinet Back Country Horsemen (CBCH) is a group of horse enthusiasts dedicated to perpetuate the use of horses in the back country. The club promotes the use of leave no trace in the back country and care of the land for the use of generations to come through education. It gives packing clinics as well as horse care clinics and vaccinations for West Nile virus. The club was formed in 1980 in conjunction with the Back Country Horsemen of Montana. Flathead Back Country Horsemen member Ken Ausk assisted in forming the club. The founding officers were Rocky Schauer, Lloyd Behling, and Geneva Lybyer. Founding Board of Directors were Alex Thompson, Glen Lackrone, and Virgil Dutton. Members included Rick and Linda Brabec, Ed Nixon, and Wayne Haines. The club also works to keep the back country trailheads, unloading ramps and trails cleared. Some of the projects the club has completed are the connection of the Cedar Lakes Trail to the Chase Cut-off Trail in the Cabinet Mountains, the building of corrals for use by the public at historic North Fork Ranger Station in the Yaak, historic East Fork Bull River Ranger Station, and a large fence to enclose the historic Fairview Ranger Station. The largest project completed by the horsemen was the Sheldon Mountain Trail Head camping facility just past the 4-mile marker, off Pipe Creek Road. The area has picnic tables, camp fire rings and braziers, rest rooms, 7 hitching rails, and parking for many horse trailers. The trail is well marked with wooden signs. Water is available for horses nearby from a cistern developed from a spring. An educational trail with a bridge, pack bumpers, and log obstacles was built to train horses for trail use. This project on U.S. Forest Service property was a result of grants from R.A.C and Montana Fish, Wildlife and Parks totaling $28,000. Current CBCH officers are Rick Brabec, President; Leslie McDougall, Secretary; and Jim Mari, Treasurer. Danny Lewis is Chairman of the Board. Presently CBCH has 25 members.

LINCOLN COUNTY REPUBLICAN CLUB

In 1989, a group of citizens met at the Venture Inn Restaurant to form the Lincoln County Republican Club with the express purpose of "emphasizing the great principles that unite us" and electing to office those Republican candidates who uphold the ideals of Abraham Lincoln. Charter members included Mike Powers, Orville Habeck, John and Teddye Beebe, Ed and Martha Jewell, Bob and Sue Kamena, Joe and Charlotte Bluhm, and Linda Gerard. Current club officers are Orville Habeck, Chairman; Alvin Benitz, Treasurer; and Linda Gerard, Secretary. The Club supports the Lincoln County Central Committee (the county's official political organization) with the annual Lincoln-Reagan Day Dinner, helps man the Republican Headquarters during state and federal election years, and informs and educates interested citizens.

LINCOLN COUNTY MONTANA GENEALOGICAL SOCIETY

The local society began in the fall of 2003 with the goal of becoming "a stepping stone to family search." The society also wanted to create a group where enthusiastic genealogists could seek and find individual ancestries together. Charter members included Ruth Taylor, president; Priscilla Pollman, Vice President; Claudine Merrell, secretary; and Charles Peek, treasurer. The group has worked with the Libby Library to acquire and explore the database Heritage Quest, a genealogy database including census and other historically relevant records. Some of the group's projects have included: indexing local newspapers for the library; indexing the 1930 census of various Montana counties for the state genealogical society; and indexing the county's cemeteries. Current projects include indexing, answering inquiries, doing personal records searches, and expanding knowledge by having guest speakers. This year's board of officers are: Ruth Taylor, President; Iva DeShazer, Vice President; Chris Dudly, Secretary; and Charles Peek, Treasurer.

KOOTENAI VALLEY PARTNERS HABITAT FOR HUMANITY

Kootenai Valley Partners Habitat for Humanity began in Libby in 1994. Affiliated with Habitat for Humanity International, the local all volunteer board advertises for, selects, and supports partner families who become proud homeowners. In 2007, the 7th house was built in South Lincoln County. In 2009, house #8 will be constructed near Troy. As is all Habitat affiliates, homes are built with low income families with each family providing "sweat equity" as their down payment. They pay for the home with a mortgage that is interest free. Labor is provided by volunteers in our communities and from our local churches. The major fund raiser for KVP Habitat is the annual Scenic Tour of the Kootenai River. Begun in 1995, STOKR raises funds and local awareness for Habitat for Humanity.

CABINET MOUNTAINS WILDERNESS AREA

The Cabinet Mountains Wilderness is located 15 miles southwest of Libby, Montana. As a designated wilderness area, no motorized access or bicycling in this area. However, horses, hiking, hunting, fishing, and camping are

Heather (from house #7) with Habitat for Humanity construction boss, Don Rigney. Photo courtesy of Habitat for Humanity.

Upper and Lower Cedar Lakes under Dome Mountain, all within the Cabinet Mountain Wilderness. Photo courtesy of Kootenai Avation.

STOKR Riders. Photo courtesy of Kootenai Valley Record.

allowed. Within the wilderness, the Cabinet Mountains range from 8,738 feet on Snowshoe Peak to 3,000 in elevation. Cabinet Mountains Wilderness is a large attraction for hikers and horseback riders and offers ample opportunities to view wildlife in an undisturbed setting.

KOOTENAI NATIONAL FOREST

Kootenai National Forest in Lincoln County offers an abundance of recreational opportunities in all seasons. Spring, summer, and autumn, the National Forest is used for hiking, camping, picnicking, and many other outdoor pass times. Many developed campgrounds and picnic areas can be found in Kootenai National Forest, some with picnic tables, toilets, fire rings, and other amenities. Some areas additionally have fishing access, such as those along Lake Koocanusa. For those who desire to go farther in, Kootenai Nation Forest has over 1,476 miles of hiking trails, some designated as National Recreation Trails. Kootenai National Forest also offers a number of winter sport opportunities. Turner Mountain operates a downhill ski location on forest land by special use permit, allowing Lincoln County residents and visitors ski slope access that is both affordable and close to home. It offers 2,110 vertical feet of runs with a high elevation of 5,952 feet. An average of 250 inches of snow falls at Turner Mountain annually. The 36 miles of groomed cross country ski trails and 162 miles of groomed snowmobile trails also attract winter use to the forest. Within the bounds of Kootenai National Forest, the Forest Service offers many cabins and fire lookouts for overnight rental. A number of private campgrounds and RV areas are also operated on Forest Service land. Kootenai National Forest sites with historical significance have also been documented. These include: sites used by explorers, fur traders, and missionaries; historic agricultural and settlement sites; former forest service sites, including old fire lookouts; and remnants of both logging and mining in the area's history.

OUTDOOR RECREATION

Along with the hiking, camping, and winter sport activities in the Kootenai National Forest, many other opportunities for outdoor recreation abound in Lincoln County. Rock and ice wall climbing is popular along the sheer walls cut away to create many of the county's highways. One popular spot is Stone Hill on Highway. 37 between Libby and Eureka. Water sports are also popular due to the great number of navigable waterways. Canoeing, kayaking, and other boating is popular on Bull Lake, the Thompson Chain of Lakes, and the Kootenai and other large rivers in the county.

NATIONAL BIKE ROUTE

U.S. Highway 2 and Highway. 37 through Eureka are both commonly used long-distance bicycle routes. Hundreds of cross-country bicyclists travel through the area each year. Wide road edges accommodate long-distance bikers and local residents are accustomed to the site of groups or single riders at road's edge. Many bicycle websites and magazines have noted the route, considered the "northern corridor" or "northern tier" of long rides.

STOKR

STOKR stands for Scenic Tour of the Kootenai River. Begun in 1995, STOKR is a bike tour that raises funds and local awareness for Habitat for Humanity. The ride consists of a 98 mile loop from Libby, through Troy and Yaak, and back to Libby down Pipe Creek Road. A shorter, Lake Creek loop is also run, as well as a second day route up Highway 37 to Libby Dam and back. It takes around 300 volunteers to make STOKR a reality each year. In 2009, nearly 300 riders took part in STOKR. Riders come from all over the Northwest and from as far away as Tennessee and Alaska. The ride is so popular that riders participate in a lottery to enter.

SCENIC BYWAYS

In 1992, the Lake Koocanusa Scenic Byway was named in part with the National Scenic Byways Program, the Federal Highway Administration, and the U.S. Department of Transportation. Scenic byways are recognized based on archeological, cultural, historic, natural, recreational, or scenic significance. Lake Koocanusa Scenic Byway follows the Kootenai River from Libby on Montana State Highway 37. It continues along Lake Koocanusa to Eureka. The byway is 67 miles long and it is open year-round.

WILDLIFE IN LINCOLN COUNTY

Flora and fauna of all sorts congregate in the primarily natural areas of Lincoln County. A wide variety of animals, birds, and fish, including bald eagles and golden eagles, are common residents to the county. Osprey, boreal owl, and common loon can also be found in the area. Rare mammals and large predators including grizzly bear, gray wolf, fisher, lynx, wolverine, mountain lion, and badger, also make their homes here, though they are rarely seen. Conversely, large mammals like black bear, moose, elk, and many kinds of deer are common residents often seen within city limits or near homes.

According the the Forest Service, most species of wildlife in Lincoln County are relatively secure given the amount of public land ownership. The Forest Service maintains habitats and makes decisions concerning land management with the many species of animals in mind.

HUNTING & FISHING

Game in Lincoln County is not difficult to come by. Hunting deer, both white-tailed and mule, as well as elk and moose is a popular and economically profitable activity in Lincoln County. Fall seasons for elk and deer are considered somewhat conservative but provide for ample game during hunting periods. It is also possible to hunt bear, mountain lion, moose, bighorn sheep, and many avian varieties in Lincoln County.

Fishing is also plentiful in Lincoln County. Rainbow, brook, brown, and cutthroat trout can all be found in the area. The primary waterway in the county, the Kootenai River, is considered a blue-ribbon trout fishing river. Kokanee salmon can also be found in Lake Koocanusa, behind Libby Dam. Many state records are held by the area. Fishing licenses are available to both Montana and out of state fishermen.

Cody Crace catches a bull trout on Lake Koocanusa. Photo courtesy of Kootenai Valley Record.

Eagle. Photo Courtesy of Libby Dam.

Joe Cox of Libby with a Rainbow Trout caught on the Kootenai River. Photo courtesy of Kootenai Valley Record.

Moose wandering through downtown Libby. Photo courtesy of Kootenai Valley Record.

Mountain Goats near Leigh Lake. Photo courtesy of Kootenai Valley Record.

Bald Eagle. Photo courtesy of For His Glory Photography.

Bighorn sheep. Photo courtesy of Libby Dam.

Lincoln County Fair

The Lincoln County Fair is the official fair for the County and is operated under the auspices of the County Commissioners for the primary purpose of education and encouraging the people of the county to raise better farm and garden products. Although entertainment is provided, the Fair is educational in all its various divisions and provides valuable training for youth and adults alike.

Current Fair Board members:
Chairman: Mike Cole, Eureka
Vice-Chairman: Valerie Hogan, Eureka
Members: Shelley Fisher and Sandra Fulgham, both of Libby
Secretary-Manager: Lynette Starling

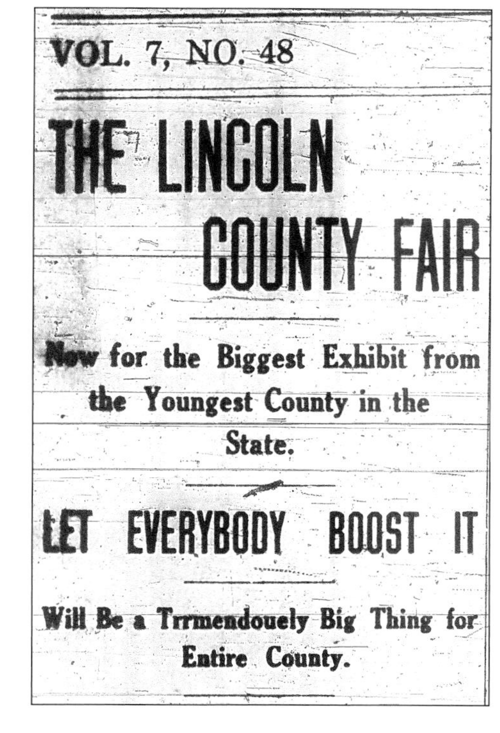

VOL. 7, NO. 48

THE LINCOLN COUNTY FAIR

Now for the Biggest Exhibit from the Youngest County in the State.

LET EVERYBODY BOOST IT

Will Be a Trrmendouely Big Thing for Entire County.

The fairgrounds are located at 900 Osloski Road in Eureka. It consists of approximately 17 acres with a rodeo arena and concession stands, horse barns and arena, an all purpose barn with a small arena, three combination display/events buildings, beef barn, swine, goats, sheep and poultry and rabbit barns. There is also a fish pond and a picnic area with a pavilion, a food court with several vendor-owned cooking and serving facilities, and large lawns used for many activities including community sports programs and camping.

The secretary/manager is the only full time employee, with part time maintenance help hired in the summer. The facility is the location of the annual county fair in August as well as many community events throughout the year. Many wedding receptions, reunions, private or corporate holiday parties, business fairs and/or workshops, and many benefit dinners and auctions for individuals and organizations are hosted there. Annual events besides the fair include the Friends of the NRA banquet in March, Rendezvous quilt show and flea market in April, the Louise Burk Memorial Breast Cancer Awareness luncheon in May, Koocanusa R.I.D.E.S. car show in June, the Tobacco Valley Rodeo in July and Fiberfest Eureka in early August. Also held in conjunction with the fair in August is The Bull Thing, an exclusively bull riding event. Local residents also use the fairgrounds for picnics, dog training classes, horse training and exercises, walking areas, and for weighing and shipping commercial livestock.

The Lincoln County Fair is a four day event held each year in August. It is well attended by residents from the whole county. There is also a large following from our Canadian neighbors and those who live between the border and the town of Fernie are eligible to exhibit in the fair. There are around 150 4-H members, leaders, and their families who end their 4-H year by exhibiting their projects at the fair and, when eligible, selling their market animals at the Livestock auction during the fair. Total judged exhibits which include open class entries as well as 4-H entries average about 1600 and increase each year. It would be impossible to count all of the volunteers who help make the fair a successful event. Division superintendents and assistants, judges, clerks, security, first aid, free entertainment and concerts, kids carnival, arena games, non-profit food vendors, parking attendants, parade directors, show directors, chaperones, booth attendants, and others are always on hand to keep things running smoothly. Community support includes not only donations of time and labor but also of funds for numerous special awards offered for the "best" in many categories and in sponsorships for parts of the event that cannot be supported through budgeted funds as authorized by the County Commissioners. The budget is supplemented with fees charged for usage of the fairgrounds throughout the year and for some fees charged during the fair. Admission is free, although a parking fee is assessed in certain areas.

The Lincoln County Fair originated in 1909, then was discontinued during World War I. A move was made to reestablish it in 1939 when the Tobacco Valley Grange sponsored it with the title of the Tobacco Valley Community Fair. The Grange hosted the fair with the exception again of some years during World War II, until 1960. At that time the title was officially changed back to the Lincoln County Fair and the Fair Board was appointed by the County Commissioners. However, the planning and operation of the fair remained with local Grange members. Scrapbooks have been preserved detailing the work involved and it is interesting to note that in 1965 sixty two Grange members spent 3508 hours planning and conducting the Lincoln County Fair. Today, the fair is operated by the Fair Board appointed by the County Commissioners.

LINCOLN TO EXHIBIT AT MANY FAIRS.

Montana Daily Record: Strawberries eight and one-half inches in circumference will be one feature of the display which Lincoln county will make at the state fair this year, Sept. 26 to Oct. 1.

Secretary Martin has received a letter from P. N. Bernard, secretary of the Eureka Commercial club, outlining the plans for Lincoln county. He writes:

"Lincoln county, the youngest in the state, is making preparations for the state fair, the Flathead county fair, the dry farming congress and the national apple show. You doubtless remember that we took five of J. J. Hill's first prizes at Billings and this fall can do better. Lincoln county is now having her berries processed at Spokane for the Great Northern exhibit car. I sent in strawberries this week that measured eight and one-half inches in circumference, to be processed at Spokane. These will be followed by a full line of all kinds of berries and fruits. We hope to have them on exhibition at the state fair. We want plenty of space and a good location, if possible."

Libby Dam and Lake Koocanusa

Libby Dam spans the Kootenai River seventeen miles upstream from Libby in the heart of beautiful northwestern Montana. The dam was constructed under an international treaty as part of a plan for the development of water resources on the Columbia River Basin. Libby Dam is a multi-purpose dam responsible for flood control, hydropower generation, recreation, fish protection, and wildlife management.

Prior to the building of Libby Dam, flooding during the spring runoff was a regular occurrence. Historically, May and June were months of sandbags and anxiety. Just between 1948 and 1961, there was over $522 million in flood damage. The U.S. Army Corps of Engineers began construction of Libby Dam in 1966, with the completion in 1972. Libby Dam is a straight-axis, concrete gravity structure solidly anchored in bedrock. It was constructed with 7.6 million tons of concrete and holds back the water of the Kootenai River with its own massive weight. The dam is 422 feet tall and 3,055 feet long.

Libby Dam backs the Kootenai River to form Lake Koocanusa which extends 90 miles upstream, making it the seventh largest reservoir in the United States. Forty-two miles of Lake Koocanusa are in British Columbia, Canada. The Kootenai River is also the third largest tributary in the Federal Columbia River Power System, contributing almost 20 percent of the total water in the lower Columbia. Because Libby Dam is the first dam in the system, it is used to store water for use during peak power needs. Water is then recycled making power 15 times on it's way to the Pacific Ocean. The first power went on line August 13, 1975. By March 1976, three more units were put on line and the fifth unit was finished in 1984.

Libby Dam from the air, with Lake Koocanusa behind it. Photo by Melody Condron.

Libby Dam operations must take into account two Biological Opinions for endangered species, Columbia River salmon and steelhead and the Kootenai River white sturgeon and bull trout. Libby Dam also provides funding for the Murray Springs Fish Hatchery located in Eureka, Montana. The Montana Department of Fish, Wildlife, and Parks, manages the hatchery which raises and stocks trout into Lake Koocanusa and many other lakes in the area.

Lake Koocanusa and the Kootenai River offer abundant recreational opportunities in both Canada and the United States. The reservoir has several private marinas and many public boat ramps. Fishing and water sports are popular year-round activities. The Kootenai River has a reputation of being a blue ribbon river for fishing. The eagle web camera is part of the Watchable Wildlife program at Libby Dam, with over 20,000 viewers from around the world annually. Libby Dam Visitor Center offers live views of the eagle camera and takes visitors an interactive journey highlighting the delicate balance of missions at Libby Dam. Free tours of the dam are offered daily during the summer and by appointment year-round.

While the main purpose of Libby Dam is flood control (to control the devastating floods of the Kootenai River and to provide 5.8 million acre feet of storage area), the dam and reservoir also serve the multiple purposes of hydropower, recreation, and environmental stewardship. Frequently, the needs of each of these Project purposes conflict with one another which requires careful balancing to ensure that as many needs as possible are met.

KOOCANUSA MARINA

Koocanusa Resort and Marina is located along Lake Koocanusa, 23 miles north of Libby. On Kootenai National Forest, the marina offers a number of amenities including boat rental, lake side cabins, RV sites, boat launch, store, restaurant, and fishing supplies. Each spring, the marina is host to the Annual Salmon and Trout Derby.

Libby Dam. Photo courtesy of Libby Dam.

Libby, Montana

The City of Libby, Montana was incorporated on November 12, 1909, making 2009 Libby's centennial as well as Lincoln County's. Libby serves as the county seat of Lincoln County and also has the largest population of the four incorporated areas in the county.

The downtown area of Libby was built in close proximity to the Kootenai River and is located 17 miles downstream from Libby Dam. The town also sits at the crossroads of U.S. Highway 2 and Montana State Highway 37. Though much of it is not within the city limits, development continues miles in each direction of the downtown area along a four lane section of Highway 2. The downtown business area stretches from Main Avenue on the west, Mineral Avenue on the east, Highway 2 on the south, and the Burlington Northern railroad tracks on the north.

Currently the City of Libby and the County manage a number of recreational paths and trails at McGrade Elementary, Asa Wood Elementary, Plummer Middle School, Libby High School, City Hall, Pioneer Park, Flower Creek, and J. Neils Memorial County Park. In cooperation with Lincoln County, the City of Libby has a five year goal is to begin to connect the individual trails into one community trail.

Kootenai Business Park, just south of town, is an industrial site with growing potential for industry and manufacturing. In 2003 the 400 acre site, formerly a lumber mill, was donated to the Lincoln County Port Authority by Stimson Lumber Company.

CITY OF LIBBY

The City of Libby manages the following departments within the incorporated area of Libby: building inspection, street maintenance, police, volunteer fire, sewage treatment, and water. City Council additionally has standing committees covering issues of local interest of other management. Libby is served by 21 full time employees, 6 part time employees, 2 temporary employees, and more than 20 volunteers. Seven positions are elected terms.

CURRENT CITY OF LIBBY OFFICERS

Mayor, Doug Roll
Council President, Charlene Leckrone
Councilmember, Bill Bischoff
Councilmember, Lee Bothman
Councilmember, Walt McElmurry
Councilmember, DC Orr
Councilmember, Peggy Williams
City Clerk/Treasurer, Glena L. Hook
Deputy Clerk, Tanya Gehrke
City Supervisor, Dan Thede
City Attorney, Chuck Evans

CITY OF EAGLES

Libby has adopted the title of the "City of Eagles" in response to the many eagle sculptures located in town. The eagles, created by local artist and teacher Todd Berget, are as large as 30′ wide. Three large eagles sit prominently over the Libby Visitor's Center / Chamber of Commerce, the gateway to downtown over Mineral Avenue, and on an island on Highway 2 when entering Libby from the south.

CHAMBER OF COMMERCE

The Libby Chamber of Commerce is an organization of businesses and individuals whose mission is to enthusiastically promote economic and community development through a positive attitude which fosters health, growth, and an improved climate for the greater Libby Area.

Eagle sculpture by Todd Berget over Mineral Avenue's gateway to downtown. Photo courtesy of Kootenai Valley Record.

The Board of Directors for 2009 consists of: Matt Hussey, past President; Cliff Gordon, President; Tami Holzer, Vice President; Bob Castaneda, Treasurer; Lisa Johnson, Secretary; Roxanne Escudaro; Allen Woods; Alana Mesenbrink; and Leslie Forester. Dusti Thompson serves as Executive Director. The Chamber, which also serves as a Visitor's Center, has 270 active members, one full time employee, and one part time employee. The Chamber brings the PRCA Kootenai River Rodeo to Libby each year, and partners with many other groups to bring events and opportunities to the area.

LIBBY MAIN STREET

Libby Main Street is a nonprofit community improvement organization that has adopted the Main Street Program, a comprehensive revitalization program designed to promote the historic and economic redevelopment of traditional business districts. In Libby, this district encompasses Mineral and California Avenues north of Highway 2. The organization's mission is to help plan and direct activities to preserve, develop, and enhance the economic, social, and cultural quality of life in the Libby area, specifically downtown. One of Libby Main Street's most recent projects is the Streetscape Project, including new lampposts and sidewalks along Mineral Avenue, among other improvements.

ASBESTOS & THE EPA

A vermiculite mine was owned and operated by W. R. Grace Company near Libby from 1963 until its closure in 1990. In 1999, the mine was blamed for dozens of asbestos-related deaths and illnesses among Libby residents and former employees due to exposure to asbestos-tainted vermiculite. The Environmental Protection Agency (EPA) was called in and Libby was added to EPA's National Priorities List in October 2002. EPA then established a program to inspect all properties in Libby for asbestos. At that time, EPA estimated that 1,200-1,400 residential and business properties needed some type of cleanup. The local economy has been helped significantly by the cleanup of asbestos in the area. However, news coverage of the asbestos cleanup and, in 2009, the criminal case brought against W.R. Grace have resulted in negative attention for the Libby community.

FLATHEAD ELECTRIC

Flathead Electric Co-op, Inc. provides electrical service to the Libby area. Flathead has been in operation since 1938, with main offices in Kalispell. It is the second largest electric utility in Montana, servicing Libby, the Flathead Valley, and much of the Montana-Wyoming border.

DAVID THOMPSON SEARCH & RESCUE

David Thompson Search and Rescue was organized in 1969 after a search for two young girls in the Ross Creek Cedars area of Lincoln County. Those who took part in the search recognized the need for an organized group that could be called up at anytime to conduct searches. This group was the start of what is now David Thompson Search and Rescue. The organization has grown in members, equipment, and skills. It continues to grow as needs and funding are identified. The organization has been called upon from its start up in 1969 until now to respond to a variety of rescues and situations.

Area agencies including David Thompson Search and Rescue train for bringing a litter down the face . Photo courtesy of Kootenai Valley Record.

VOLUNTEER FIRE

The City of Libby Volunteer Fire Department and Lincoln County Rural Fire Districts provide code management, fire protection, and prevention to residents in and around Libby. The department operates from one station, located on 6th Street between Mineral and Montana Avenues. The department operates with three class A engines, three water tenders, one 4x4 wild land engine, a utility van, hose/boom truck combination and a 1500 GPM trash pump. Thirty volunteers make up the volunteer fire service. Tom Wood is the current Chief, with Assistant Chiefs Bill Watt and Curt Jones. Jason Place is Fire Investigator and Bill Watt is Fire Marshall.

RAIL & AIR

Libby is home to both a small airport and an Amtrak rail station. The Libby Airport offers charter service, flight school, rental aircraft, and scenic flights with Kootenai Aviation. Libby's Amtrak station serves travelers once daily in each direction (east and west) on the Empire Builder line.

Mineral Avenue in downtown Libby. Photo by Melody Condron.

KVRZ 88.9 supporters David Friedman, Leo Marnell, John Herrmann, Brian Sherry, Glenn Garrison, Ralph Stever, Dan Taasevigen, Rick Vogel, Julia Cozzi, Glen Gill, Moira Blazi, Burton Stoltz, Susan Sandahl, and Terry Walen. Photo courtesy of Kootenai Valley Record.

RADIO MEDIA

Libby radio station KJRZ 105.3 provides entertainment as well as information to the Libby area. Segments like "What the heck is going on?" and community interviews make the radio station an important asset in Libby communications. Jim Miles is Director of Operations for the station. Other contributors include: Jim Nelson, Music Director; Keith Meyers, Public Affairs Director; Wendy Martin, On-Air Personality; and Miranda Raab, On-Air Personality. KLCB 1230-KTNY 101.7 has been an active radio station in Libby for 59 years. Popular segments including Libby Logger Sports updates and KLCB Swapshop make the station popular. In addition, radio personality Duane J. Williams interviews guests to keep the public informed of upcoming events.

The newest area radio station, KVRZ started providing radio service to Libby, Troy, and areas of Bonners Ferry, ID in 2008. Live shows include Moira's Kootenai Talks and John Herrmann's Jazz Hour. As a nonprofit community radio station, KVRZ has developed many organizational sponsors in order to get the station started.

PRINT NEWS

Libby has three local newspapers, each serving Libby and the Kootenai Valley into Troy. The *Kootenai Valley Record*, located in the Printing Press print shop on Mineral Avenue, publishes weekly every Monday. The *Montanian*, located at 312 Mineral Avenue, publishes weekly every Wednesday. The *Western News*, located at 311 California Avenue, published twice weekly each Wednesday and Friday.

FINANCIAL INSTITUTIONS

There are four financial institutions to choose from in Libby. All are very active in the community and provide services that meet the needs of Libby residents. They are: First National Bank of Montana; Lincoln County Credit Union; Glacier Bank; Kootenai Valley Credit Union; and US Bank.

A Historic Timeline of Libby

by Mark J. White

1801-1803 - Le Blanc and La Gasse, traders for the Northwest Fur Company, winter in the Kootenai in the Tobacco Plains Country. They are the first recorded non-native Americans in the Kootenai. They are later killed by the Kootenai Indians due to a misunderstanding.

1808 - On May 05, David Thompson comments on the area that would later be the site of the present day Libby, Montana in his journal: "fine Woods everywhere for Building & fine low Points, but the Country in every other respect forbids any Settlement/hereabouts at the last Rivulet [Libby Creek] of 15 yards across on the left both Sides of the River/have extensive low lands, between the Mountains, seemingly swampy & more extensive on the left than on the right, latter part of the day, the /River quite Rocky & Hills dreary."

1808-1809 - During the winter, Finan McDonald constructs a trading post on the north side of the Kootenai River, across from the later site of Libby. The Northwest Fur Company begins trading with Native Americans at this place of business, which was the first of its kind in northwest Montana.

1821 - The Hudson Bay Company and North West Company merge as the Hudson Bay Company.

1821-1839 - Hudson Bay Company intermittently operates the seasonal 'Fort Kootenai' near the Big Bend of the Kootenai River and the Fisher River.

1839-1859 - Fort Kootenai is moved into the Tobacco Plains and operates south border of the British Possessions (Canada) until the 1860s when it moves north of the line.

1845 - During the summer, Father Pierre De Smet passes by what would later be Libby.

1859 - On October 11-12, the Palliser expedition, consisting of John Palliser, James Hector, and Thomas Blakiston, passes by the Libby area. This British expedition explored the Kootenai River area.

1864-1865 - Wild Horse Gold Rush occurs in British Columbia. Most miners use the Moyie River Wild Horse Trail, while others use a trail on the north bank of the Kootenai River to Wild Horse. A ferry is established near the later site of Jennings by Ed Warren but it is abandoned within a year due to miners preference of the Moyie Trail route.

1867 - In August, a party of twelve miners working on Libby Creek during the summer discover gold. Four of the miners are sent to Spokane Bridge for supplies. On their return three are killed by Kootenai Indians near the mouth of Libby Creek on August 14, 1867. Joseph Herring survives a shoulder wound for 23 days until discovered. One of the miners killed, Stephan Allen, names Libby Creek after his daughter Elizabeth or 'Libby' Allen.

1867-1868 - By September, 500-600 miners are working on Libby Creek. By 1868, the 'Discovery' mining camp has been renamed Libbysville and a voting precinct by that name is established for Missoula County. The numbers of miners begins to decrease after the initial rush because the placers are not as rich as originally anticipated. The mining camp was the ancestor of the present town of Libby.

1868-1869 - The July 31, 1868 edition of the Montana Post (Vol. 4. No. 43) reports that 100 miners are at work on Libby Creek averaging 6 to 8 dollars a day to the hand. The mining camp is called Libbysville. The Libbysville election precinct of Missoula County is created on June 13, 1868 but is discontinued on May 4, 1869.

1871 - The Libby Creek Voting Precinct of Missoula county is created on August 7, with the election to be held at Luke Nolan's house. John Fisher (who the Fisher River is named after) and Thomas Kelly are appointed judges.

1871 - On August 1, Libby Creek Election Precinct is discontinued.

1876 - Placer mining activity comes to a temporary end on Libby Creek but John Fisher continues to prospect on the creek to this time.

1885 - Thomas Shearer finds gold on Libby Creek. On his return to the Thompson Falls area he interests other miners to head back to Libby Creek. A small rush ensues. A miners' meeting is held on Libby Creek on September 15, naming the Libby Mining District.

1887 - Lake City (not to be confused with Lake City later established at the mouth of Lake Creek near Troy) or "Old Town" is established below the mouth of Ramsey Creek. The Thompson Falls to Libby Creek Trail is constructed up the Vermilion River, through Silver Butte and the West Fisher to Libby Creek.

1887 - Chinese miners are allowed to lease placer mining claims in the area. John Leigh locates quartz claims on Leigh Creek.

1887 - Robert Rennie begins prospecting the creek which would bear the misspelling of his name, Rainy Creek.

1889 - In this spring, Mrs. Planina E. Field comes to Libby Creek to live with her husband at Shaunnessy Hill. She is the only woman in the Libby Placer Camp.

1889 - In August, a forest fire starts from locomotive sparks. The August 14, edition of the *Missoulian* says of the fires: "They were the worst on Vermillion, Lyons, and Libby Creeks and also extended to Granite Creek, and in all of these localities it was necessary to drive out the livestock. The flames leaped over the Clarkes Fork in a twinkling, and often when dry timber was struck the flames would reach a height of over 100 feet."

1889 - In October, the Snowshoe Mine is located by A.F. Dunlap and J. Abbot. The mine becomes a major silver and lead producer for the Libby area during the late 1890s and operates intermittently until 1964. Production for the mine totaled 145,000 tons of ore valued at $1,211,000.

1890 - In November, Thomas Bryant's sluice boxes are robbed and a Chinamen is blamed. A miners meeting is held and all Chinese in the Libby Mining District are ordered out of the area.

1891 - Miners move to the mouth of Libby Creek and establish ranches in anticipation of the construction of the Great Northern Railroad and possible compensation for right of way through these lands. Ed Traner is the first white child born at Old Town at the site of the sawmill. He dies of tuberculosis in Hunter, B.C. in August of 1911 according to the August 31 *Western News*. Old Town begins to move after the Great Northern depot is located further west. The original site of the town consisted of approximately 50 rough buildings in about the location of the old sawmill log pond. The old town buildings were washed away in the flood of 1896.

1891 - On September 18, a post office is established at Old Town at what would later be the Libby mill. Robert Cantwell was postmaster.

1891-1892 - The Great Northern Railroad is built into the area and during the winter of of 1891-1892, the Libby Townsite Company brings in the first sawmill. It is used to cut timber to build Libby in its present location.

1892 - On May 3, the first train arrives at Libby Creek on the Great Northern Railroad.

1892 - On June 8, Missoula School District 63 is created. The area of the school district starts from the confluence of Rainy Creek and

Kootenai River, west to Pipe Creek, to the mountains dividing Lake Summit, to the range dividing Fisher and Libby Creeks.

1892-1893 - The earliest paper to publish in Libby is the *Libby Miner*. The editors of the newspaper were Edwin S. Doyle and John W. Pace. The first edition is published on October 09, 1892. The sole surviving edition is Volume 1, Number 07 dated November 19, 1892. The November 3, 1893, edition of the Kalispell Interlake notes the following on the demise of the *Libby Miner*: "The Libby Miner has proved to be a dismal failure. Deputy Sheriff McFarrin attached the plant yesterday for the sum of $376.95 the amount due Marder, Luse and Co. Editor Doyle it seems could not gather the wherewith and was obliged to succumb to the inevitable."

1893-1895 - Repeal of the Sherman Silver Purchase act leads to the collapse of the silver mining industry in Montana. A financial panic ensues. Libby is hard hit as it is a silver mining camp and financial panic leaves most of the people in town unemployed. The population turns to hunting deer for hide. Hundreds of deer hides were shipped out of Libby and Troy during this period with deer carcasses left to rot. Rod and Gun clubs around the United States protest and more stringent laws are enacted.

1895 - The *Silver Standard* newspaper begins publishing in Libby with the first edition coming out on July 13. The newspaper was out of existence in the same year.

1895 - The Chicago and Montana Mining Company purchases Snowshoe Mine and begins developing the mine.

1896 - On May 11, Libby Rod and Gun Club formed. W.A. Hillis-President, J.T. Hillis-Vice President, and D.P. Boyle-Treasurer.

1897 - The *Montanian* (formerly the *Thompson Falls Montanian*) moves to Libby in May of 1897. D.A. Hendricks is editor of the newspaper. This paper was published in Libby until 1903.

1898 - Pacific Northwest Mining Company, an English syndicate, purchases Snowshoe Mine and continues development.

1899 - A large sawmill is built on Flower Creek by the Pacific Northwest Mining Company. A pole road is built to Parmenter Creek and logs brought to the mill via horse drawn wagons with flanged wheels. It is the first large mill established at Libby.

1901 - The Pacific Northwest Mining Company sawmill is closed in March. The mill is disassembled and sawmill machinery is shipped out of the area.

1901 - On December 18, the first Kootenai Reserve is established by the U.S. Geological Survey and temporarily withdrawn and held under the Department of the Interior. The withdrawal is in effect until 1905.

1903 - The Bonners Ferry Lumber Company logs along the Kootenai River and sends the logs down to their mill in Bonners Ferry, Idaho. The first drive is not very successful due to logging crews' inexperience on the river; many logs are not recovered until the drive of 1904.

1904 - On May 29, Libby Creek is renamed Libby by the Great Northern Railroad. The town of Libby was already recognized by the government and the U.S. Post Office but the Great Northern called the place "Libby Creek" from 1892 to 1904.

1904 - The Bonners Ferry Lumber Company utilizes contractors to cut saw logs along the Kootenai River and purchases much of their timber from homesteads there.

1906 - Construction of the Dawson Lumber Company sawmill begins. This is the first successful sawmill to operate in the Libby vicinity. Railroad logging begins in the area in 1907 with the construction of a logging railroad along Libby Creek. Julius Neils and Weyerhauser interests busily acquire timberlands in the area at about the same time.

1909 - On September 7, Libby becomes an incorporated town. The first town council is held on November 12 at Plummer Hall. E.W. Doe becomes the first mayor of Libby.

1910 - In August, major forest fires burn many acres of the Kootenai including the West Fisher and upper Libby Creek drainages.

1911 - On July 1, Libby becomes the permanent county seat.

1911 - In February, the Libby Lumber Company acquires the Dawson logging operations. The J. Neils Lumber Company are partners in the venture with Thomas Shevlin, Sr.

1915 - Due to disagreements in management of logging operations, the assets of the Libby Lumber Company are divided among the shareholders and Julius Neils separated his company's interests from the Libby Lumber Company.

1919 - On January 1, J. Neils Lumber Company reacquires most of the assets of the Libby Lumber Company owned by the Shevlin interests.

1915 - Edward Noah Alley discovers the properties of vermiculite in an old mining adit on Rainy Creek. A lighted candle causes the material to expand on the tunnel wall.

1923 - Mining of zonolite (vermiculite) begins on Zonolite Mountain.

1920-1929 - A timber recession affects Montana's sawmills. Brooks-Scanlon closes at Eureka putting local economy in Eureka into downturn. Small portable sawmills then operate in the area. Baird and Harper mill closes at Warland in 1926. Sandpoint Lumber and Pole Company closes down in Troy in 1928. J. Neils Lumber Company is the sole large mill to survive in Lincoln County.

1930-1932 - J. Neils Lumber Company operates during lean times, keeping employees working half-time.

1957 - St. Regis Timber Company acquires the J. Neils Lumber Company mill and lands in Libby.

1962 - In September, St. Regis opens a new plywood plant at the sawmill in Libby.

1963 - W.R. Grace purchases Zonolite Mine and becomes an important employer. The material mined is called vermiculite.

1983 - Rupert Murdoch attempts a hostile takeover of the St. Regis Company but fails. St. Regis is acquired by Champion International. Rapid harvest of timber lands takes place and a 50 year rotational cycle of timber is liquidated prior to 1993.

1990 - W.R. Grace closes the Rainy Creek mining operations.

1993 - Champion divests itself of its Libby holdings by selling timberlands to Plum Creek Timber and selling the mill to Stimson Lumber Company. A ten year timber contract is made between Plum Creek and Stimson with timber being provided to the Stimson operations in Libby. The mill now has no timberlands.

2002 - On October 28, Stimson Lumber announces the closure of its plywood plant in Libby, putting 300 employees out of work. Only a 20 man finger joining operation remains. Libby is now without a large operating mill for the first time since 1906. The plywood plant closes after December 20.

2003-2004 - Plum Creek begins actively selling former timber lands of the earlier Libby Lumber Company, J. Neils Lumber Company, St. Regis, Champion International for subdivision development.

2008 - On September 10, the Stimson fingerjointer at the old Libby sawmill site runs it last shift. The last remnant of the former Libby mill operations from 1906 to 2002 is closed.

2008 - In November, Doug Roll is appointed Mayor when previous Mayor, Tony Berget, is elected County Commissioner to District 1.

Libby Medical

ST JOHN'S LUTHERAN HOSPITAL

St. John's Lutheran Hospital has proudly served the citizens of Lincoln County for the past 56 years. The current hospital, a 25-bed, critical access hospital, was built in 1952 at the behest of the community. Founded as a non-profit organization, which continues to this day, St. John's is devoted to providing quality healthcare to all, regardless of their circumstances. Because of the changing demands and needs of the community, St. John's has continued to evolve and develop since its creation. The Hospital has been expanded or remodeled three times since being built in order to improve the existing facilities and provide more modern care to Lincoln County. Currently, the hospital maintains continuously staffed facilities of 30 active or consulting physicians, visiting specialists, and out-patient services. A plan is additionally underway for a new hospital.

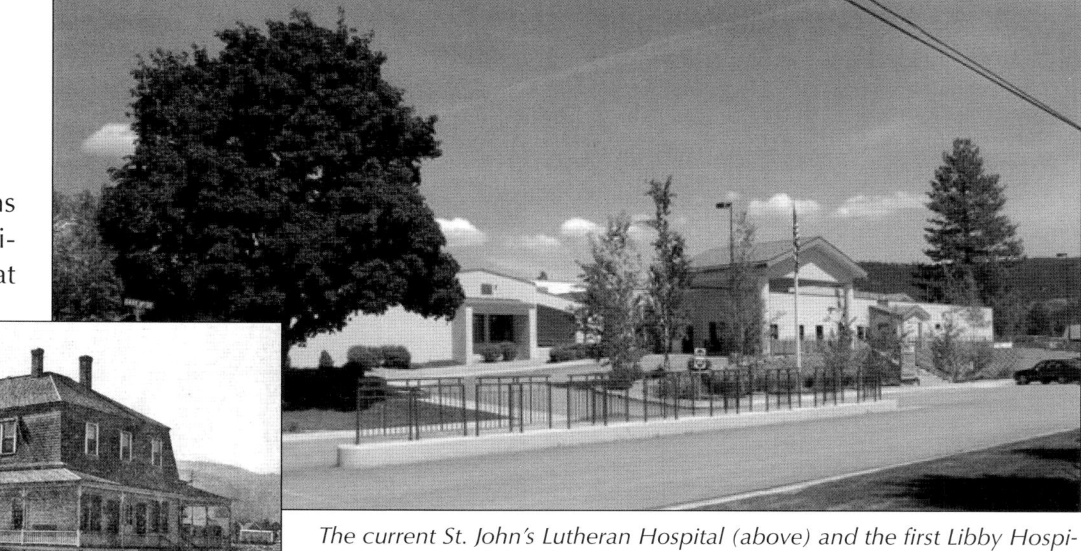

The current St. John's Lutheran Hospital (above) and the first Libby Hospital, circa 1925 (left). Photos courtesy of St. John's Lutheran Hospital.

In addition to serving the community medically, St. John's is an anchor employer, the largest private employer in the county. The Hospital also contributes to community growth and development by sponsoring community events and activities such as the Annual Health Fair, Cancer Support Groups, and annual discounted health screenings.

Jan Kendall, St. John's Lutheran Hospital Auxiliary President, hands KC Hoyer a check for $1,000 toward the Digital Mammography campaign. Photo courtesy of Kootenai Valley Record.

ST. JOHN'S HOSPITAL AUXILIARY

St. John's Hospital Auxiliary is an altruistic working organization. The main purpose of the organization is to support the hospital with monetary donations for specific equipment needs and to supply time and energy for services at the hospital. The auxiliary runs a gift shop, works in various areas of the hospital, and has purchased over $28,000 worth of equipment during 2008/2009. They purchased the first mammogram machine for St. John's with no monetary help from other sources. Fundraisers for the auxiliary include Nordicfest Swedish Meatballs, Annual Spring Style Show, Festival of Trees bakesale, chili feed, and rummage sales. Current officers for the auxiliary are Janet Kendall, President; Bev Swing and Judy Perry, Co-Vice Presidents; Lis Osteen, Treasurer; and Sandy Nelson, Secretary. There are currently 49 members.

St. John's Annual Health Fair at the Libby Memorial Center. Photo courtesy of Kootenai Valley Record.

VOLUNTEER AMBULANCE

Libby Volunteer Ambulance is a non-profit, volunteer-manned service. Six vehicles are located in the new ambulance building, built in 2008.

Libby Schools

LIBBY SCHOOL DISTRICT

Libby School District is made up of Libby Senior High School, Libby Middle School, Asa Wood Elementary, Central Alternative School, Plummer Center, and the District Offices. Enrollment for the 2008-2009 school year for students Pre-K to High School was 1,272. The District employs 99 certified instructors, 60 classified instructors, and 8 administrators. In addition, many parents and volunteers are involved in the schools. For Elementary and secondary students, the District offers a complete course of study reflecting current research on effective curriculum and instruction. Libby Senior High School requires 23 credits to graduate under a General Diploma, and 25 credits under a College Prep Diploma, as compared to 20 credits required by the State Board of Public Education. When earning a College Preparatory Diploma, the student completes a demanding academic schedule in preparation for college admission. High school students can receive duel credit for college classes. High School sports are popularly attended and participated in and the Libby Loggers are represented in football, volleyball, tennis, and more. It is possible for Libby students to earn a one year Vocational Certificate or a two year Associates of Arts Degree while in high school. Central School offers classes in an educational setting that adapts various methods for those students who learn differently from students in the traditional school environment. Approximately 35-50 students attend the Central School. Currently, Plummer Center is used by Kootenai Valley Head Start.

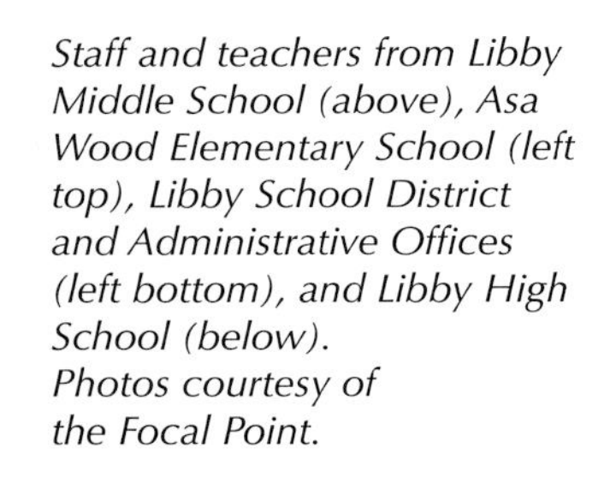

Staff and teachers from Libby Middle School (above), Asa Wood Elementary School (left top), Libby School District and Administrative Offices (left bottom), and Libby High School (below). Photos courtesy of the Focal Point.

KOOTENAI VALLEY CHRISTIAN SCHOOL

Kootenai Valley Christian School is founded to provide an inter-denominational Christian center for academic excellence, to provide a community to model godly lives and principles for the students, to assist the families and churches in challenging the students to grow and mature into Christ-centered people. Enrollment consists of grades from Pre-School up through High School. For the academic year 2007-2008, enrollment was 116 students, with 10 full time and 6 part time staff members and a wealth of volunteers.

FLATHEAD VALLEY COMMUNITY COLLEGE

The Lincoln County Campus of Flathead Valley Community College provides students with opportunities to start an undergraduate degree, earn a technical degree, retrain for a new profession, or explore personal interests through non-credit courses. The Libby campus includes: art, computer, and science labs; Glacier Bank Adult Basic Education Learning Center; and two state-of-the-art interactive teleconferencing labs. Patrick Pezzelle is the Director of the Lincoln County Campus.

Libby Churches

ASSEMBLY OF GOD

Assembly of God was founded in 1936 by Richard Philp and Fred Dalton. Current leadership includes Senior Pastor Kevin Lindgren, Youth Pastor Dave Ginther, and Children's Pastor Bob Vande Sandt. Current attendance is about 175 people, including children. Church activities include ministry to all ages. The church's vision is to share Christ's love with the greater community of Libby.

CHURCH OF JESUS CHRIST OF LATTER DAY SAINTS

Church of Jesus Christ of Latter Day Saints in Libby was first organized in 1950 by LDS Missionaries. Early on, the congregation met in the community room located in the basement of the old Library. At that time there were 15 members. Construction of a building on Highway 2 south started in 1961. The completed structure, finished in 1985, includes gym, chapel, classrooms, kitchen, library, and family history center. The congregation raised money for the building with book sales, smorgasbord dinners, and fundraisers at Logger Days. One fundraiser called for the use of the World's largest frying pan, now on display in the Heritage Museum. The Libby LDS Church has also committed to many community projects, including: Habitat for Humanity; Family History Library; and Boy Scout Troop 70. The church has also hosted a number of preparedness seminars over the years, teaching people about safety, first aid, food storage, financial planning, and how to store and dry foods. They have additionally hosted many bazaars featuring handmade quilts, afghans, and baked items. Many of our young men and a women have served two year missions all over the country and in many foreign lands at their own expense. In addition, some of the elderly patrons of the church have previously served in this way. Current membership exceeds 400.

FIRST BAPTIST CHURCH

First Baptist of Libby was founded by pastor Matthew Thornycroft who served from November 11, 1965 to May 1970. Early services were held at the Moose Hall. Merle Milner became pastor in June of 1970. Soon after, in 1972, construction was started on a permanent building. Pastors serving since that time were David Anderson (1978-1982), Michael McLaughlin (1982-1985), Robert Roberts (1985-1987), and Robert Noller (1987-2002). In 1987, the property for the church was completely paid for and is now owned outright by the congregation. Current pastor is Joseph Slaughter. He and his wife, Brenda, have been with the congregation since 2002. Current membership is 16.

FAITH BIBLE CHURCH

The goal of Faith Bible Church is to be a Christ-centered Bible-teaching church whose mission is exalting Jesus Christ, evangelizing and discipling people in service for Him, and connecting with each other. The church was founded as an independent Bible church in 1955 by Louis and Nora May Auge, Ernie and Ethyl Hamilton, Clarence and Irene Kutz, and Albert and Lois Oursland. In 1979, the church joined the Evangelical Free Churches of America denomination. The current pastor is Laurie Stuck who came to the congregation in February of 2007. The church offers Sunday worship services, Sunday school, and Wednesday night Awana Clubs for ages on Wednesday and other small groups meet together throughout the week. The church is located at 239 Education Way.

FIRST CHURCH OF THE NAZARENE

First Church of the Nazarene was founded in May 25,1952. The current Pastor is Donald L. Moore who has been a senior pastor for over 30 years. The church has five employees and membership is 113. The church plans a number of events, including Vacation Bible School for children each summer, special functions for Easter and Christmas, "a truly dynamic Ladies Bible Study," Roundup Barbecue coinciding with the Libby Rodeo, and "A Brotherhood of Men" men's ministry.

OTHER ACTIVE CHURCHES IN THE LIBBY AREA

Christ Lutheran Church ELCA
Church of Christ
Church of God
Family Baptist Church
Family Worship Center
First Presbyterian Church
Jehovah's Witnesses Kingdom Hall
Kootenai Valley Church
St. John's Christ Lutheran Church LCMS
St. Joseph Catholic Church
St. Luke's Episcopal Church
United Methodist Church

ST. JOSEPH'S COUNCIL OF CATHOLIC WOMEN

The first organized group of Catholic women met between 1902 and 1905 formed from the dozen or so Catholic families in the area. Their purpose was to provide religious education for the children, help needy families with bundles of clothing, and host socials and fundraisers. They were known as the Ladies of the Catholic Sunday School. In September 1906 the "06 Club" replaced the Ladies of the Catholic Sunday School to raise money for church needs and for the construction of the first Catholic Church, built in 1910 by Frank Pival. The 06 Club was the forerunner to the Alter Society when the women began taking care of the altar linens and cleaning the church and rectory. The Altar Society evolved into the Catholic Women's Club; it was present when the current parish hall was built in 1951. In the 1960s the Catholic Women's Club joined the National Council of Catholic Women (CCW). Father Jozef Perahubka, originally from Poland, who has been pastor of St. Joseph's and of the Immaculate Conception mission in Troy has been a great proponent of the Council of Catholic Women.

Community service has included: "baby shower for infant Jesus" to benefit the Pregnancy Care Center; Catholic Relief Service *Water for Life* to help victims of natural disasters; baking for Red Cross Blood Drives and STOKR; and offering community meals once a month. The women also organize the annual parish Fat Tuesday, Fall Harvest Dinner, Christmas Bazaar, and many receptions and funeral luncheons. Current officers are: Ricki Yeager, President; Rhea Bernardy, Vice President; Sandy Romey, Secretary; and Marge Kroeger, Treasurer. There are about 12 active members and 45-50 volunteers.

Libby Groups & Organizations

AUSTIN REEDY AMERICAN LEGION POST 97

The Austin Reedy American Legion Post #97 was organized on October 25, 1920. The charter members were Vernon Crotteau, Cecil C. Gompf, Irving E. Adams, John H. Koehler, Harold W. Miller, Graham Fletcher, Vern Fairbanks, Erford E. Jaqueth, R.C. Ellis, R.M. Griffin, F.W. DeLapp, F.M. Cowell, Joe Sheffield, Ray Siegmund, Hugo Peters, and R.C. Elton. Current officers include: Don Auger, Commander; Larry Kind, Vice-Commander; Larry Stroklund, Adjutant/ Finance Officer; Ray Dedic, Sergeant-at-Arms; Bernadette Breeden, Historian; Harold Cole, Chaplain/Service Officer; and Richard Darsow, Public Relations Officer. Trustees are Joe Kelly, Jim Wardensky, and Richard Darsow and current membership is 240.

Post involvement in the community has included: providing the color guard for all Libby parades; providing military funeral honors for all veterans in south Lincoln County that request it; maintaining highway fatality makers (white crosses) in Lincoln County; providing a van and drivers to transport veterans to the VA Medical Center in Spokane; sponsoring Boy Scout and Cub Scout units; sponsoring an American Legion Baseball team; sponsoring American Legion Boys State and Girls State delegates; providing an American Legion Libby High School college scholarship; sponsoring the American Legion Oratory contest; organizing Yellow Ribbon, Blue Banner, and 9/11 events; and providing Memorial Day and Veterans Day ceremonies at the Libby Cemetery. The Post also provides a local American Legion club, Sons of the American Legion Organization, and Women's Auxiliary to the Libby Community.

COMMUNITY THRIFT

Libby Community Thrift was organized in the late 1960s to organize to raise money for the community through a donation thrift store. In 2008, donations totalling $10,236 were presented to 16 area organizations. In addition, volunteers have participated in the Festival of Trees and have created floats for the Nordicfest parade. Current leadership includes: Roberta Taylor, President; Anita Short, Vice President; Yuki Warnell, Secretary; and Martha Smith, Treasurer. Board members are Marlene Nelson, Joan Clough, and Linda Schikora.

Community Thrift presentas a donation to St. John's Lutheran Hospital. Photo courtesy of Kootenai Valley Record.

FOOD PANTRY, INC.

The Libby Food Pantry was founded on June 28, 1982. The founding Board of Directors were Mark G. Payne, Laura Endicott, Helen Coverdell, Wanda Beaudoin, and Penny Robbe. The current Board of Directors are: Charles Woods, President; Mervin Fenimore, Vice President; Kathy Lauer, Treasurer/Coordinator; Larry Hebenstreit, Secretary; Chloe Adamson, Director; Joyce Lelm, Director; and Syneva Pitman, Director. Libby Food Pantry is an all-volunteer organization and currently has 28 members. The pantry served 3,332 people in 2008 and expects to serve more in 2009.

GIRL SCOUTS

Libby Girl Scouts has been active for over 80 years. There have been anywhere from two troops at a low point to twenty-two troops during the Libby Dam-building years. Girls from kindergarten through high school are able to join this international organization. The Libby Service Unit is made up of Troop leaders who work directly with the girls. There were four active troops in Libby during the 2008-2009 school year and girls aged 5 to 15 participated.

KOOTENAI VALLEY QUILT GUILD

Kootenai Valley Quilt Guild was founded January 1987. The guild started with 22 members and now has approximately 50. Current leadership for the Kootenai Valley Quilt Guild includes: Cindy Peek, President; Karen Hutchinson, Vice President; Devi McCully, Treasurer; and Renee Grotjohn, Secretary. Every year the guild provides comfort to those that have lost their homes to a fire by providing them with a quilt. The guild holds an annual quilt show at Nordic Fest in September, where a drawing for one of the guild member's quilts raises money for the organization. The guild has also provided quilts for the Pregnancy Care Center and lap quilts to the Libby Care Center for residents in wheelchairs. Teaching is also part of the organization, and guild members offer quilting classes most months of the year. In the autumn, members travel to the Spokane Quilt Show for educational purposes and to envision new projects. Other community services include: two scholarships given each year to quilting-minded students; adopting a magazine for the library every year; cash donation to the Heritage Museum; and displaying quilts at the Heritage Museum each summer.

IGNITERS CAR CLUB

The Ignitors Car Club was founded in 1961 by a group of eighteen-year olds. It is the oldest car club in Montana and the tenth oldest active club in the country. Originally, meetings were held behind the *Western News* building. The founding group held dances at the old Moose Lodge to raise money for the current building. George Enders donated an acre of land on Hogan Drive where the building now resides.

The club started holding car shows in the early 1980s and as few as a dozen cars attended. The first few shows were less than fifty cars and required a lot of leg work in getting business' support to park. In the mid-nineties, Grace Rantala became the first woman to hold office in the club, first as Vice President, then as President. During that time, membership went from a few dozen to over a hundred. Igniters provides service to the community in many ways, including: helping four other cities form their own clubs, holding fundraisers to benefit the Food Pantry, Care Center, and adopted families during the holidays; donating child car seats and child booster seats to several families; and, during Gary Rantala's term as President, offering the Humanitarian Award. The club has also contributed to other projects. Steve Curl donated a 1957 Nash to make a tribute to Bart Teske. Marge Kroeger, Gary Rantala, Todd Berget, Jim Reigh, Eric Wilson, Bert Wilson and others helped to fix the car and post it on top of a pole at the drive-in. "Bart the Car" is set at an angle to look like car on the TV show *Third Rock from the Sun*. Club members participate in fixing up "lost cause" and difficult car projects, attending out-of-town shows, cruising, having potluck at the club house, and holding dances throughout the year.

LIBBY DAM GOOD SAM CHAPTER

The Libby Dam Good Sam Chapter is a group of campers and travelers who caravan together to places of interest. First organized in 1976, the founders of the group were Mr. and Mrs. Roy Cook, Leroy and Betty Baker, Irving and Myrna Balls, and Ivan Williams. The first elected president was "Pop" Stewart. Service to the community has included: keeping highways clear of trash; collecting aluminum can tabs for organizations including Ronald McDonald House, Search and Rescue, Ruth Baenen Memorial, and Libby Care Center; and hosting a Fireman's Park Picnic for disabled achievers.

LIBBY ROD & GUN CLUB / LIBBY SCATTERGUNS

The Libby Rod and Gun Club is a storied organization that is more than 100 years old. A shooting range for members is located near the airport in Libby on Farm to Market Road. As a committee, the scatterguns operate under the constitution and by-laws of the Rod and Gun Club. The committee provides shotgun shooting sports such as Trap, Skeet, and Sporting Clay. All labor provided for construction and improvements at the club is made possible by volunteers and capital for construction materials was provided through various grants such as the Friends of the NRA and Montana Fish, Wildlife and Parks.

MASONIC LODGE #85 AF & AM

Libby Masonic Lodge #85 is located at 1218 Utah Avenue in Libby. The Lodge was organized in 1911 and received its charter on September 19, 1912. D. Nelson Bland is the current Worshipful Master of the Lodge (2008-2009). He was also Master in 1986 and 2006. Other current officers are: Bruce Carrier, Senior Warden; Harold Gemmel, Junior Warden; David Stephenson, Senior Deacon; Raymond Dedic, Junior Deacon; Eldon Phillips, Senior Steward; Larry Merchant, Junior Steward; Charlie Eanes, Chaplain; and Chuck Racicot, Secretary and Treasurer. The first Master of the Lodge was Louis Klenck, who served from 1911 to 1913.

The Masons are the world's oldest and largest fraternal organization with Lodges in most countries around the world. The oldest known records of meetings are in England. Prior to 1717, there were at least four lodges there, which affiliated with each other forming the Grand Lodge of England in 1717. In the USA, each state has its own Grand Lodge, which governs the Lodges within the state. Masons contribute more money each year to charitable causes than any other organization in the world. Shrine Masons operate 22 hospitals in North American for burned and orthopedically impaired children. The Scottish Rite Masons operate over 150 Language Disorder Clinics, Centers, and programs for children. Other Masonic organizations sponsor a variety of philanthropies, including scholarships. The Masonic Lodge is dedicated to making good men better men and, by helping others, making a difference for good in the nation and world. Libby Lodge currently has 58 members.

RAYMOND A. BELANGIE #3250 KNIGHTS OF COLUMBUS COUNCIL

The Raymond A. Belangie Council #3250 Knights of Columbus Council in Libby celebrates its 60th anniversary in 2009. It was formed on June 26, 1949 with Dr. Paul Seifert elected as first Grand Knight. When formed, the Council numbered 38 members. Presently, the Council counts 103 members on its roster and is very active in the Libby/Troy Catholic Community. Grand Knight Mire Cirian presently leads Council #3250, aided by trustees John Schneider, Neal Kerzman, and District Deputy Kevin Miller.

Through the years, the Council has continued in its stated mission of supporting its parish priest and the local parish, St. Joseph's. The Council has supported the community of Libby in many ways such as: improvements and additions to the playground equipment at Asa Wood School, financial and maintenance support at the Pregnancy Care Center, sponsorship of free movies at the Dome Theater, and sponsorship of two meals during Nordicfest (the fishboil and the Swedish pancake breakfast).

Sons of Norway volunteers Carol Burriss, Joyce Lelm, and Katie Dwello (left to right) making Vikings on a Stick for Nordicfest. Photo courtesy of Kootenai Valley Record.

SONS OF NORWAY

Norhaven Lodge 536 was founded in the early spring of 1974 by Harold Hatlen and Ed Prestegaard. Norhaven had 198 charter members when it was officially instituted on April 27, 1974. A contest was held to name the lodge and the winning entry was Norhaven, submitted by Hilda Hatlen. The title comes from the "Nor" in Norway and Haven, a safe place.

The lodge today has about 40 members and current officers are: Freda Howard, President; Dan Howard, Vice President; Jean Sonju, Secretary and Financial Secretary; and Don Westfall, Treasurer. Norhaven Lodge offers lanaugage classes for lodge members and the public. They are involved in the Adopt-A-School Program at the Kootenai Valley Christian School and collect soup labels, box tops for education, and used ink cartridges in addition to holding a monthly presentation on

Spinning Squares. Photo courtesy of Spinning Squares.

Scandinavian countries and culture. The lodge also hosts a food booth at Nordicfest every September. Other activities include an annual $500 scholarship to a graduating Libby senior, and sessions on making lefse, rosettes, and vikings-on-a-stick throughout the year.

SPINNING SQUARES

The Libby Spinning Squares is a group of square dancers who get together regularly. The group was formed in 1965 by Bob and Betty Olson, Red and Bogie Post, Fred and Delores Keiffer, Lyle and Myrna Coon, and Cliff and Joanne Coon. Bill and Billie Melcher were the advisors who helped with the constitution and bylaws and taught the first lessons using records. The 2009 officers are: Verna Johnson and Ted Jewell, Co-Presidents; Clarence Johnson and Ken Kehn, Co-Vice Presidents; Rhonda Taigaafi, Treasurer, and Jo Wilson, Secretary. The membership stands at 48. Libby Spinning Squares holds two dances a month, most months of the year. In addition, special dances are held at Logger Days, the Dam Dance at Libby Dam, and for other occasions. They also teach square dancing. Themes for the dances include Oktoberfest, Fabulous 50s, Roaring 20s, Halloween, Christmas, Mexican, Western, Valentine, Luau, and Crazy T-Shirt.

U SERVE TENNIS

U Serve Libby, Inc. is a tennis club in the process of building community courts for the City of Libby. It was founded March 30, 1987 under the leadership of Clarence Knutson, Jay Dinning, and Lee Chandler. U Serve Libby, Inc. was formed to meet the expenses of the Libby High School tennis team when funding from the school was cut back. U Serve raised enough money to cover coaching, transportation to meets, equipment, court use, and occasionally, uniforms.

In recent years, the school began funding the tennis team completely. This allowed U Serve Libby to concentrate on a project that was proposed in 2001: building community tennis courts. Funds are being raised to complete six tennis courts on East Spruce Street near City Hall. Lincoln County and the City of Libby have donated services to clear and prepare the land. The county has also contributed funds toward the project. Local businesses and individuals have made over $50,000 in contributions toward construction. Three grants have also contributed to the building fund. The courts are due to be completed when adequate funding is available, tentatively summer of 2009. After the completion of the courts, U Serve Libby, Inc. will manage the courts, sponsor tournaments, and schedule programs such as Junior Team Tennis, lessons, and clinics.Current leaders are Sandy Hauck and Laurie Mari. U Serve Libby, Inc. is an all-volunteer organization. Membership varies year to year, but typically there are 5-8 active members.

VFW LADIES AUXILIARY

In 1945 Harper-Erdman VFW Post 1548 voted to form the Ladies Auxiliary to the Post. The auxiliary was instituted on June 10, 1945, with 33 members. First officers were: Mabel Solem, President; Irene Zollars, Senior Vice President; Flavia Becker, Junior Vice President; Mildred Flesher, Secretary; Lucy Vartanian, Treasurer; Ella Ayotte, Chaplin; and Phoebe Voves, Conductress. Gloria Shrewsberry is the only charter member alive in 2009. Currently, there are 108 members and officers are: Stella Sharp, President; Lila Campbell, Senior Vice President; Nancy Sutton, Junior Vice President; Mavis Johnson, Secretary; Connie Thompson, Treasurer; LoRee Hook, Chaplin; Teddye Beebe, Conductress; and Maria Wegner, Guard. The Auxiliary joins the Post every year to sponsor scholarships in the Voice of Democracy Essay Contest at the High School level and the Patriot's Pen Essay Contest at the Middle School. In addition, they sponsor scholarships for the patriotic art contest at the High School.

Rick Klin of the Polar Bear Club. Photo courtesy of Kootenai Valley Record.

OTHER ACTIVE GROUPS, CLUBS, & ORGANIZATIONS IN LIBBY

4-H (numerous groups)
American Field Service
Boy Scouts
Cabinet Oddfellows
Eagles Lodge
Elks BPOE
Kiwanis
Kootenai Bird Club
Kootenai Fly Fishers
Kootenai Heritage Council
Kootenai Valley Mycological Club
Kootenai Winter Sports
LaLeche League
Libby Lions
Libby Red Hats
Libby Saddle Club
Libby Senior Center
MIA Writers Group
Montana Athletic Club
Pioneer Society
Polar Bear Club
Red Hat Rebels
Rotary International
Society of American Foresters
Toastmasters
Veterans of Foreign Wars

HERITAGE MUSEUM

In 1973, a group of citizens formed Museum, Inc., a non-profit corporation. The main purpose was "the recovery of and preservation of historical culture of the Lincoln County area" with the immediate need of a place to house the historical collection of the late Roy Porter.

Hundreds of people participated in the building's construction. From the felling of the first tree, on to the hauling of the logs, the peeling, chinking, decking the roof, pouring the cement floor, and building exhibits, community support for the project was evident. Special grants and assistance from the Montana Bicentennial Commission, a Bicentennial levy from the Lincoln County Board of Commissioners, the St. Regis Co., Montana Arts Council, U. S. Forest Service, private businesses, and individuals helped pay for the museum. Grants from the Institute of Museum and Library Services and the State Historical Records Advisory Board helped set up and continue the Archives, which houses numerous paper collections and photographs. Since its inception, The Heritage Museum has been run completely by volunteers. A least 40 are needed to keep things running smoothly. Its only funding comes from donations and grants.

Bruce Davis with antique drag saw. Heritage Museum opening day. Photo courtesy of Heritage Museum.

The Heritage Museum is open for the summer season, June through August. Opening Day each year is a celebration of times gone by, with entertainment, demonstrations of antique equipment, food in the historic Sylvanite cookhouse, and operating vintage vehicles. There are changing exhibits at the museum from year to year in addition to art, quilt, and photography displays in the Tower Gallery. Original Board of Directors at May 22, 1973 founding were: Douglas Porter, John W. Davidson, Bettie Doetch, and Emmett Harmon. Current Board of Directors are: Eileen Carney, Don Shea, Becky Timmons, Jay Goley, Mark Morain, August Hardgrove, and Iva DeShazer.

Libby's Heritage Museum. Courtesy of Heritage Museum.

Libby's Memorial Center. Photo courtesy of Memorial Center.

MEMORIAL CENTER

The Libby Memorial Center is operated by the Kootenai Heritage Council with the mission of preserving the Heritage of Lincoln County, Montana and to enhance culture, education, social, and economic well-being through all forms of artistic activity and performing arts. To that end, the Memorial Center offers a wide variety of theater performances, special events, conferences, shows, and musical performers. As one of the largest venues in Libby, it also hosts private weddings and numerous fundraisers.

HISTORIC DOME THEATER

The Dome Theater was originally built in 1910 and was called the Kootenai Theatre and Opera House. The original structure was a wood frame building that was later stuccoed. Early owners were A.M. Hoffman and W.F. Kientz. The original theater burned down on January 20, 1948.

The owners at the time of the fire were Mrs. Arthur J. Neils and Mrs. A.J. Agather. The theater was rebuilt on the original site and called the Dome Theater, reopening for business on June 29, 1948. Other early owners include: the Woods Family, 1960s; Dave and Phyllis Weisbeck, 1970s; Leo and Emelia Huber, 1979-2002; Bert and Marguerite Wilson, 2002-present. Currently the theater offers movies nightly, is involved in numerous special and fundraising events, and maintains seven employees.

Historic Dome Theater. Photo by Melody Condron.

A Year in Libby

Over 100 special events happen in and around Libby every year. All event types are represented, including theater, lectures, shows, and musical entertainment. In addition, Libby is host to many annual events and traditional festivals.

March

Irish Fair at Libby's Memorial Center

April

St. John's Lutheran Hospital Health Fair at the Memorial Center
Home & Garden Expo at Libby's Memorial Center

May

Wings Walk in Libby and Troy
STOKR Race, county-wide
Salmon and Trout Derby at Koocanusa Resort & Marina

June

IncrediBull Riding
Logger Days

July

Junior Fair
PRCA Kootenai River Rodeo at the J. Neils Complex
St. John's Lutheran Hospital Fundzies Golf Tournament

August

Relay for Life at Asa Wood Elementary School
Ignite the Nights

September

Nordicfest
Koocanusa Resort Fish Fry at Koocanusa Resort & Marina
Kiwanis Demolition Derby
Heritage Museum Chili Cook-Off

December

Tree of Life
Parade of Lights
Achievements Craft Bazaar
St. John's Lutheran Hospital Festival of Trees

Events in Libby

LOGGER DAYS

Each June, Libby hosts a three-day weekend of family events celebrating the timber and logging heritage of the region. Beginning on Thursday, the event features logging events, demonstrations, and competitions, including a lumberjack relay for those skillful in setting chokers, chain sawing, ax throwing, and both single and double buck sawing. There is also the large-scale adult water fight, carnival, parade, lip sync contest, a 5 and 10k fun run, vendors, and games. In addition, the Bull and Bullette of the Woods —where boxers compete atop a giant log—has become a popular Logger Days tradition. Children under 12 can compete to be Wimp of the Woods in a pillow-fight competition. 2009 marked the 51st annual Logger Days celebration.

NORDICFEST

Nordicfest is an annual event celebrating the Scandinavian heritage of many of Libby's residents. The two-day celebration includes a fjord horse show, lutefisk dinner, youth runnerfell, Hardanger display, Scandanavian Varpa, art show, quilt show, vendors, live music, and a parade. Organized by the Sons of Norway, many people visit Nordicfest annually just to partake in the regionally famous Viking on a Stick offered by the Sons of Norway food booth each year.

PRCA KOOTENAI RIVER RODEO

The Kootenai River Rodeo is a Professional Rodeo Cowboy Association organized by the Libby Area Chamber of Commerce and held the last weekend in July in J. Neils Memorial Park. The event features vendors, food booths, entertainment, kids' rodeo activities, and, of course, rodeo events.

IGNITE THE NITES

Ignite the Nights is a car show hosted by the Igniters Car Club and held downtown on Mineral Avenue for two nights every August. A neon lights contest, burn-out contest, flame-throwing contest, Friday night cruise, and car show are all part of the event.

RELAY FOR LIFE

Libby's Relay For Life is one of many in a nation-wide fundraiser for the American Cancer Society. The first Relay in Lincoln County happened in 2007, under the direction of Diane Rewerts. Participants are sponsored to walk the track at Asa Wood Elementary overnight, with supporters staying nearby to cheer them on. In 2007, the event raised approximately $36,000, and in 2008 the amount totalled $47,000. The 2009 Relay for Life committee is made up of: Keith Meyers, Chair and Entertainment/MC; Tara Niemi, Co-chair and Corporate; Cathy Ann Jenkins, Registration and Accounting; Elizabeth LaMonica, Team Development; Jessica Munts, Team Development in Troy; Karen Repine, Logistics; Debra Erickson, Luminaria; Judi Bloomer, Survivor; Sandy Elmore, Relay Store; Brooke Helzer, Prizes; Melody Rohrer, Online / Tech; Mary Pfeifer, Publicity; Darlene Nelson, Food.

Libby Events

PRCA Kootenai River Rodeo. Photo courtesy of Kootenai Valley Record.

Jim Mari at the Heritage Museum's annual chili cookoff. Photo courtesy of Heritage Museum.

Blake Knapp, 6, leads the survivor's lap in the 2008 Relay for Life. Photo courtesy of Kootenai Valley Record.

Chad Miller competes in the 2008 Nordicfest Scandinavian Varpa (rock throwing contest). Photo courtesy of Kootenai Valley Record.

Waterfight at Libby Logger Days. Photo courtesy of Kootenai Valley Record.

Kelda Latham dispatches Brandie Ehlenfeldt in the 2008 Bullette of the Woods. Photo coutesy of Kootenai Valley Record.

Norhaven food booth at Nordicfest. Photo courtesy of Kootenai Valley Record.

CABINET VIEW COUNTRY CLUB

The Cabinet View Country Club in Libby offers 18 holes, surrounded by the beautiful Cabinet Mountains. At par 72, the course offers a challenge to golfers of all levels. The course features five ponds, many bunkers, and other natural highlights. Built in the 1950s by community volunteers, the property is still partially maintained by volunteer members today. A strong membership has made many events at the club a possibility, including a City Tournament, WMCPGA Pro Am, and Apple Open. Libby High School's golf team also uses the course, encouraging junior players to stay involved in the sport.

Pavilion at Riverfront Park in Libby is yet another community gathering spot. Photo courtesy of Kootenai Valley Record.

FARMER'S MARKET

The Libby farmer's market happens throughout the summer, every Thursday afternoon between Fireman's Park and the Libby Area Chamber of Commerce. Local artists, bakers, and those with fresh eggs and produce have the opportunity to sell their wares locally.

LIBBY CREEK GOLD PANNING AREA

For those wishing to get back to the days of gold panning, Libby Creek Recreational Gold Panning Area offers visitors a chance to pan for their own gold on the creek where over 500 miners set up camp in the 1860s. Any gold found at the panning area can be kept by the gold panner. Located 23 miles south of Libby, the area is part of the Kootenai National Forest.

Middle Thompson Lake. Photo by Debbie Munro.

Chain of Lakes

A growing area in the county, the Chain of Lakes region is full of many opportunities for fishing, camping, and water recreation. In the winter, the lakes are ideal for ice fishing. Located in the southeast corner of Lincoln County, almost to Flathead County, lakes include the Thompson Chain of Lakes (Upper, Middle, and Lower), Loon Lake, Horseshoe Lake, and Crystal Lake. Most businesses in the region—which is serviced by Highway 2—are seasonal and supported by summer camping and recreation.

Happy's Inn is a mid-point for many traveling between Flathead and Lincoln Counties on Highway 2. Marked on the map as Happy's Inn, the name is both place and that of a business in the area. The business of Happy's Inn offers restaurant, cafe, bar, gambling, convenience store, gas, diesel, horseshoe pits, and an outdoor patio.

Some private homes exist in the area, as do many private campgrounds. Larger tracts of private land exist in this region of the county than most others. More available land, combined with a closer proximity to the Flathead Valley and larger city of Kalispell have marked the area for development. According to the 2009 Lincoln County Growth Plan, the Chain of Lakes Homeowners Association and Plum Creek collaborated to work out a Neighborhood Plan concerning where new development will be allowed in the area. The growth plan additionally discusses Plum Creek's plans to split their land holdings into 4-5,000 new lots in the future. In 2008, there were approximately 260 homes in the Chain of Lakes region.

Eureka, Montana

The City of Eureka is located along the Tobacco River. It is reached either by Highway 93 via Whitefish and Flathead County, or from Libby on scenic Highway 37. Visitors from Canada cross at the Port of Roosville just eight miles away from Eureka, entering directly onto Highway 93.

The region surrounding Eureka is often called the Tobacco Valley, named for a plant resembling tobacco that was plentiful in the valley. Eureka has a visitor-friendly downtown area, located along the main thoroughfare of Highway 93, called Dewey Avenue locally. The Cutting Board Restaurant on Dewey Avenue was recently awarded "Best Burger" in a national hometown grill-off on Live with Regis and Kelly for its Bubba Burger. Other businesses, including art galleries, coffee shops, yarn shop, thrift store, and organic grocery, are all grouped in this very walkable area. Several buildings in downtown Eureka are listed on the National Register of Historic Places. The city is additionally home to Eureka Riverwalk, a 1-mile paved trail, and the 6-mile long Tobacco River Trail. Riverwalk begins at Eureka's Historical Village near the end of the downtown area.

Recent census estimates put the region's population at approximately 5,400 people. Population in the area has been increasing since 1990, with the last 2-5 years seeing a sharper rise in numbers. According to the 2009 Lincoln County Growth Plan, the region is growing because of its proximity to Whitefish, Glacier National Park, and Glacier International Airport. Indeed, those who enjoy living in a rural area within reasonable driving distance of a larger city and transportation feel at home in Eureka. Many city-dwellers also purchase second homes in the region, making some of Eureka's locals summer-only residents.

The valley is much more suitable to agriculture than other areas of Lincoln County, due to its wide valleys. The thick forests of south Lincoln County give way to the wide open fields when entering the region. When arriving from the Port of Roosville or Libby, visitors also pass the Lincoln County Fair Grounds. Indeed, ranching is still one of the primary industries in the region, along with timber and tourism. As in many areas, the timber industry is in decline. However, tourism is on the rise and many Eureka businesses are eager to provide amenities to visitors. An increase in dining and lodging establishments has occurred to meet the need.

CITY OF EUREKA

Dave Newburn, Mayor
Ethel White, City Council President
Jim Bolen, City Council
Rachel Duram, City Council
Gary Dedina, City Council

EUREKA CHAMBER OF COMMERCE

The purpose of the Eureka Area Chamber of Commerce is to promote and enhance the economic vitality of the community. Their mission is to support membership through business promotion, networking opportunities, educational programs, visitor information services, and community events which reflect unique Northwest Montana culture.

2009 Board Members are: Clover Kincheloe of Silver Fish Gallery, Board President; Shelly Gilman of 1st Interstate Bank, Board Vice President; Tammy Lawler of Glacier Bank, Board Treasurer; Wayne Robinson of Robinson Associates; Kymberlie Shoemaker of LCCU; Vicki Tisdell of 1st Interstate Bank; Randy Wilson of Interbel; Mark Griffin of Big Sky Wireless; and Sherry Newcomb of Sherry's Jamboree of Gifts. Randy McIntyre is Executive Director. The Chamber and the Visitor's Information Center are run by Randy as the full time employee and Rita Stevens as a part-time summer employee. There are many volunteers and committees. Current chamber membership is 158.

The Chamber sponsors events including Rendezvous and the Annual Salmon Fest. Both are community events and bring huge crowds to the area. The Chamber has monthly luncheons and mixers open to everyone.

PORT OF ROOSVILLE

The border crossing at the Port of Roosville is open 24 hours per day, 7 days per week, allowing for travel between Lincoln County, Montana, U.S.A. and British Columbia, Canada. The location of the Port in close proximity to Eureka allows for many Canadian travelers to visit the region, especially in the summer months. Many Canadians visit to fish and hunt since Montana laws are less conservative than British Columbia's in this area.

Dewey Avenue in Eureka. Photo by Melody Condron.

A Brief History of the Tobacco Valley

by Darris Flanagan

The beautiful Tobacco Valley was the original home of the Ktunaxa or Kootenai Indians. They were fishermen and hunters, but are best known for having a distinct language of their own. As the tribe grew they expanded out to other parts of Montana, Idaho and British Columbia, but the Tobacco Valley was the home of their "Big Village." Three times a year, members from other branches met at the "Big Village" to depart for their buffalo hunts to the plains. They rode and packed as many as 700 horses for the spring hunts when the whole village made the journey. A fall hunt occurred, as did a winter one when they traveled on snowshoes the seventy miles to the plains. The meat and all supplies were carried on their backs on their return.

It was the first documented white man in this area, David Thompson, who named the area the Tobacco Valley, because he found the Kootenai Indians growing a form of tobacco near the mouth of the Tobacco River. The North West Company employed Thompson as a surveyor, geographer, astronomer and, most important to them, as a trader to the Indians. He was followed by numerous trappers and traders, but few stayed long except those who worked at the Hudson Bay's trading posts along the Kootenai River.

THE NATIONAL HOTEL

CUNNINGHAM & DOXSIE Proprietors

EUREKA MONTANA

Special atention given commercial men and tourists.

Every comfort and courteous service. Large sample room to show goods.

In about 1880, the first resident to built a year around wooden structure home was Sophie. There is no woman more famous or fascinating in Tobacco Plains history and maybe Montana history than Sophie Morigeau. She amputated her own rib, ran a pack train in the wilds of the west, operated a trade post, and owned a cattle ranch. Over the next two decades settlers and homesteads slipped into the area to join her. Many were stockmen who found the grasses to their liking. The first of these cowmen was William Fergerson who purchased the home and trading post of Sophie, who then moved near the lake that now bares her name. Fergerson was followed by many others and by 1890 farming homesteaders found the area to their liking. They took up a claim on forty or one hundred sixty acre parcels. They were self-sufficient farmers out of necessity, as supplies were only available after a long pack trip.

Sophie and the Fergersons ran a trading post beginning in 1882. Supplies were hauled by pack train from as far as Fort Colville. It was the steamboat traffic on the Kootenai River that allowed the Tobacco Valley settlers to get supplies without the time consuming trip to the outside world. In 1892, White's Landing became the stopping point for the steamboat trade supplying the Tobacco Valley. White's Landing survived until the Jennings to Fernie Railroad opened.

The people in the Tobacco Valley wanted a community center and the area around the Sophie's original trading post gradually fulfilled the desire. When a post office was established in 1894 the town was called Tobacco. Almost immediately after that, a lodging house and store was built just south of Tobacco by William Mills and others and Mills' Springs came into existence. The two towns were so close that visitors thought of the two as one. Both became ghost towns with the advent of the railroads. In the southern part of the valley Stryker and Marston were stopping points along the Fort Steele Road. Eventually, Marston became a town comparable to Tobacco and followed it into ghost town status. Stryker is, of course, a town today.

The Jennings-Fernie Railroad Line led to two new towns Hayden and Gateway. Gateway, the border crossing survived until 1936 when Great Northern closed the rail line and the crossing was moved to Roosville. Hayden's short life was as a supply point during construction of the Columbia Falls-Rexford branch of the Great Northern Railroad. Along the railroad line developed the towns that exist today of Rexford, Eureka, Fortine, and Trego.

Not until the railroad advanced into the valley did we make use of our most abundant resource, timber. More homesteaders followed the railroads to settle the valley, but the biggest influence of the railroad was it opened up markets for our lumber. At one point Eureka had the largest mill in Montana. All went well until 1924 when the mill closed. The Tobacco Valley was in the depression years before the rest of the country. Rural residents survived by selling butter, cream, and apples to Spokane residents by way of the Great Northern Railroad.

Like a miracle, just a few years later, a new industry began which was a savior for many. The Christmas tree industry developed because

Northwest Montana Doug fir trees hold their needles long after they were cut and they became a favorite of consumers. Buyers from the rest of the nation wanted our trees. By the 1940s Eureka was known as the Christmas Tree Capitol of the World. Almost two million trees were shipped out of the Tobacco Valley each year. There was hardly a person who did not make money from the industry. On October 1, 1952, the valley had its most famous visitor, President Harry S. Truman, who spoke at the depot and talked about our Christmas Tree industry.

During the 1940s and 1950s, dozens of tie mills sprang up through out the valley. They cut ties for the railroads. They were soon joined by new bigger permanent lumber mills who used the Great Northern to ship their products to the rest of the world. In the 1960s the construction of Libby Dam led to new growth. One of the consequences of the dam was that the old town of Rexford was moved and rebuilt. Other Kootenai River towns were not as lucky. In the southern end of the valley a seven mile long tunnel was constructed through Elk Mountain so the railroad could be rerouted. The Trego/Fortine area grew overnight with the tunnel workers. The population of the whole valley skyrocketed.

By 1973 the tunnel and dam were completed. The Great Northern Railroad no longer traveled into Eureka except for a local that hooked up the railcars of lumber still being produced. Many of the dam workers left for other opportunities, but a few stayed and became permanent residents. A slow, but steady, decline in the timber industry followed. The Christmas tree industry also decreased to almost nothing. By 1990, many feared for the future of the valley.

Today the valley has only one major sawmill whose future often appears to be in doubt. Several times a week a local still transports our only lumber to Whitefish to hook unto the main rail line. For better or worse, the last five years has seen tremendous growth of the real estate market. As a result the construction industry has replaced the timber industry as a source of jobs for many workers. The present economic crisis is a major concern for the valley. We have diversified our economy with some tourist trade, small industrial plants, computer transactions and businesses that reach their own notch in the world economy. With our eyes to the future in we have built a new modern high school to better prepare our youth to function in that world.

IMPORTANT DATES IN TOBACCO VALLEY HISTORY

1808 ~ On August 26, David Thompson visits Tobacco Valley
1845 ~ Father De Smet visits the Tobacco Valley
1892-1902 ~ Steamboats trade on the Kootenai River
1896 ~ The Fort Steele Road opened between Flathead and the Tobacco Valley
1902 ~ Jennings to Gateway railway opened
1904 ~ First Train through Tobacco Valley on Great Northern tracks from Whitefish
1926 ~ Beginning of Christmas Trees Industry.
1952 ~ On October 1, Truman's train stopped in Eureka
1970 ~ First train through Elk Mountain tunnel

Arriving in the Tobacco Valley via Highway 37. Photo by Melody Condron.

LINCOLN ELECTRIC COOPERATIVE

Lincoln Electric Cooperative (LEC) energized its first lines on November 7, 1949 serving 28 member/owners in the Bissell area. LEC now provides electric service for nearly 3,900 members in Flathead and Lincoln Counties. There are 21 full-time employees with 10 elected members on the board of trustees. In 2002, LEC, along with InterBel Telephone Cooperative formed Eureka Rural Development Partners, Inc. (ERDP) to build economic opportunity for the Tobacco Valley and surrounding communities. In 2005 significant upgrades were made in Lincoln County at a cost of more than $1,455,000. These include providing service to 164 new members, clearing electric line hazards, testing and treating poles, and many other upgrades. LEC's mission statement is to provide reliable energy, at reasonable rates, with exceptional member service and commitment to the communities we serve.

TOBACCO VALLEY NEWS

Tobacco Valley News is Eureka's sole newspaper serving the Tobacco Valley. It is an independent newspaper, published weekly under the direction of Managing Editor Robin Newman. Tobacco Valley News has been in publication for decades and is the trusted source for local news in the region.

TOBACCO VALLEY COMMUNITY DEVELOPMENT COUNCIL

Tobacco Valley Community Development Council is concerned with economic and community development in the Tobacco Valley. More than 40 people take part in committees with focuses including housing, business development, tourism, business expansion, and infrastructure. The organization hosts an all-organization meeting near the beginning of each year, and a home business expo, as well as a wine and cheese reception in conjunction with the Eureka Chamber. Current Board Members include: Eric Heyn, President; Jon Leonard, Vice President; Mike Henry, Treasure; Tracy McIntyre, Secretary; RayLynn Hays, Public Relations; Valene Goff; Lee Parks; Ethel White; and Leslie Graves.

TOBACCO VALLEY IMPROVEMENT ASSOCIATION

The Tobacco Valley Improvement Association (TVIA) is an organization devoted to preserving history and enhancing arts in the community through charitable and educational opportunities to both residents and visitors.. TVIA is an all-volunteer, nonprofit group consisting of three boards: Parent Board, Board of Arts, and Board of History. The organization manages both the Historical Village and the Creative Arts Center. The Tobacco Valley Improvement Association was formed in 1945 by a group of local residents from the communities of Eureka, Fortine, Trego, and Rexford. Originally, the goal of the organization was to tie together the interests of the north Lincoln County communities in order to promote growth, development, and cooperation. Some of the projects completed by early members include: the recruitment of a resident physician; fundraising to build a nursing home; and monitoring and representing the community's interests in matters related to the construction of Libby Dam. In all practical aspects, TVIAs earliest activities were similar to those of a chamber of commerce. In 1970, TVIAs newly created Board of History formally acquired ownership of the historical structures and artifacts now on display at the Historical Village. The Board of Arts was also created in the early

EUREKA, MONTANA: CHRISTMAS TREE CAPITAL OF THE WORLD

by Darris Flanagan

The first Montana Christmas trees were cut in 1924 and shipped from Warland, MT. Few people paid attention to that shipment of trees, but the Christmas tree industry was underway. The industry grew tremendously fast. Within a few years, Christmas tree yards opened throughout Western Montana. Montana trees were special because of the climate; Doug fir held their needles long after they were cut. The industry was ideal for rural areas like Lincoln County because it allowed additional use of equipment and hired help. In 1948 one third of the income of many farmers/ranchers came from Christmas trees. Most outdoor work was concentrated during the summer months and so a seasonal peak and slump in employment resulted. Christmas trees supplemented the other work rather than adding to the seasonal summer peak. The industry's jobs were good for almost three months.

While the industry was important to many sections of the state it was definitely centered in Northwest Montana and Eureka in particular. During the Christmas tree boom few records were kept other than those by the railroads. In 1936 Montana shipped a little over 1,200,000 trees, over half of them from Lincoln County. A scant five years later over 3,000,000 trees were exported out of Montana. The upward trend continued with 1,800,000 trees shipped from Eureka alone in 1948, needing more than three hundred railcars to export them. Total cut for Montana that year was 3,098,886 trees so roughly two-thirds of them were shipped from the Tobacco Valley. No state shipped more trees than Montana so Eureka could honestly claim the title Christmas Tree Capital of the World, which was first attached to the town during the 1930s. In 1970, a researcher concluded that over 80 million trees had been cut from the Eureka area in the three preceding decades.

Colliers Magazine in their December 4, 1948 issue published an article titled "Christmas Tree Capital" complete with color pictures. The article described how the residents of Eureka had been busy for months, cutting, tying, and shipping Christmas trees. It was this national article which further cemented Eureka's title as the Christmas Tree Capital of the World. After the magazine appeared, Eureka residents constructed billboards on roads leading into town highlighting the title. The 4.2 million trees cut in 1956 was the high point of the industry and due to many reasons including artificial trees, more tree plantations close to major cities, and desire for other species than doug fir lead to a decline almost as fast as the rise of the industry. By the 1980s, the title Christmas Tree Capital of the World was lost. The last tree yard in Eureka operated in 1994 and the Christmas Tree industry was basically finished.

1970s, tasked with reviving and increasing interest in the arts.

Today, TVIA continues to support community development through the three boards. In addition, it annually grants awards to community members for their contributions to the community.

HEALTH RESOURCES

A new emergency and medical clinic was added to the Tobacco Valley in 2000 to meet the growing population's needs. In addition, Eureka is within easy driving distance to North Valley Hospital in Whitefish, MT.

EMERGENCY SERVICES

Eureka emergency services include Volunteer Ambulance, Volunteer Fire, and Can-Am Search and Rescue. Ambulance crews in Eureka are all volunteer and are often needed to transport residents to North Valley Hospital in Whitefish or Kalispell Regional Medical Center during medical emergencies. Can-Am Search and Rescue is responsible for north Lincoln County's search and rescue efforts, assisting David Thompson Search in Rescue in the south when needed.

Eureka Volunteer Fire Service, beyond managing the Eureka area, also assist TFS Fire and West Kootenai Fire Services, and Eureka Volunteer Ambulance when needed. In addition, they perform vehicle rescue work. The Fire Department started about 1912. Previously located adjacent to Riverside Park, the new (2005) Fire Hall can now be found at 10 Utility Way. There are presently 25 active firemen and 10 living retired firemen in the area. Current officers are: John Livingston, President; Ron Komac, Chief; Ron Morgan, Jr., 1st Assistant Chief; John Hannay, 2nd Assistant Chief; Craig Eatop, Secretary; and Dave Lyons, Jerry Bonner, Ron Hvizdak, Mike Hansen, and Wilber Keller, Board of Directors.

Eureka Library. Photo by Melody Condron.

FINANCIAL INSTITUTIONS

Whitefish Credit Union opened a newly constructed office building in the 100 block of Dewey Avenue in April, 2009. JoAn Cuffe is manager and loan officer. Office staff includes Marilyn Parrish, Desiree Bean, and Karri Stenslie. WCU was chartered August 29, 1934, with assets of $25. In addition, each of five Whitefish railroad workers put in $25. As of February 2009, assets total $1.1 million. The dividend paid to members on December 31, 2008 ranked number one in the nation for all federally insured savings accounts. Typically, it ranks number one in Montana and among the top 10 in the nation. The Eureka office opened April 10, 2002, at 202 Dewey Avenue in a rented office.

Other banks in the region include Glacier Bank and First Interstate Bank.

CHRISTIAN RADIO KEUR-LP

Eureka Christian Radio, KEUR-LP 107.7 FM is Eureka's only radio station, "Sharing the Message of God's Love." Eureka Christian Radio first went on the air in 2004 after many months of preparation involving local, State, and the Federal governments of the US and Canada. Using call letters KEUR-LP and broadcasting at 107.7 on the FM band, the radio's signal covers not only Eureka, but Fortine, Trego, and nearby Elko in Canada. As the only radio station in north Lincoln county, the station's goal is to serve area residents by providing a distinct blend of Christian programming. Format includes talk, information, music, and inspiration. Programming is designed to reach into the hearts and lives of the listeners, addressing everyday problems and needs.

EUREKA LIBRARY

As part of the Lincoln County Public Libraries, the Eureka Library ministers to the media and information needs of the Tobacco Valley by offering free lending services, as well as both adult and children's programming. As part of the Montana Shared Catalog Partners Group, Eureka Library patrons can borrow freely from many other libraries in western Montana, including Whitefish, Kalispell, and Missoula.

New (2009) Whitefish Credit Union. Photo by Melody Condron.

KEUR-LP 107.7 FM radio towers. Photo by Angela Poch.

Eureka Schools

EUREKA SCHOOL DISTRICT

The Eureka Public School District serves children and families from not only Eureka, but Fortine, Trego, West Kootenai, and Rexford. Schooling for grades K-12 are provided for at Eureka Elementary, Eureka Junior High, and Lincoln County High School (LCHS). The elementary school serves students in kindergarten through 4th grade. Eureka Junior High, serves grades 5-8. The building currently housing the Junior High was built in 1929, with an addition in 1967, and was used for most of that time as Lincoln County High School. In 2004, a modern high school was built nearby and the older building was re-purposed as the Junior High. Eureka's high schoolers, the Eureka Lions, participate and compete in a full sports roster including basketball, cross country, football, golf, softball, tennis, and wrestling. Other high school activities include Tech Club, Key Club, Pep Club, Lion Leaders, Speech, and Drama.

EUREKA VALLEY CHRISTIAN & EUREKA HOMESCHOOLERS

In addition to Eureka School District schools, the Tobacco Valley is home to the Eureka Valley Christian School and an active group of homeschooling families.

Eureka Valley Christian is a private school offering education with a religious perspective to students from the Eureka area. The school serves about two dozen students from kindergarten through 8th grade.

Eureka homeschoolers include about 25 families that meet and cooperate in homeschooling efforts. Annually, the group organizes a spelling bee, musical, science fair, geography bee, harvest festival, talent show, dances, and many field trips.

Eureka Churches

THE CHURCH OF JESUS CHRIST OF LATTER DAY SAINTS

The first printed copies of the Book of Mormon became available to the public in 1830 and the Church of Jesus Christ of Latter Days Saints was formally organized on April 6, 1830 with its main focus on family and compassionate service. The Church in early Eureka met in various buildings and homes, even meeting a few times at the Morgue for Sunday School. The first Branch President was Garland Bryce Hibbert in 1954. Today, the 271 members have a new building on Osloski Road and current Branch President is Rick Peterson.

As a Christian Church with a lay ministry, all the members have the opportunity to give of themselves. The Church sponsors an annual Christmas Experience, annual live Nativity for the public, blood drives, kidsville at County Fair time, quilt making for the needy or ill, humanitarian kits, and compassionate service for those who need meals. In addition to teaching the Gospel of Jesus Christ, church Missionaries help at the Senior Citizens Center, food pantry, shoveling snow, stacking firewood, and walking the dogs at the animal shelter.

HOLY CROSS LUTHERAN CHURCH

Holy Cross Lutheran Church began in 1948 as a mission outreach at Warland, MT from St. John's Lutheran Church in Libby. In the spring of 1951, the mission moved to Rexford and on June 29, 1955, the organization of the church was completed with a move to Eureka. In the fall of 1955, there was a mission up Pinkham and the Eureka parsonage was dedicated in May 1956. A Trego church was started in 1958 and then merged with Eureka in 1967. Ground breaking for the new church in Eureka was in May 1959. In October 1963, the church started a kindergarten in

Lincoln County High School. Photo by Melody Condron.

Eureka and later one in Trego. The program lasted for ten years. Many pastors have served Holy Cross Lutheran: Pastor Albert Pullman 1954-1964; Richard Thompson, 1964-1970; David Boehnke, 1970-1976; Terry Martin, 1977-1978; Melvin Ghodes, 1978-1980; Dudley Johnson, 1981-1984; Wayne Berkoben, 1984-1993; James Wilson, 1994-1997; and Christopher Tabbert, 1998 to present. Holy Cross has a baptized membership of 225.

OUR LADY OF MERCY CATHOLIC CHURCH

The Catholic Church's presence in the Tobacco Valley dates from Father De Smet's historic 1845 trip through the region. A short time after, a log church was built in the area. The church was tended by numerous priests, several of whom were from Canada. In 1903 the first diocesan priest from Helena was assigned to the valley. Father McGlynn began construction of a frame building which served as church until 1967 when the present church was built. Eureka's Catholic Church now stands at 500 Dewey Avenue in central Eureka, a mission church served by the Whitefish pastor/priest Fr. Patrick Patton. Staff consists of: Dan Casazza, resident Parish Administrator and Permanent Deacon; Lisa Stein, part-time office manager; Shelly Clark, Director of Faith Formation; and Bob Wuebler, Music Director. Parish size is approximately 120 families. Each year, the Catholic Church plans multiple community and parish events, including Community Valentine Luncheon, a burger booth at the County Fair, and multiple Christian related activities. Religious education is available for grades K-12 as well as for adults.

ST. MICHAEL AND ALL ANGELS EPISCOPAL CHURCH

St. Michael and All Angels Episcopal Church in Eureka continues to hold services in its original building, dedicated October 3, 1915. Funds for construction were provided by May L. Malkoff in memory of her husband, Michael. Lumber came from the Weil Lumber Company of Eureka. The beautiful altar and altar rail were sent by express from New York to arrive in time for the wedding of the lumber company owner's daughter. Current leaders in the church are: Reverend Pattiann Bennett, Rector; Jack Smiley, Senior Warden; Doug Merrill, Junior Warden; Claudia Evans, Clerk; and JoAn Cuffe, Treasurer. Also on the Board of Vestry are BeeGee Cole and Mike Cuffe.

SEVENTH-DAY ADVENTIST CHURCH

The Eureka Seventh-day Adventist church started as a small company in 1996 and became an official church in July 2000. Current leadership: Pastor Lonnie Liebelt; John Krum, head elder; Larry Ewing, elder; Paul Rayne, elder; Tom Waters, elder; Sandee Olson, Treasurer; Veronica Skelton, Head Deaconess; Pam Brown, Clerk; Donna Stafford, Sabbath School Leader; Wayne Castellarin, Building Committee Chairman; and Angela Poch, Personal Ministries Leader. Current membership is about 55 members plus visitors and seasonal friends. Seventh-Day Adventist offer many services to members and the public, including food baskets for the needy, marriage seminars, health programs, cooking schools, door to door outreach, evangelistic series, and personal Bible study. The church additionally offers a monthly newsletter and is actively involved in Eureka's only radio station, KEUR 107.7 FM.

OTHER CHURCHES IN THE AREA

Assembly of God
Chapel of Praise
Eureka Christian Center Four Square Gospel
First Church of God
Gideons International
Jehovah's Witnesses Kingdom Hall
Kootenai Christian Fellowship
Valley Baptist Church

Photo of Eureka Seventh-Day Adventist by Angela Poch

A view of the beautiful Tobacco Valley from Eureka Seventh-Day Adventist Church. Photo by Angela Poch.

Eureka Groups & Organizations

FRIENDS OF THE SHELTER

Friends of the Shelter (FOS) was founded in 1995 in response to the identified needs of Lincoln County's animal control facility in the north end of the county. Founded as Friends of the Shelter/Tobacco Valley Animal Shelter (TVAS), FOS volunteers sought to raise money to assist in building improvements, help meet the medical needs of impounded animals, and increase adoptions for these animals. Original founders of the group were Randy and Steve Turpie. FOS has provided spay/neuter programs, education, foster care and facilitated adoptions. In 2008, the group entered into a contractual agreement with Lincoln County to operate the shelter facility. Land was donated for a new shelter by Dona and Keith Taylor and volunteers are working to raise the funds to so that the original organization goal of building a shelter can be realized. Current leaders are: Lori McNicol, Board President; Sue Fanning, Vice President/Treasurer; Jane Hamilton, Secretary; and Wendy Anderson, Shelter Director. Wendy is the only paid employee and is part-time. In addition, FOS has many volunteers who give of their time and resources. There are currently about 15 active volunteers who help at the shelter. They directly interact with the cats and dogs which includes grooming, walking the dogs, and cuddling with the cats. Volunteers wash the bedding and decorate for holidays. These frequent visits help keep the animals socialized which greatly increases their odds for adoption.

GIRL SCOUTS

Girl Scouting has been present on and off in the Tobacco Valley for as long as any current residents can remember. Clara Fleming was an active Neighborhood Chairman and hosted vigorous program for girls in the 1950s and 60s. To ensure the continuance of the Girl Scout program in the area, she remained Neighborhood Chairman for many years after her own children were grown. Catherine Schroeder led troops transitioning from Brownies to Juniors and on through Intermediates and Senior Scouts during this time. Ms. Schroeder's Senior troop presented the flag at the dedication of the Koocanusa Bridge. There came a lull in membership during the 1970s. However, in the early 1980s, Sally Steward and Mary Wetzel decided to reinstate girl scouting in the Eureka area. With help from the Girl Scout office in Missoula, they were able to establish several Brownie troops in the area, including Trego. Judy Lou Kilroy became Neighborhood Chairman during this time and is credited with growing scouting to its largest number of registered girls. Currently Rebecca Sorensen is Service Unit Leader and has been for the past seven years. This year there is one active Brownie Troop, one Junior Troop, one Cadette Troop, and one mixed level troop in the West Kootenai.

HIGH COUNTRY HORSEMEN

The Tobacco Valley High Country Horsemen (TVHCH) was organized in 1983 as a riding group to help further mountain trail riding and help maintain and develop backcountry trails. Original officers were: Clarence Ness, President; Dr. Mintz, Vice President; and Debbie Parish, Secretary/Treasurer. Current officer are: Bob Jacobs, President; Tammy Bozarth, Vice President; and Dorene Fish, Secretary/Treasurer.

Their organizational mission includes educating and encouraging the public in wise use of the back country and assisting government agencies in the maintenance and management of trails and resources. TVHCH has helped restore remote cabins and maintain and plan trails. The group promotes the leave no trace user philosophy. TVHCH also sponsors and runs the 4-H obstacle course at the Lincoln County Fair. Membership is open to all riders of all ages and levels of riding/packing abilities. Currently we have approximately 40 members.

Tobacco Valley High Country Horsemen. Front row: Brenton Pluid; Kneeling: Bob Jacobs (president) Barb Pluid, Pat Jacobs, Lisa Brown; Standing: Leonard Peterson, Michael Peterson, Mark Peterson, Jay Lee, Becky Sorenson, Sandra Lawler, Tammy Owen. Photo by Katherine Hoagan.

K7EUR AMATEUR RADIO CLUB

The K7EUR Tobacco Valley Amateur Radio Club, Inc. (TVARC, Inc.) was founded in July 2005 by Craig and Wendy Eaton, Bob and Pat Jacobs, Scott Colgrove, Don Johnson, Greg Fisher, and Johnny Armstrong. The club was incorporated October, 2008 and became a nonprofit organization. The purpose of TVARC, Inc. is to foster electronics and radio experimentation, provide emergency backup communications, encourage private citizens to train and practice operating radio equipment, and conduct club programs and activities to advance the general interest and welfare of Amateur Radio in the community. Current officers (with radio call signs) are: Johnny Armstrong, President - K7BIR; Don Johnson, Vice President – WR7DW; Greg Fisher, Secretary – KE7DNO; Gayle Newman, Treasurer – N7RYE; Bob Jacobs, Trustee – KE7DNI; Scott Colgrove, Trustee – AB7SC; and Rick Peterson, Trustee – N7AMP. Officers of Incorporation were: Chuck Newman – W7CAN; Johnny Armstrong – K7BIR; and Greg Fisher – KE7DNO. The club currently has 27 members and offers a training class, in progress, with 12 potential FCC licensed ham radio operators and members.

Original founders of K7EUR Tobacco Valley Amateur Radio Club, pictured in 2005. Photo courtesy of Scott Colgrove.

RODEO ASSOCIATION

The current Tobacco Valley Rodeo Club has been active in the area since about 1982, though rodeos have been going on in the region since the late 1940s. Organizing the rodeo has always been a volunteer effort. It was first known as the Eureka Rodeo, but in 1982 it became The Tobacco Valley Rodeo Association. The club has included residents of Roosville, British Columbia in addition to local residents.

Our current group has three board members with Mike Cole as President and BeeGee Cole serving as Secretary/Treasurer. Mike organizes the event and lines up sponsors, with the help of many volunteers. The Association plans Eureka's rodeo, the 4th weekend in July, and The Bull Thing, held the Saturday night of the Lincoln County Fair every August.

SCRAPS AND THREADS QUILT GUILD

Scraps and Threads Quilt Guild was organized May 23, 1996. The original twenty five members elected Bunny Franklin as President, April Heyn Vice President, Claudia Evans as Secretary, and Audrey Smith as Treasurer.

The Guild meets monthly at the First Baptist Church in Eureka for meeting and potluck lunch. The Guild sponsors classes—taught by both local and professional teachers—to teach new techniques. Guild members also participate in a number of fundraisers and make many charity quilts each year. In addition, the Guild sponsors an annual Quilt Show in conjunction with Rendezvous. Current officers are: Donna Caffee, president; Melody Casey, Vice President; Pat Holder, Secretary; and Terrie Phillips, Treasurer.

SENIOR CITIZENS ASSOCIATION

The Tobacco Valley Senior Citizens Association was incorporated by the State of Montana on October 10, 1972 with 30 paid memberships. The goals of the Association were: to promote the social and recreational activities of its members and any other programs adopted by the organization; work toward a health service program; and arrange transportation if needed to visit other senior citizens clubs. The first officers were: Lee R. Matthews, President; J. Alfred Peltier, Vice President; Mary Moses, Secretary; and Amel Swing, Treasurer. Original Board of Directors: Howard Helms, Addie Scott, and Roy Brock.

The Senior Citizens Association building was built in 1906 as a Christian Church. It was used by the Methodists and in 1953, the Baptists. In 1972, the Baptists sold the building to the newly formed Tobacco Valley Senior Citizens Association for $5,000.

Events and activities, other than events booked by non-members, include: a "Cabin Fest" hobo stew, pie, and ice cream social in February; breakfast during Rendezvous and Quilt Show weekends; a food booth at the Lincoln County Fair; sponsoring cookie day in December; Christmas bazaar; and Eureka Style Antique Roadshow dinner party with a free Christmas Day dinner (a new event in 2008). The Association manages a staff of seven with the help of thirty volunteers. Membership varies from year to year with an average of 150 members.

TOASTMASTERS

Toastmasters International was founded in 1924, and the Tobacco Valley Toastmasters began holding regular meetings in 2008. The mission of a Toastmasters Club is to provide a mutually supportive and positive learning environment in which every member has the opportunity to develop communication and leadership skills which in turn foster self-confidence and personal growth. Members learn skills such as how to run a successful meeting, be more confident in front of an audience, and become active listeners. Current leaders are: Eileen Barrett, President; Lisa Stewart, Vice President of Education; Deborah Wagner, Vice President of Membership; Jackie Beyer, Vice President of Public Relations; Jon Leonard, Treasurer; Angela Miller, Secretary; and Gene Tunick, Sergeant-At-Arms.

VETERANS OF FOREIGN WARS POST 6786

The Veterans of Foreign Wars (VFW) Post 6786 was chartered May 2, 1946. Charter members were : Frank A. Bean, Dale A. Broderick, Harrold W. Collison, George W. Davis, Thomas A. DeShazer, Willis B. Elliot, William R. Ellis, Gayle A. Eskilsen, Robert W. Eskildsen, James D. Fleming, Orvile G. Fuller, John D. Gaertner, Moritz J. Gehre, John D. Helms, Roy C. Huggman, Merton A. Hunsinger, James L. Hurst, Robert B. Linton, Frederick R. Marvel, Paul D. Marvel, George E. Miller, Otto Olt, Norbert L. Shuck, Thomas L. Skelly, John W. Vukonich.

The post currently employs eight people. Total membership of the post is approximately 150. VFW Post 6786 will perform military services for any Veteran who passes away locally. They also perform military honors at numerous events such as: Memorial Day, Rendezvous, Lincoln Electric Annual Meeting, InterBel Coop Annual Meeting, and The Bull Thing.

The VFW Medical Locker has many items lent out free to whoever needs them, such as hospital beds, wheel chairs, walkers, etc. In addition, the Service Officer will help any veteran to apply for Veteran's benefits. VFW Post

Tobacco Valley Senior Citizens Association. Photo courtesy of Senior Citizens Center.

6786 donates time, money, and other effort to numerous causes in the community. The Post has been awarded the National VFW Service to the Community Award two times, 2004 and 2008; the award is given to only the top 1% of the posts world wide (67 out of over 6,700 posts).

Officers in 2009 are: Ken Utter, Commander; Stan Burns, Senior Vice CMDR; Carl Woltz; Junior Vice CMDR; Howard Aemisegger, Quartermaster; Gary Crandall, Adjunct; Jonathan Cook, Surgeon; Jim Kuchenski, Chaplain and past commander of 16 years; Pete Klinke, Judge Advocate; Roger Shelley, Service Officer; and Jim Follensbee, Daryl Handy, and Robert Seidel, Trustees.

VETERANS OF FOREIGN WARS LADIES AUXILIARY

The Veterans of Foreign Wars (VFW) Ladies Auxiliary was chartered October 12, 1953. Charter members were: Lillian Bean, Beatrice Burch, Marjorie M. Collins, Cora A. Fuller, Lola Marie Gropp, Mildred J. Harris, Vera Mae Holder, Helen Hume, Mary Irwin, Jessamine Morrison, Betty Jane Phillips, Marion J. Scott, Jennie Sederdahl, Gloria Jean Taylor, Madeline J. Utter, Mae Utter, and Esther Utter Carvey.

The Auxiliary has as their main purpose to help the VFW. In addition, all members are active in the community, through the auxiliary and otherwise. The Auxiliary completes a special project every year on Make a Difference Day in October. They are active with the Patriot's Pen and Voice of Democracy in the local schools. They have raised thousands of dollars for the Cancer Aid and Research Fund, National Home for Children and Families of Veterans, Heritage House in Helena, Families in Partnership, Eureka Volunteer Fire Department, Eureka Volunteer Ambulance, and ALERT helicopter. They have also contributed thousands of pounds of food to the Food Pantry. In addition, they help fund the VFW Medical Locker with Make a Difference funds from one year. Auxiliary also sends lap robes, knee warmers, and cookies to the Columbia Falls Veterans Home each year. At Christmas, they buy gifts and make fruit baskets for all of the Vets at Columbia Falls and Mountain View Manor in Eureka. For their service, they have won the 2009 Auxiliary Award for the state of Montana.

Ladies Auxiliary Current Officers in 2009 are: Lis Blair, President; Charlene Carvey, Vice President; Eva Anderson, Junior Vice President; Marilou Payton, Secretary; Marilyn McKenzie, Treasurer; Chris Case, Chaplain; Ester Moody, Guard; and Linda Ivers, Kay Handy, and Susan Crandall, Trustees.

WEEDETTES

The Weedetes Garden Club was organized in the summer of 1963 with Dorothy McFadjean as president. Current officers are: Linda Jett, President; Joanna Nelson, Vice President; and Beckie Evins, Secretary/Treasurer.

Continuing projects include planting and monitoring flower beds at the entrance of town, maintaining Clara Fleming Memorial Garden at the Historical Village, caring for the Memorial Rose Garden at the Eureka Library, taking care of the cemetery's potters field, awards at fair, and assisting residents with floral arrangements at the Mountain View Manor and Garden contest. Present membership is 19.

OTHER ACTIVE GROUPS, CLUBS, & ORGANIZATIONS IN EUREKA

- American Legion
- Blazing Red Hats
- Boy Scouts
- Eureka Food Pantry
- Friends of the Library
- Friends of the NRA
- Koocanusa R.I.D.E.S.
- Kootenai Valley Rangers
- Lions Den Boosters Club
- Eureka Masons
- Mountain Bluebird Trails
- Music Boosters Club
- Tobacco Valley Fiber Guild
- Tobacco Valley Rod and Gun Club

Eureka Recreation

MURRAY SPRINGS FISH HATCHERY

Murray Springs Fish Hatchery offers visitors a chance to see raceways where fish are grown for release into nearby Koocanusa tributaries and many waterways in the Flathead Valley and beyond. Rainbow trout are raised in the hatchery from broodstock and are released when they reach one to two years old. Westslope cutthroat trout are also raised at the hatchery. Both are released to increase fish available to Montana anglers and improve native species' numbers. The hatchery was built by the U.S. Army Corps of Engineers in the late 1970s. In 2008, it released 232,000 rainbow trout alone. The hatchery coordinates the "planting" of fish by helicopter into over 100 lakes in a three year period.

STONE HILL

Stone Hill is a popular climbing area located on Highway 37, three miles south of Eureka. Accessibility is part of what makes the climbing area so popular: located above Lake Koocanusa along Highway 37, the area has ample parking and is clear of spring snow before many other climbing spots. Rock is relatively solid, and the cliff offers buttresses for both beginners and expert repellers and climbers. In the winter, expert climbers can be seen climbing the icy cliff face. Views from the top of the cliff are stunning, with Lake Koocanusa stretching out below.

Rockclimber at Stone Hill. Photo courtesy of Rexford Ranger District.

TEN LAKES SCENIC AREA

In 1984 the Wilderness Study Act recommended the Ten Lakes Scenic Area for wilderness designation. However, since 1971 is has been a designated Scenic Area. Whatever designation, the area offers significant recreation benefit to north Lincoln County. Glacier-cut valleys and cirques define the region, and many basin lakes run along the border between Montana and British Columbia, Canada. These lakes give the area its name. Lake hikes, fishing access, mountain lookouts, and trails of many lengths make Ten Lakes an appealing recreation destination close to Eureka.

Rexford Ranger District. Photo courtesy of Rexford Ranger District.

REXFORD RANGER DISTRICT

Rexford Ranger District includes 311,000 acres of the Kootenai National Forest. It is responsible for management and stewardship of a variety of natural resources including: vegetation, wildlife, and fish habitat; soils and water resources; and recreation opportunities. Important activities include timber harvest, prescribed burning, and wildfire suppression, as well as with recreation activities like oversight of hunting and fishing, water sports, hiking, bicycling, horseback riding, sightseeing, and winter activities like snowmobiling and ice fishing. The Rexford Ranger District office was based out of the town of Rexford from 1915 to 1959, when the construction of Libby Dam required both the town and administrative site to be moved. The station can now be found on Highway 93 in Eureka. The first ranger was Barney Mooney, who worked out of his home to patrol the Pinkham and Yaak districts. The first ranger station was constructed in 1925 in Rexford. The Ranger District employs 41 full time employees and 35-45 seasonal employees or volunteers. The current Rexford District Ranger is Glen McNitt (1998 to present) and current Kootenai Forest Supervisor is Paul Bradford (2006 to present). The National Forest has and will continue to be an important partner with Lincoln County as we move forward into the next 100 years.

CREATIVE ARTS CENTER

The Creative Arts Center, under the guidance of the TVIA Board of Arts, offers various classes and performances in accordance with their mission: to provide opportunities for attaining knowledge and skills that promote well-balanced human development advancing a sense of community, and outlets for expression, through involvement in the arts. The TVIA Board of Arts is committed to the philosophy that the study and practice of art is essential to one's educational experience in order to be a more balanced individual and contributor to society and the world. Recent classes have included karate, reiki, yoga, watercolor, and dance.

TOBACCO VALLEY HISTORICAL VILLAGE

The Tobacco Valley Improvement Association empowered the Board of History, chartered in 1971, to preserve historic information, buildings, and culture. The Board of History's mission is to: encourage and act on the publication of historic works; restore and preserve historic buildings, artifacts, and monuments in our possession; and retain a living link with past cultural forms through interpretation, display, and programs at the Historical Village in Eureka. William Fewkes, Clara Brock, Cathryn Schroeder, Martha Parrish, Jack Parrish, and Joe Pitman were some of the founding members.

The Historical Village is a collection of historic buildings and artifacts from the Tobacco Valley area. Properties, which include ten structures and their contents, are maintained and administered by volunteer workers and fundraisers inspired by concern to preserve the history of the Tobacco Valley area. This unique collection of structures and artifacts was made possible by generous donations from a number of private donors and the Lincoln Electric Cooperative.

Volunteers at the village offer interpretative and public programs such as the annual second grade field trip in the spring, conduct research and create exhibits from our extensive collection. The Historical Village is also a source of visitor information for the Tobacco Valley and the grounds are available for both private and public events including Rendezvous, Eureka Montana Quilt Show, Salmon Days, and Shakespeare in the Park.

Historical Village. Photo courtesy of Historical Village.

All buildings and artifacts on site date back to the 1880s. They include a general store which serves as a museum, schoolhouse, library, church, two log cabins, hand-hewn house, railway depot, caboose, and fire tower. Interpreters are on-site and all buildings are open to the public from Memorial Day until Labor Day. A large collection of archival materials donated by organizations and residents of the Tobacco Valley is stored in the Fewkes General Store. Current officers are: Lynda Young, Chairman; Joan Shirley, Secretary; and Gayle Newman, Treasurer. In 2008, the Historical Village had over 70 volunteers. There are no paid employees.

LINCOLN COUNTY FAIR

Eureka is host to the Lincoln County Fair each year and is proud to have the opportunity to show off the many talents and interests of county residents. More information on the Lincoln County Fair can be found in the County section on p. 31.

A Year in Eureka

Eureka has many annual community events, especially in the summer. The widest attended are the Lincoln County Fair (see p. 31) and the very popular Rendezvous Days. Below are some of the annual events the city is host to:

April

Rendezvous Days

May

Louise Burk Memorial Luncheon

July

Wood Rocks! Festival
Tobacco Valley Rodeo
Classic Car Show
Chautauqua

August

Fiberfest
Lincoln County Fair
Eureka Montana Quilt Show
The Bull Thing
Shakespeare in the Park

September

SalmonFest

October

Home Business Expo

Events in Eureka

RENDEZVOUS DAYS

2009 marks the 31st Annual Rendezvous Days in Eureka, and 200 years since David Thompson explored the area. The event offers Dutch Oven cook-off, sand drag racing, greenhorn shooting competition, roughstock rodeo, live music, kickoff dinner, craft fair, quilt show, parade, and antique car show. Events take place in Historical Village, Lincoln County Fairgrounds, Lake Koocanusa Arena, Riverside Park, and in between, making it a city-wide celebration.

FIBERFEST EUREKA

Eureka's 7th Annual Fiberfest takes place in 2009. The event is a celebration of fiber arts and production and offers vendors, classes, demonstrations, finished products, animal and fleece judging, and fiber animals of all kinds.

EUREKA MONTANA QUILT SHOW

During the annual Eureka Montana Quilt Show (EMQS), upwards of 450 quilts line the Dewey Avenue and the Historical Village all the way to Memorial Park. Vendors, raffles, quilting instruction, event T-shirts, and display of a featured quilter. The event is popular with downtown businesses, who participate by allowing quilts to be hung along the front of their buildings. In addition, it brings many visitors to Eureka from all over the region.

LOUISE BURK MEMORIAL
BREAST CANCER AWARENESS LUNCHEON

The Louise Burk Memorial (LBM) luncheon was founded in May of 1998, by County Commissioner, Marianne Roose, in memory of her mother, Louise Burk. Louise was a long time Tobacco Valley resident who died of breast cancer in 1989. Lynette Starling, longtime family friend, serves as cochairman. The luncheon is held every year on the Friday before Mother's Day at the Lincoln County Fairgrounds. A program featuring the latest information about breast cancer is presented at the luncheon as well. Memorials and donations are also given throughout the year. The main purpose of the luncheon is to provide education and information about breast cancer and to help men and women become aware of how they can help themselves through self exams, annual clinic exams, and mammograms. 2009 will be the 11th annual luncheon. In the past ten years the LBM luncheon has donated over $48,000 to the WINGS foundation. WINGS helps all types of cancer patients from Flathead and Lincoln Counties with non-medical expenses. The 2009 LBM Committee consists of: Marianne Roose and Lynette Starling, cochairmen; Daisy Yerian and SheeLa Beeman (Louise's daughter and granddaughter), luncheon salad bar/homemade donuts; Jolene Workman and Debbie Henry, silent auction; Karen Suchy, bags, brochures, booth displays; Eldora Spier, ticket chairman; and Vicki Lyons, decorations.

SALMONFEST

The Annual SalmonFest is held the weekend following opening day of "Snagging Season," when salmon are swimming upstream through the Tobacco River. A relatively new event, started in 2008, the event features food, games, arts, and crafts while watching the upstream-swimming salmon.

West Kootenai

What once was the Kootenai River in north Lincoln County is now Lake Koocanusa, wider and deeper due to the presence of Libby Dam, downstream. Half-mile long Lake Koocanusa Bridge, located just south of Rexford on Highway 37, is the only bridge over the 48 miles of Lake Koocanusa on the American side. On the west side of the bridge, just south of the Canadian border, is a small, predominantly Amish community called West Kootenai. The area is remote and beautiful, surrounded by National Forest and sparse population. Few amenities exist in the area. Area businesses rely heavily on wood, including North West Log Homes, Montana Millwork (siding), Montana Woodwork (post and pole furniture), Weeping Willow Woodwork, Beebe's Log Furniture, Eli Beechy's gazebo construction, custom logging and sawing, and wood carving. The area is also home to New Horizon's Youth Ranch, Miller's Green House, two taxidermists, and a few other construction-related or home-based businesses.

Available history of the area is limited. The Truman family homesteaded on the West Kootenai in the early 1900s and are still living near the original homestead. They are some of the oldest residents but for Native American residents. The current Sturdevants' Ranch still stores hay in a 1930s barn built by Wallace Butt. During the 1970s, there were 11 families living on the Kootenai. This includes the Amish community, who bought a large acreage of West Kootenai in 1975. There are now 33 Amish households, from families with eight or nine children, to bachelors living in small cabins. The Amish have their own school, with 17-20 students every year. The playground equipment is from the old Tooley Lake School. The students' desks are from the old Eureka Roosevelt building. Currently, there are about 170 households in the region, plus an additional 30 or so who reside in the area during the summer.

In the summer, dinner is served every Friday evening at the Kootenai Kraft and Groceries Amish Store, owned by Andy Yoder and family. Every Saturday, all year, there is coffee hour at the Amish store. West Kootenai's oldest resident, Robert "Pop" Ressler, celebrated his 91st birthday in 2009. Summer activities include creek fishing, swimming in Lake Koocanusa at the gravel pit, hiking, and boating. Summer haying continues to be done, though the large cattle herds are gone. Most hay is cut for horses and small family herds. There is an annual West Kootenai residents and friends picnic in July.

Hunting deer, elk, and moose is popular in the autumn. Activities in the winter include cross-country skiing and ice fishing.

There have been many new additions to the area. In 2006, the Uncommon Threads Quilt Guild was formed. They meet at the West Kootenai Community Church. Also in 2006, West Kootenai Fire Protection was formed. A small community cemetery has been added. Alkali Shooting Range began in 2008 at Alkali Lake, within walking distance of the community. The Range expects to offer four or five shooting events in the summer months.

The Amish community meets at different homes for Sunday church, in the Amish tradition, with Andy Yoder as Bishop. There is also West Kootenai Community Church at the end of West Kootenai Road. The social hall is frequently rented out for meetings and social gatherings. The newest church is the Lakeside Christian Church on West Kootenai Road, with Roman Kauffman as Pastor.

Lake Koocanusa Bridge. Photo by Melody Condron.

West Kootenai is also home to a Wildlife Management Area, created in cooperation with Montana Fish, Wildlife, and Parks Department. The area provides management for winter range of elk and deer in the area.

AMISH AUCTION

The largest event in West Kootenai by far, the annual Amish Auction draws bidders from thousands of miles away. The auction supports the one room schoolhouse the serves the students of the Amish community in West Kootenai. The event has been going on for over twenty years. Auction items vary widely but always include handmade items, cabin kits, playhouses, quilts, and furniture. Donuts and coffee are served in the morning and a homemade dinner in the evening. The auction begins in the morning and lasts until everything is sold.

WEST KOOTENAI VOLUNTEER FIREFIGHTERS

The West Kootenai Fire Protection Company (WKFPC) was started in March of 2005. The nonprofit company was formed to provide fire protection for the residents of the West Kootenai. It got its start when TFS Fire Department sold an old engine to this community for one dollar. The founding members for the company were Barb Morgan, Jim White, Jim Treweek, Stuart Hall, Steve Justus, and Greg Belisle. Original firefighters were Stuart Hall, Steve Justus, Jim White, Mike Wilson, Bob Krepp, Jenny Ressler, Joel Young, Bill Beeler, Judy Hal, and Bill Greenlee.

Current Board Members are: Dwayne Dodd, President; Carole Johnson, Vice President; Steve Justus; Lee Ressler; Jim White; and Don Hallock. Current firefighters are Chief Stuart Hall, Assistant Chief Jason Miller, Joel Young, Greg Miller, Greg Belisle, Jenny Ressler, Landon Hofer, Steve Justus, Tom Tokos, Jim White, Wes Clemmens, and Todd Savage.

Each year the WKFPC holds fundraisers, including an annual dinner and breakfast events at the Amish Store. Raffle tickets for items such as rifles, quilts, and Amish furniture are sold during the Friday evening Amish dinners and at other county-wide events. Bricks being used in the building of the new fire hall are also being purchased. Construction of a fire hall is expected to begin in 2009.

Rexford

by Julie Smith

The smallest of the four incorporated areas in Lincoln County, Rexford is a small town along the banks of Lake Koocanusa. Rexford is located just off of Highway 37, eight miles west of Eureka. Rexford has a few businesses and about 150 full-time residents.

Rexford has the unique distinction of being the only community on the Kootenai River which was established anew on the banks of the Lake Koocanusa. When Libby Dam and its rising waters became a reality, the community incorporated the town and then negotiated with the Army Corps of Engineers to relocate. A bench above the confluence of Tobacco and Kootenai Rivers was established for the new town site. There, lots were surveyed, water and sewer lines were put in place, and underground electrical service was provided to each lot. Streets in the new town were named for communities now under the reservoir waters: Gateway, Ural, Warland, Tweed, Rondo, and Hayden.

Oddly, moving for Libby Dam was the second move for Rexford. The original town moved from the banks of the Kootenai River, which was south of the site of "Old Rexford" to be near the newly constructed railroad in 1901. The river site had provided access to steam boats and commerce on the river before the railroad era.

The water and sewer utilities are the main source of revenue for the town. Rexford also owns the building leased by the U.S. Post Office, which provides additional monies. These revenues enable it to be one of the few Montana towns without a municipal tax.

A new grade school building greeted students after our move and existing teachers from the old town were moved to the new school grounds. The school district has since consolidated with Eureka, and the school is now owned by the town.

In earlier days, folks in Rexford made a living in the timber industry, farming, and ranching. More recently, timber and lumber jobs have all but disappeared and incomes for the town people are varied, including teaching, banking, Forest Service, medical, and service industry employees. The railroad, which was an early employer, no longer runs through the town; the rail bed is now a 'rails to trails' path for hikers and bikers, connecting Rexford to Eureka along the banks of the Tobacco River. "Old Rexford," which once had two grocery stores, gas stations, barber shops, library, a blacksmith, and other businesses, also provided convenient access for West Kootenai and Pinkham Creek residents for their necessities. The Catholic Church and Fewkes General Store were moved to the Eureka Historical Village and saved from the rising waters. At the time of Libby Dam's construction, Rexford Ranger District was moved to Eureka, contributing to the downsizing of our town.

Because of the recreational opportunities resulting from close proximity to the Lake Koocanusa, Rexford now has two RV parks, a vacation rental unit, and a town park with available camping spaces for locals and tourists. The Frontier Bar serves their famous steaks and chicken, known far and wide in Northwest Montana. Bikers and sightseers drive the U.S. Highway 2/37/93 loop from the Flathead to enjoy the atmosphere and good food provided by this establishment. The community hall and school building are available for church gatherings, family reunions, or other groups needing a meeting facility. The Rexford Bench Campground, managed by the Forest Service, has excellent camping facilities and is well used throughout the summer season. A swimming beach with picnic area and bathhouse, boat ramp, and hiking trails bring guests from a wide ranging area. Many Canadian families have purchased homes and/or lots in Rexford because of the superb recreational activities.

Recently, in an effort to rejuvenate town spirit, the local ladies have organized a weekly craft/visiting day to share local news and ideas. They have also opened one of the former classrooms in the school for an exercise group, complete with treadmill, stair-steppers, and other machines for locals to use an enjoy. Plans for annual clean-up days with potluck lunches are designed to bring everyone together and create a closer community. We now look forward to a continued improvement for our little town, and envision a community of friends and neighbors united in our quest to keep our "New Rexford" legacy alive and well in the coming years.

Upper Pinkham

BRIEF HISTORY OF THE UPPER PINKHAM SCHOOLS AND COMMUNITY CENTER

by Madeline Utter

According to old school records there was a school held at upper Pinkham in 1910. It was a little log cabin and the teacher was Estella Milnor from Eureka. She boarded in Bill Workman's home. In February of 1911 School District 18 was formed. Trustees appointed by the county superintendent were C.W. Workman, Henry Stacy, and Frank Slick. The Clerk was N.E. Workman. The school had 20 pupils.

The next year, when the O'Brien family moved up the creek, the school was bursting at the seams. Frank Slick sawed lumber in his saw mill to build a larger school on land donated by Andy O'Brien in 1912. Enrollment jumped to 30 registered children and it became known as Upper Pinkham School.

Down the road where Slick's Gulch road went up the hill, another new school was built in 1915 on land from Will Stacy's homestead. Both one-room schools were painted white with green trim, including the two outhouses in back. The same school board governed both upper and lower schools of District 18 and a teacher was hired for each. There were 60 pupils in the combined schools the first year, and 72 the following year. Double schools were kept open until 1922 when fewer students attended the larger, lower school. In 1955, the District was consolidated and children were bussed to Eureka for schooling.

The school building still stands and is used as a Community Center. Upkeep of the building is done by the Pinkham Moose Horn Club. Current Leaders are: Don Stacy, President; Tom Wilson, Vice President; and Madeline Utter, Secretary and Treasurer.

Trego

Trego is a former Great Northern Railroad station located 15 miles south of Eureka. It is reachable by Highway 93 from Eureka or Whitefish. As with many towns in the region, the boom of lumber and railroad industry have left the area. However, Trego remains a lovely small town with lots of natural recreation opportunities and local community spirit. A general store, post office, K-8 school, RV Park, Civic Center, and Volunteer Fire Service can all be found in Trego.

TREGO CIVIC CENTER

The Trego Civic Center was founded in 1947 by community members. The land was donated by William and Madeline Opelt. It is located on Fortine Creek Road near the post office and consists of a 40 x 60 foot framed building. It has indoor accessible bathrooms, a kitchen, and an entryway leading to the large hall. The Civic Center has also made room on the property for a building to house the Trego-Fortine-Stryker (TFS) Volunteer Fire Department.

Current President is Fern Sartori. Other members on the 2008 board include: Dave Guild, Vice President; Shawn Sloan, Secretary; Mike Gamblin, Treasurer; Lynn Johnson; and Marcy Butts. There are almost 200 members, many of whom volunteer to help at the Civic Center's annual events. It is a self supporting operation. Grants have been received over the years to update and improve the facility.

The Civic Center is the hub of Trego. It sponsors a number of annual events including the Easter Egg Hunt, Bike-A-Thon, Halloween Party, and Winter Pinochle. It is also available for rental. It is proudly home to the TFS Volunteer Fireman's Ball and Christmas Bazaar, both held annually for many years. Current rentals have included Sunday worship, portraits, line dancing, and yoga, as well as weddings and anniversary celebrations. In addition to these many events, the community pulls together throughout the year for fundraisers at the Civic Center to help individuals or families in need.

TREGO-FORTINE-STRYKER VOLUNTEER FIRE DEPARTMENT

The Trego-Fortine-Stryker (TFS) Volunteer Fire Department was incorporated on May 8, 1970 with board members David Curtiss, Ted Burk, Chet Apeland, Jack Dickenson, and Howard Mee. On August 21, 1987, the certificate of incorporation was amended to show nonprofit status. TFS Volunteer Fire Department provides structural suppression protection and education to citizens of three unincorporated communities (Trego, Fortine, and Stryker), outlying residential areas and subdivisions, and the forest land that encompasses their 167 square mile service area. There are currently six trucks in three stations with 12 active firefighters. On May 3, 1990, county commissioners Morey Dolezal and Noel Williams passed a resolution to form the Trego-Fortine-Stryker fire service area. Current officers are: Isaiah Williams, President; Dale Baldwin, Vice President; and Dawain Burgess, Fire Chief. The TFS Volunteer Fire Department contracts with the Trego-Fortine-Stryker fire service area to provide structure protection. Primary fundraisers are an annual Firemen's Ball, held at the Trego Civic Center around the third Saturday in June, and their yearly rifle raffle.

TFS Volunteer Fire with a new truck received in 2008. Shown are students of a driver training class. The firemen are (left to right): Glen Dorband, Danni Dorband, Isaiah Williams, Ed Burlingame (instructor), Robert Braun, Liz Williams, and Bill Huyck. Photo courtesy of Elizabeth Williams.

TFS Volunteer Fire Department controlling a grass fire. Photo courtesy of Elizabeth Williams.

Fortine

Fortine is located 11 miles south of Eureka and 39 miles north of Whitefish, 3 miles off of Highway 93. The town site has been established since 1905 and is found in close proximity to the Burlington Northern Santa Fe railroad tracks. The town has a post office, golf course,Community Church, and Ranger Station. Census estimates put Fortine's population at about 170 people. With its close proximity to Ten Lakes Scenic Area, Fortine has high recreation value. It's short distance to Trego—they are connected by about 4 miles of county-maintained Ant Flat Road—makes it easy for the two towns to share a fire service (TFS Volunteer Fire, p.61).

FORTINE RANGER DISTRICT

The earliest Rangers, on what is now the Fortine Ranger District of the Kootenai National Forest, were Joe Eastland and Fred Herrig. They were appointed by the Department of Interior in 1900-1901 to the Lewis and Clark Forest Reserve, Northern Division. Joe Eastland's headquarters was at Bunch Grass on Grave Creek and Fred Herrig built his cabin at Ant Flat in 1902, later to become the Ant Flat Ranger Station. In 1908, the Reserve was divided into two National Forests; the Blackfeet and the Flathead. The current Fortine District was then part of the Blackfeet National Forest. As the National Forest program expanded under the Department of Agriculture, Herrig was given additional men to add to his staff. The Bunch Grass Ranger Station, manned by Joe Eastland, was terminated and Eastland moved to Ant Flat to work with Herrig. In 1933, the Blackfeet Forest was eliminated and the Fortine District was reclassified as part of the Kootenai National Forest. Ant Flat, located near the small towns of Trego and Fortine in northern Lincoln County, remained the District Station until the new headquarters were constructed at Murphy Lake in 1963. An addition and remodel to the facility at Murphy Lake occurred in 2006.

Betty Holder is the District Ranger. The Ranger District consists of approximately 30 permanent employees, several of which are shared with the neighboring Rexford Ranger District, located in Eureka, MT. In the spring/summer/fall field season around 50 temporary employees also join the Fortine Ranger District. Volunteers also host at the some of the campgrounds and various groups volunteer in trail or recreation facility maintenance.

The Fortine Ranger District includes approximately 250,000 acres of National Forest system lands. Fire management remains as important today as in the past even though equipment and training have modernized fire-fighting techniques. Timber stand management now consists of timber stand improvement, tree planting and a variety of timber harvesting methods. Sales of sawlogs, small non-sawlog material, Christmas trees, firewood, and trees for landscape planting occur every year. The District also has an active invasive species treatment program. Lands and programs are managed for wildlife, grazing, heritage resources, and other special uses. Recreation includes driving for pleasure, wildlife viewing, water based recreation on numerous lakes, campgrounds, dispersed camping opportunities, hunting, fishing, berry-picking, cabins, lookouts, and miles of trails for hiking, horseback riding, and biking. Winter recreation in the form of snowmobiling, cross-country skiing and snowshoeing are also popular. The district's vast lands of lakes, mountains, valleys, and creek drainages and its forest products and versatile work programs play a substantial part in the modern conservation of the area's public resources.

FORTINE COMMUNITY CHURCH OF THE CHRISTIAN MISSIONARY ALLIANCE

The Fortine Community Church has a long, rich history, being originally founded by several families who lived and homesteaded in the Fortine area in the early 1930s. They saw the need to meet and worship together. The church became affiliated with the Christian and Missionary Alliance in 1944 and incorporated as a Christian and Missionary Alliance Church in 1946.

Pastor Cade Bichel is the most recent pastor of the church, having begun his preaching ministry at Fortine in June of 2006. He is one of the a long line of pastors there who has sought to meet the religious and practical needs of the people in the community.

The church currently has two part-time office secretaries and a janitor on staff. The average attendance for Sunday worship is 85, and the church has maintained a variety of ministry outreaches to the community including AWANA for young children, youth group, Wednesday evening prayer meetings, and Vacation Bible School in the summer.

Fortine Community Church. Photo by Sherry Santine Hearn.

Stryker

Stryker is a small outpost with a post office and many residences. Located along the Burlington Northern Santa Fe tracks, 20 miles south of Eureka, Stryker shares a fire service with Trego and Fortine (TFS Volunteer Fire, p.61). Residents visit Fortine and Trego for basic amenities or travel a farther distance to much larger Whitefish or Eureka.

Troy, Montana

Only 14 miles east of the Idaho border, Troy is the "Gateway to Montana" for thousands of tourists who enter the state on U.S. Highway 2. Located on the banks of the Kootenai River 18 miles west of Libby and at the head of Bull Lake Road (Highway 56), the region is a jumping off point for visitors to the Bull Lake region or Yaak River Valley. Residents of the Yaak River Valley also come to Troy for amenities since it offers the closest post office and large grocery store. It is the smallest of the three primary regions in Lincoln County, with approximately 970 people living in the area. A growing proportion of residents are retirees.

The city offers many recreational opportunities in town as well as in the vase forest areas surrounding it. Roosevelt Park, Troy Museum, Troy Airport walking path, Visitor's Center, and the Timberbeast FOLF course keep visitors busy. A five year plan for the region includes connecting a number of walking paths from the Visitor's Center to Roosevelt Park.

Beyond residential and city buildings, Troy is also home to a number of dining establishments, a bowling alley, two hardware stores, and a few specialty and gift shops. Kootenai Drug and Hardware and Stein's Market are located in a plaza close to the Visitor's Center along Highway 2 and provide for most residents' and visitors' basic needs.

For many years, the largest industry in the Troy region was and remains mining. Revett Minerals, Inc., through subsidiary Genesis, Inc., owns and operates the current Troy mine. It also operated a previous mine in the area, active firm 1981-1993. Troy's mine is estimated to produce two million ounces of silver and seventeen million pounds of copper per year when producing at full capacity. It employs approximately 22 salaried workers and 150 hourly workers.

Logging and lumber trades have also played a part in the Troy region. Chapel Cedar in Troy is one of the few remaining mills in the county. A family-owned and operated mill, Chapel Cedar sells cedar products, custom milling, planing, and fencing.

View up Kootenai Avenue in downtown Troy.

Troy City Building. Photo by Melody Condron.

Other major employment sectors include education and retail. Tourism-focused businesses like outfitters and campgrounds are also on the rise to meet the demand of summer's high traffic. Many travelers are on their way to Glacier National Park from Idaho, Oregon, and Washington. Others come directly to Troy for the region's many trails, ample fishing opportunities, and low population.

CITY OF TROY

The City of Troy manages the following departments within the incorporated area: City Hall; Troy City Court under Judge John Duehr; Troy Volunteer Fire Department; Parks and Recreation, including management of Roosevelt Park; Police Department; Power and Light; and Public Works.

Jim Hammons, Mayor
Don Banning, City Council President
Laura Schrader, City Council
Larry Coryell, City Council
Larry Baker, City Council
Sandra Johnson, City Clerk / Treasurer
Tracy Rebo, Deputy Clerk
Sandi Sullian, Customer Service Representative
Ron Higgins, Building Inspector.

TROY CHAMBER OF COMMERCE

The Troy Chamber of Commerce supports economic development in the Troy Area through support of businesses and local events, and the planning of Troy's largest annual event, the Old Fashioned 4th of July celebration. Troy's Old Fashioned 4th of July brings over 5,000 visitors to Troy every summer. In 2008-2009, the chamber financially and otherwise supported many events, including: annual Timberbeast, Roosevelt Park Easter Egg Hunt, Kootenai River Bluegrass Festival, and the 12 Days of Christmas, encouraging local holiday shopping. Current leaders are: Melody Condron, President; Sue Mendive, Vice President; and Steve Bowen, Secretary / Treasurer. There are no paid employees. The Chamber has a current membership of 50.

A History of Troy, Montana

by Jim Calvi

Troy, Montana began as a small miner's camp on the Kootenai River at the mouth of Lake Creek in about 1886. At that time the camp was known as Lake or Lake Creek Camp. Between 1888 and 1889, the mouth of Lake Creek was visited regularly by surveyors looking the surrounding area over for a possible railroad route. Surveying work increased between 1889 and 1891 after the Kootenai River route was selected by the Great Northern Railway for an extension of their line to the Pacific Ocean. The miner's camp grew into a large railroad grade construction camp with a population of over 1800 men. By June of 1891, the new town of Lake City boasted a post office, general store, two restaurants and sixteen saloons surrounded by tents and hastily constructed log cabins. In April, 1892 the railroad crews moved west and the town was nearly deserted. Following the departure of the crews, the town site of Lake City was sold, mapped and in October, 1892 dedicated as Troy, Missoula County, Montana.

The need for a freight division point, between Kalispell and Spokane, Washington prompted the GN to select an area a mile west of the new town of Troy for a large railroad yard. In the fall of 1892, work gangs again moved into the area and by January, 1893 work on the Troy Freight Division Yard was completed. Although Lake City, now called Troy, once again came to life, it would be short lived. As work on the new railroad yard began, work also began on another town, one nearer to the new railroad yard and known as West Troy. By the end of 1893, most of the remaining businesses in old town had moved into West Troy. Within a few years, West Troy was simply called Troy.

Troy was a railroad town which slowly grew and in 1915 with a population of 320 people, voted for incorporation. Within a few months, officials were elected and sworn into office and the Town of West Troy was established. In 1926, the town council changed the town's designation from "town" to the "City" of West Troy, Montana.

In 1889, a major mining claim was located six miles south of Troy, on Callahan Creek known as the Banner and Bangle (B&B) mine. Across the creek from the B&B, was another mine, which would later be known as the Big Eight. Both of these galena properties looked good and considerable development work was done between 1890 and 1915. The owners of the B&B decided in 1915 to initiate major mine development work which included building a large concentrator in Troy, a concrete dam and powerhouse on Lake Creek, and over six miles of narrow gauge railroad connecting the mine with the mill. By the end of 1915, Leo Greenough, president of the B&B, purchased the mining property and reorganized it with his family holdings in Idaho. The Banner & Bangle Mining Co. became the Snowstorm Silver-Lead Mining Co.

The Snowstorm mine was finished and in operation by the end of 1916, The new mine immediately contributed to the economy of Troy as well as doubling of the town's population. The well established railroad town had become a mining town as well. The Snowstorm demand for miners soon found itself competing with Butte and the Coeur d'Alene Mining districts for men.

By 1920, the population of Troy numbered 763 people, as the Forest Service advertised a large sixty million board foot timber sale twelve miles up Callahan Creek. The successful bidder was the Sandpoint Lumber & Pole Company which began immediately buying land near the Snowstorm concentrator. Two years later a new sawmill was under construction and the demand for labor increased the town's population once again. The new sawmill of the Sandpoint Lumber & Pole Co. was in operation by the end of 1923. To reach the timber sale, the company added onto the narrow gauge railroad line from the Snowstorm mine. Troy's prosperity now included a third major industry and for awhile the town was the richest in Lincoln County. However, the late 1920s were not good to the town of Troy.

In 1926, with the town's population estimated at 1700 people, Great Northern decided to close its freight division yard in Troy. Technology had caught up to the Troy Yard as trains now could easily travel between Whitefish to Spokane in a day. The loss of its railroad industry after thirty four years, did not appear to seriously hamper the town's outlook. However the next year, things began to take a serious turn for the worse.

In May, 1927, the Snowstorm Silver-Lead Mining Co. concentrator in Troy burned to the ground, effectively closing the mines. Instead of rebuilding the concentrator, the company put its mining holdings in Troy up for sale. Large scale mining remain elusive in the Troy area until ASARCO opened their mine in 1980.

The final catastrophic blow arrived in Troy in February, 1928, when the sawmill of the Sandpoint Lumber and Pole Co. burned to the ground. With only one more year on their timber contract, the company did not rebuild the sawmill. By 1929, the sale was over and the tracks were pulled from the South Fork of Callahan Creek.

With the scarcity of money created by the Great Depression of 1929, Troy's prosperous years were over. This was evident when the 1930 U.S. Census indicated that the town's population had dropped to 463 people.

For the next thirty years Troy's businesses catered to homesteaders, ranchers, forest service and tourist traffic off Highway 2. Although the economy eventually stabilized, the town was left with many vacant business buildings.

During the early 1950s, the forest service provided a boost for Troy when large areas of dead and dying spruce were offered for sale. This in effect, reestablished logging in the Troy area. By 1954, J. Neils Lumber Co. of Libby was constructing a large sawmill facility along the Kootenai River in Troy. However, in 1957, J. Neils merged with St. Regis Paper Co. who took over operation of the sawmill in Troy. This sawmill provided employment and the demand for loggers found a ready local labor market. The Troy St. Regis sawmill persisted until the 1970s when it closed.

During the late 1970s, the American Smelter & Refining Co. (ASARCO) began construction of a milling plant and major mine development work south of Troy in the Bull Lake Valley. Production work began in 1981 and the operated until the mine closed in 1993.

By the 2000 U.S. Census, Troy's population was just under a thousand people. The city now caters to the needs of a larger rural area, from the Bull Lake Valley to the Montana/Idaho state line, northward into the Yaak River Valley.

A Timeline of Troy History

1808 - May 6, David Thompson and party pass through the site of Troy on first trip down the Kootenai River

1889 - November 8, Montana Becomes the 41st State. Troy area is now administratively a part of Missoula County

1889 - November 29, Welcome Guest & Northern Belle lode claims (later known as the Big Eight) located

1890 - November 22, J.G. Van Dyke arrives from Bonners Ferry with a pack string; the trip took him nine days

1890 - December 9, George Potter locates the Herykaha Placer Claim, now part of West Troy

1891 - March 2, the Spokane and Kootenai Placer Claim is located, the site of Lake City (Troy) and now a part of West Troy

1891 - March 21, H.T. Fairlamb buys out his partners in the Spokane and Kootenai Placer Claim and begins developing Lake City

1891 - August 7, the road from Lake City to Smead's Spur on the Clark Fork River, near Noxon is completed

1891 - August 21, Snowball Fraction Claim was located - now a part of West Troy

1891 - October 14, Lake City Post Office Commissioned with Tom Dobson the first postmaster

1891 - December 4, Missoula Placer Claim is located - now part of West Troy

1892 - April 13, H.T. Fairlamb sells the Spokane and Kootenai Placer Claim to William O'Brien for $123.90

1892 - June 12, William O'Brien files a Cert. of Dedication on Spokane and Kootenai Claim and Lake City, calling the new town Troy

1892 - August 8, Troy Fraction Claim is located, now part of West Troy

1892 - August 17, First scheduled Great Northern passenger train passes through Troy

1892 - September 9, Pine Tree Placer Claim is located, now a part of West Troy

1892 - October 10, Declaration of Occupancy is filed on the West Troy town site

1892 - December, Troy's population is estimated at 225 people

1892 - December 2, First building lots located in West Troy

1893 - February, Troy becomes administratively a part of Flathead County, Montana

1893 - June 13, Banner and Bangle Lode Claims are located in Callahan Creek.

1893 - December 11, Lake Creek Road declared a Flathead County road

1894 - April 30, First Troy Wedding - Annie Stanley marries John Cummings in Troy's log schoolhouse

1894 - May, Douglas Leslie Wood is born, first birth in Troy

1894 - September 25, First Church Service held in Troy by Rev. Ellis of Helena

1894 - September 28, First issue of the *Troy Times* Newspaper published

1894 - October 7, D.T. Wood secures the "Johnson Bldg" and opens a store

1894 - October 14, The Troy Mining and Improvement Company is organized to sell mining property and real estate in Troy

1894 - November 1, Troy's first school begins

1895 - July 21, Work began on the Troy Ferry across the Kootenai River

1895 - August 29, About 60 feet of the Lake Creek Bridge destroyed by fire

1895 - October 23, Troy Mining, Power & Development Co. signs Articles of Incorporation

1896 - March 1, The Troy-Sylvanite Wagon Road declared a public highway by the Flathead County Commissioners

1896 - March 21, West Troy, Flathead County, Montana approved as a town

1896 - March 23, Map of West Troy filed with Flathead County, containing 168.299 acres

1896 - April 19, The Banner and Bangle Mining Company is formed

1896 - November 6, Rev. Berk disappears while hunting south of Troy, body is never found; Preacher Mountain named for him

1897 - February 19, Big Eight Mining Company incorporated

1900 - May, U.S. Census shows Troy's population at 242 people

1906 - August 26, Troy's first major fire destroys-three business buildings including the Windsor Hotel, loss set at $10,000

1909 - July 1, Lincoln County formed

1910 - May 20, First issue of the *Troy Herald* Newspaper is published

1910 - August, Wildfires threaten town, GN railroad cars standing by to evacuate the town's population

1910 - August, The new Lincoln County Jail in Troy completed.

1911 - May 8, First silent movie shown in the old Woodmen Hall

1911 - July 14, First Automobile arrives in town by way of the Yaak

1911 - July 28, Last issue of the *Troy Herald* Newspaper was published

1911 - August 25, Robert Gregg files on Lake Creek Water Rights

1912 - June 5, First Addition to West Troy approved

1913 - May 1, Kootenai Valley State Bank opens-for business in Troy

1914 - October 2, First Issue of the *Troy Echo* Newspaper Published

1915 - May 15, The "Princess Theater" begins showing movies on a scheduled basis

1915 - July 21 Troy Votes for incorporation, town's population at 320 people

1915 - September 2, Town of Troy's first election to vote for town officials following incorporation

1915 - September 9, First Meeting of the Troy Town Council

1915 - December 22, Greenough Investment Company purchases the Banner and Bangle Mining Company for $150,000

1916 - March 21, Leo Greenough purchases Lake Creek water rights and begins building a dam, flume, and power house

1916 - April 5, Work begins on the Snow Storm Concentrator Building

1916 - June 7, Work begins on the Snowstorm Railroad up Callahan Creek, connecting the mine with the concentrator.

1916 - September 22, Snowstorm Mine Consolidated has over 500 men working on concentrator and new facilities in Troy

1916 - October 30, Second Addition to West Troy approved

1916 - December 1, Troy Telephone Exchange opened

1916 - December 15, Concrete work on Lake Creek Dam completed

1917 - January 15, Stanfield Addition to West Troy approved

1917 - April 23, The Snow Storm concentrator begins operation

1917 - May 1, Work begins on enlarging the Troy railroad yard to 13 miles of rails, holding over 900 railroad cars

1917 - May 8, Prince's Addition to West Troy approved

1917 - June 22, "Wobblies" create problems at the Snow Storm mine and concentrator.

1917 - July 12, U.S. Troops arrived in Troy to control "Wobblies."

1917 - July 16, A jailed man sets the Troy Jail on fire and dies in the fire before he could be released

1917 - August 1, Town of Troy issues permit to William MacDonald for right to install electric lines in town.

1917 - October 1, Kidder Addition to West Troy approved

1917 - November 6, English Addition to West Troy approved

1917 - December 1, Kootenai Electric and Power Co. turns on the lights for the first time in Troy

1918 - March 16, Kinzie Hall, the largest building built in Troy, opens for business

1918 - April 11, Robert Webster Mechen is killed in World War I, Troy's only war loss. He worked for GN in Troy.

1918 - May 24, Kootenai Power and Light Company completes installation of first electric street lights in town

1918 - July 1, North Troy and Lawrence Additions to West Troy approved

1918 - November 1, First Spanish Influenza death reported in Troy

1920 - April 23 Sandpoint Pole and Lumber Company awarded a 60 million board foot timber sale in Callahan Creek

1920 - May U.S. Census shows Troy's population at 748 people

1920 - July 2, Papineau and Keenana Garage opened - now the Troy City Hall Building

1920 - September 30, Doonan Addition to West Troy approved

1921 - May 5, First issue of the *Troy Tribune* Newspaper is published

1922 - May 27, Linger Longer Beach opens with dance at Savage Lake

1922 - June 23, Sandpoint Pole and Lumber Company begins work building a sawmill along Callahan Creek in Troy

1922 - September 3, Sandpoint Pole and Lumber Company railroad makes first run up Callahan Creek to Camp #1

1922 - December 6, Post Office moves to new brick building leased by D.W. Fewkes on Second Street

1923 - May 1, Sandpoint Pole and Lumber Company's sawmill begins limited production

1923 - October 3, Third Addition to West Troy approved

1924 - August, Current City of Troy Jail finished

1924 - November 24, The Lincoln Theater opens, showing "The Virginian"

1924 - January 19, T. S. King sells Fred B. Callow, a half interest in the original town site of Troy (Lake City), for $2,250.00

1925 - January 9, The first "3D" movie is shown at the Princess Theater, the "Plastigram."

1925 - June 1, Callow Addition to West Troy approved

1925 - August 5, Troy Town Council votes to drop the title "Town" and assumes that of "City"

1925 - August 5, Water from O'Brien Creek turns into city water mains

1926 - March 15, Troy Great Northern Railway freight division yard closes for good

1926 - March 26, Big Eight railroad spur completed and begins shipping ore to the Snowstorm concentrator in Troy

1926 - April 9, Troy Great Northern Division Yard is briefly reopened

1927 - May 6, Snowstorm Concentrator burns to the ground

1927 - May 13, Last issue of the *Troy Echo* Newspaper published

1927 - October 12, Troy Fire Department Incorporates, now called the Troy Fire Department Relief Association

1928 - February 17, City Dog Pound Building behind the City Hall opens for business

1928 - July 27, The Sandpoint Pole and Lumber Co. sawmill burns to the ground

1929 - June 27, First Airplane lands in Troy, piloted by Paul Shepherd

1929 - October 11, Logging completed, the Sandpoint Pole and Lumber Co. begins removing rails from the South Fork of Callahan

1929 - November 12, Kinzie Hall is destroyed by fire, was the largest building in Troy

1930 - April 15, Troy Great Northern Depot moves 100' to the west

1930 - May 16, U.S. Census lists Troy's population at 493 people

1931 - May 1, The abandoned Sandpoint Pole and Lumber Company planer shed burns down

1931 - October 9, The big "T" on the mountain above Troy completed by high school students.

1931 - November 18, The first lighting of the natural Christmas Tree in Troy

1932 - February 6, First "talkie" shown at the Lincoln Theatre with the movie "FLIGHT" starring Jack Holt, Lila Lee, and Ralph Graves

1933 - June 9, Last issue of the *Troy Tribune* published

1934 - June 21, First issue of the *Troy Ranger* Newspaper was published

1935 - August 29, Last issue of the *Troy Ranger* Newspaper was published

1936 - April 6, Lincoln County sold to Troy, Tracts A, B, C & D

1936 - May 31, Herykaha Placer Tracts Addition to West Troy approved

1940 - May U.S. Census shows Troy's population at 796 people

1941 - August 7, Fire destroys a part of Yaak Ave.; the Great Northern Hotel, Paddy's Bar, and Ernie's Market were destroyed

1950 - May, U.S. Census lists Troy's population at 770 people

1956 - November 8, J. Neils sawmill in Troy begins operation

1957 - January 1, J. Neils merges with St. Regis Paper Co, Troy sawmill now operated by St. Regis

1960 - May, U.S. Census lists Troy's population at 855 people

1970 - May, U.S. Census lists Troy's population at 1,046 people

1977 - December, Troy City Hall moves to its current location, in the old Kootenai Valley Garage building

1994 - Lincoln Theater is remodeled, now seats 170 people

HISTORIC TROY PHOTO KEY

This historic photo shows Troy in 1916. The photo key below outlines the different buildings, some of which are still present in Troy today.

1. Fast Rooming House
2. U.S. Forest Service Warehouse (Railroad Yard)
3. Chinese Restaurant
4. Petty's pool hall
5. & 6. Hotel Doonan, Bar & Restaurant
7. Troy Pharmacy
8. Princess Theater
9. Callow's Mercantile
10. Troy Barber Shop
11. Morrison's Barber Shop
12. Kootenai Valley State Bank
13. D.T. Wood Mercantile
14. D.T. Wood's Palace Saloon
15. Papineau's Buffet
16. Windsor Hotel
17. Troy Cafe
18. G.N. Depot (Railroad Yard)
19. Montana Rooming House
20. Troy Townsite Office
21. Callow's Warehouse
22. Troy Livery
23. W.F. Doonan Home
24. & 25. Regensberger Rentals
26. G.N. Rooming House
27. Methodist Church
28. Hen Houses (chickens)
29. Troy City Hall
30. Log Cabin House
31. Cabin
32. Log Cabin
33. House
34. Cabin

Troy in 1916 showing most of the business district, taken from the hillside across the Kootenai River. Buildings identified by Jim Calvi. Photo courtesy of Jim Calvi.

HEALTH & INFRASTRUCTURE

Locally, Troy residents can visit the Troy Medical Arts Building for their medical needs. The Lincoln County Community Health Center holds offices there, with larger facilities in Libby. Medicine Tree Clinic also offers on-site care, appointments with physicians, x-rays, and completion of minor procedures. For medical emergencies, Troy's Volunteer Ambulance transports individuals to St. John's Lutheran Hospital in Libby, 18 miles away.

NORTHERN LIGHTS, INC.

Northern Lights, Inc. member-owned cooperative, based in Sagle, ID, serves the Yaak area and Bull Lake Road with power needs, delivering electricity to over 2,600 miles of line throughout Montana, Washington, and Idaho. Formed in 1935, Northern Lights, Inc. is the oldest rural electric cooperative west of the Mississippi River.

Within city limits, Troy has its own electrical distribution system. Electricity is dependent on the Bonneville Power Administration. Troy's Power and Light Department consists of Clint Taylor, Power Manager, and Bob Boren and Tim Shaver, Power Department Workers.

FINANCIAL INSTITUTIONS

Troy is served by First National Bank of Montana and Lincoln County Credit Union. First National Bank is located along Highway 2 in the main business district and Lincoln County Credit Union is located in Stein's Market. Both institutions are committed to Troy's improvement and are actively involved in the community. Both heavily support Troy's Old Fashioned 4th of July and other events throughout the year.

HISTORIC BAR STREET

Along the Burlington Northern Santa Fe rail lines, Yaak Avenue, locally called "Bar Street," features a number of historic bars and saloons. The bars once greeted train passengers who stopped in the area. Though many have been remodeled, some have maintained the western facades distinct in early frontier trail stops. Among other historic features, the Home Bar has a carved bar-back dating to the early days of Troy.

TROY SENIOR CENTER

The Troy Senior Center serves the needs of senior citizens in the Troy area. In addition, the dining room has become the best place for larger gatherings in Troy, including luncheons, weddings, anniversaries, dinners, and other celebrations.

TROY LIBRARY

A branch of Lincoln County Public Libraries, the Troy Branch Library serves the needs of Troy patrons through access to materials, public use computers, wireless Internet, and other informational resources. As part of the Montana Shared Catalog Partners group, the Troy Library can freely borrow from many other libraries throughout western Montana.

Medicine Tree Clinic building is one of Troy's early homes. Photo by Melody Condron.

Historic Bar Street. Photo by Melody Condron.

Troy Senior Center. Photo by Melody Condron.

Troy Library, a branch of the Lincoln County Public Libraries. Photo by Melody Condron.

TROY VOLUNTEER FIRE

Troy's Volunteer Fire Department is managed by the City of Troy. Current Fire Chief is Larry Chapel. Fire Marshall is Darren Coldwell. Other firemen in the volunteer service include: Kevin Anderson, 1st Assistant Chief; Terry Steiger, 2nd Assistant Chief; Mike Cratty, 1st Assistant Fire Marshall; and Jeff Bonifas, 2nd Assistant Fire Marshall.

Troy Schools

Troy Public Schools manages three schools: W.F. Morrison Elementary; Troy Junior High School; and Troy Senior High School. Administrative offices are held at 236 Spokane Avenue. Administrative staff include: Brady Selle, Superintendent; Mary Brown, District Clerk; and Susan Duve, Accountant. Total enrollment is approximately 460 students.

TROY ATHLETIC CENTER

In May, 2009, Troy's new Athletic Center was opened to the public. The Athletic Center houses the Kootenai ROCKS climbing wall, basketball court, locker rooms, concession area, and a number of other all-purpose rooms. Racquetball courts are also in the process of being built within the facility. The Troy Athletic Center came about to meet the needs of Troy Schools and students for improved athletic facilities. The gym replaces the old High School gym at the High School and will be home to Troy Trojan basketball home games. Significant local effort went into the center, which was erected in under a year. Volunteer labor from city workers and others kept costs manageable. While the Center is owned by Troy Schools, the school district has expressed a desire to make the facility public friendly. The public will have ample opportunity to use the building in the future.

W.F. MORRISON ELEMENTARY

Morrison Elementary School is located at 501 E. Kalispell Avenue. Lance Pearson is Principal. Morrison serves Troy students from Kindergarten through 6th grade. In 2008, New Horizons after school program also became part of the after school experience for some Troy students. Programs include art, games, learning activities, guests, and other fun activities. Morrison is host to many events each year, including book fairs, science fairs, plays, talent shows, dances, fundraisers (for the school and others), and the Boy Scout Christmas Bazaar. In the summer, Morrison offers free breakfast and lunch to children, summer school, elementary tennis, and limited computer lab usage. New Horizons is also be offered as a summer program at Morrison. Approximately 220 students attend Morrison Elementary each year.

TROY JUNIOR & SENIOR HIGH SCHOOL

Troy Junior and Senior High Schools are located at 118 E. Missoula Avenue. Jeff Ralston is Principal. The Junior High School is comprised of grades 7 and 8, and 9th through 12th grade are at the Senior High School. Significant upgrades have been made to the school buildings and facilities recently, including the Troy Athletic Center and new science lab. Approximately 175 students attend the Senior High School; the Junior High School serves approximately 75. Both schools are actively involved in sports at both a regional and state-wide level.

Grand opening of Troy's new Athletic Center, opened in 2009. Kootenai ROCKS climbing wall can be seen in the far corner. Photo by Melody Condron.

New science lab facilites at Troy High School. Photo courtesy of Kootenai Valley Record.

Troy Churches

COMMUNITY BAPTIST

Troy Community Baptist Church was formed in 1996 under the leadership of Chuck Gray. In April of 1999, Cathy and Cameron Harrison Foote and family were called to pastor. They began serving the church on June 1, 1999.

Starting with a group of six in attendance, the church has grown to around 120 in attendance, with over 200 members in 2009.

With the growth came changes and a new building. The spacious 12,000 square foot building was raised with the help of Volunteer Christian Builders of Texas. Troy Community Baptist Church is located at 725 East Missoula Avenue in Troy, and offers ministries for all ages. Staff includes: Cameron H. Foote, Pastor; Thomas Hampton Rowe and Ron L. Adair, Associates; and Cecil Foote and George Thompson, Deacons.

FAITH CHRISTIAN CENTER

The property and buildings located at 87 Amber Road in Troy, Montana, now owned by Faith Christian Center, was purchased from the Pentecostal Church of God of America, Inc., in 1980. The Fellowship had four pastors in the next eight years.

In October of 1988, a governing body consisting of Vern Hutt, Marie Hutt, and Janet Moore petitioned Martin and Linda Bower to be the pastors. They have remained and are still serving in that capacity in 2009. Janet Moore is a lifetime member of the Fellowship now living with her children in Arkansas. Leroy and Wilma Beebe were ordained around 1995. Leroy passed away in the spring of 2008. Wilma is still a member of the Fellowship. Donald and Lois Natale joined the Fellowship in June of 1999, and were ordained December 1999. They presently serve as worship leaders and assistant pastors.

Faith Christian Center is Full Gospel in belief and supports missions monthly to Transki, South Africa and northern India.

The Fellowship is currently involved in a building program to provide a new sanctuary. New Sunday school rooms will be housed in the full basement of the new addition.

THREE LAKES COMMUNITY BIBLE CHURCH

Three Lakes Community Bible Church grew out of a home Bible study conducted by Rocky Mountain Bible Mission in the homes of Marvin Kates and John Ring near Milnor Lake. The Bible study group, which started in September of 1972, was outgrowing the Ring's trailer so the suggestion was made to start a church. The Kates donated property and construction began in April 1975.

Pastor Clarence Kutz was the Bible study teacher, but he passed away from leukemia in October of 1975. His son-in-law, Dave Nelson, had been teaching the youth group and became the pastor. He has remained pastor and is in that position in 2009. The original Executive Council consisted of George Jordan, John Ring, Ivan Varner, Raymond Sampson, and David Nelson. The current Council includes Raymond Sampson, Ellis Stewart, Jerry Davis, Gay ("Stump") Heiselman, and David Nelson. There are also two associate pastors: Denny Noble, visitation; and John Demmendaal, youth. Debbie Dare has served for many years as the church custodian.

In 1978, Three Lakes started Elohim Bible Camp 13 miles south of the church on Highway 56. The camp is now run by Rocky Mountain Bible Mission. In 1979, Three Lakes Christian School began and ran until 1992, with a peak enrollment of nearly 90 students in K-8. Sunday School is also offered, with average attendance of 80-85. An AWANA children's program is conducted on Wednesday nights along with youth group during the school year and a family Bible study during the summer. Many home Bible studies are also conducted throughout the area each week.

OTHER ACTIVE CHURCHES IN TROY

Assembly of God
Church of God
Church of Jesus Christ of Latter Day Saints
Holy Trinity Episcopal
Immaculate Conception Catholic Church
Kootenai Chapel
United Methodist

Troy Community Baptist's new building, built in 2009. Photo by Susan Nikolaus.

Troy Groups & Organizations

KOOTENAI ROCKS CLIMBING WALL CLUB

Kootenai ROCKS Climbing Wall Club was formed in May 2008 and raised $56,796 in one year to construct a climbing wall in the Troy Activity Center. "Our mission is to provide a link between outdoor education and a healthy lifestyle. Our focus is on safe and rewarding recreation for youth and community members to develop confidence, strength and problem solving skills." The club consists of 43 student and adult members: Justin Randall, Makaylin Randall, Jasmine Johnson, Jeffery Johnson, Ray Maas, Callan Peel, Kevin Peel, Mazzy Hermes, Holli Higgins, Michaela Curry, Lexi McCann, Michael Goe, Taylor Brown, Allie Goe, Tana Thill, Tom Roeder, Katie Lundin, Kellie Lundin, Makayla Osterberg, Anna Valentine, Patrick Valentine, Jeffrey Rebo, Azure Stever, Cody Williams, Sophie Pearson, Jesse Pearson, Kyle Hermann, Ashley Neely, Tyann Hermes, Chris Hermes, Shana Bernall, Ben Bernall, Josh Boyd, Chris

Members of Kootenai ROCKS Climbing Wall Club, formed in 2008. Photos courtesy of Tyann Hermes.

Boyd, Sarah Canepa, Shane McMillen, Timory Peel, Lance Pearson, Ousie Pearson, Ben Valentine, Shawna Kelsey, Michelle Carlson, Kristen Thrall, Matt Thrall, Hana Coy, Shawna Charbonneau, Jill Dieser, Brenda Goe, Jeremy Lizotte, Hannah Hernandez, and John Peel.

The wall was installed in February 2009. Donors include: Kootenai ROCKS Climbing Wall Club, Morrison Elementary Club Funds "In memory of Bill Ackley," Kootenai Drug True Value, Plum Creek Foundation, Troy Parks and Recreation, Larson Lumber, Seifert Family Foundation, Lincoln County Combined Campaign, Lincoln County Credit Union, Lincoln County Community Foundation, Troy Booster Club, Lippert Log Construction, Troy Area Community Association, John and Timory Peel, Sharron Sverdrup and Dave Friedman, Troy Softball Association, Troy PTA, First National Bank, R Place, Granite Concrete, Shana & Ben Bernall, Sarah Canepa, Bill Harwood, Tony Smith, June McMahon, Ralph Stever, Al Randall, Booze N Bait, Mazzy Hermes, Marcus Hermes, Ed Stamy, Darrell and Connie Hand Family, Homesteaders Ranch and Feed, Cabinet Resource Group, Josh and Kris Boyd, Chance Bernall, Montanore Minerals Corporation, Heather McDougall, Black Diamond Equipment, and Eldorado Wall Company.

FINE ARTS COUNCIL

Troy Fine Arts Council was founded as a non-profit in September 1994 to promote a cultural climate in Troy. Founders include Jennifer Seifert, Terrel Jones, Sherry Lersbak, and Peg Fleming. Current officers are: Tyann Hermes, President; Kristen Thrall, Vice President; and Betty Phillips, Secretary.

Since inception, Troy Fine Arts Council has been involved with a number of projects, including: Missoula Children's Theatre, 1993-present; ethnic dinners, 33 since November 1997; cultural cinema, 31 films between 2003-2008; Montana Repertory Theater; Neil Lewing workshop/performance, 2005; Drum Brothers workshops, 2004; Mud Bay Jugglers School performance, 2004; New Old Time Chautauqua, 2003 and 2007; Artrain 1998 and 2001; Artists in Residence, 11 visits in schools; Arts in the Park; Ceramic Tile Bench Project, 2006; hip hop dance classes, 2006; Disc Golf; Music in the Park, 2006-present; Beth Nixon Puppet Project, 2007; Kootenai River Bluegrass Festival, 2008-present; and financial support to Libby's Memorial Center.

FRIENDS OF THE LIBRARY

Troy Friends of the Library supports the Troy Library by hosting and planning library programs, raising funds for special projects, and supporting the activities of the library in general. Troy Friends have supported Summer Reading, Magazine Sponsorship, and the Annual Lincoln County Poetry Contest. In addition, Troy Friends of the Library decorates the library for holidays and participates in upkeep of the front garden. Programs planned by the group include High Tea, classes on Medicinal Herbs, and presentations on international travel.

GLASS ART GUILD

The Troy Glass Art Guild was formed in 2005 by a group of local glass artists. The purpose of the Guild is to support art awareness and the creative growth of local artists in all forms of glass art and other mediums. Together with the Troy Museum, the group sponsors Arts on the Grass, an art fair on the Troy Museum lawn. 2009 will mark the fourth year this very popular event will be held at the Troy Museum. Some of the art featured at Arts on the Grass includes paintings, log creations, photography, stained glass, pottery, leather work, and various forms of glass art.

The current officers of the Troy Glass Art Guild are: Sharon Denton, President; Monica Anderson, Secretary; and Dale Peterson, Treasurer. Other active members include Beth Schweitzer, Betty Phillips, and Arlo Reilly.

GIRL SCOUTS

Troy Girl Scouts are currently active, with three troops: Daisies for Kindergarten-1st grade; Brownies for 2-3rd grades; and Juniors for 4-5th grades. Girls participated in the Gift of Caring in 2009, donating cookies to local heroes including Troy teachers and Volunteer Fire. In 2008, troops participated in a downtown clean-up for Earth Day. Troops have cooperated with the Libby Girl Scouts for events and attend a number of field trips and sleepovers. There are currently 24 registered girls and 8 registered adults in the Troy area.

OTHER ACTIVE GROUPS, CLUBS & ORGANIZATIONS IN TROY

Boy Scouts
Tender Lovin' Quilt Guild
Troy Business and Professionals Club
Troy Snowmobile Club
Veterans of Foreign Wars
VFW Ladies Auxiliary

Annual Quilt show put on by Troy's Tender Lovin' Quilt Guild on July 3 & 4 each year. Photo courtesy of Kootenai Valley Record.

Recreation in Troy

TROY MUSEUM & VISITOR'S CENTER

The idea of a museum was started by the Troy Woman's Club in 1973. Nola Sloan was the person who got the museum going. It was sponsored by the Troy United Methodist Church. This first museum was on the corner of 4th Street and Highway 2 and the building belonged to Bill McGlumply of Libby. The ladies of the museum decided they needed a permanent place for a museum so they lobbied the county and the current museum's property was given to them. Martin McCann sold them the old "train mens" building from the old railroad depot in 1978.

The museum is volunteer-run and lots of Troy residents have participated in keeping it open. The museum features all Troy-related historical items. In addition, the Museum area is home to the FOLF course, public rest rooms, public posting area, picnic tables, and parking area available to visitors. The wooden visitor's sign in front of the museum was carved entirely by chain saw by Dave Clarke of Eureka. The Troy Museum and Visitor's Center also cooperates with the Troy Glass Art Guild to host the annual Arts on the Grass. Current leaders for the Visitor's Center are: Beth Schweitzer, President; Donn Ross, Treasurer; and Patti Haaland, Secretary.

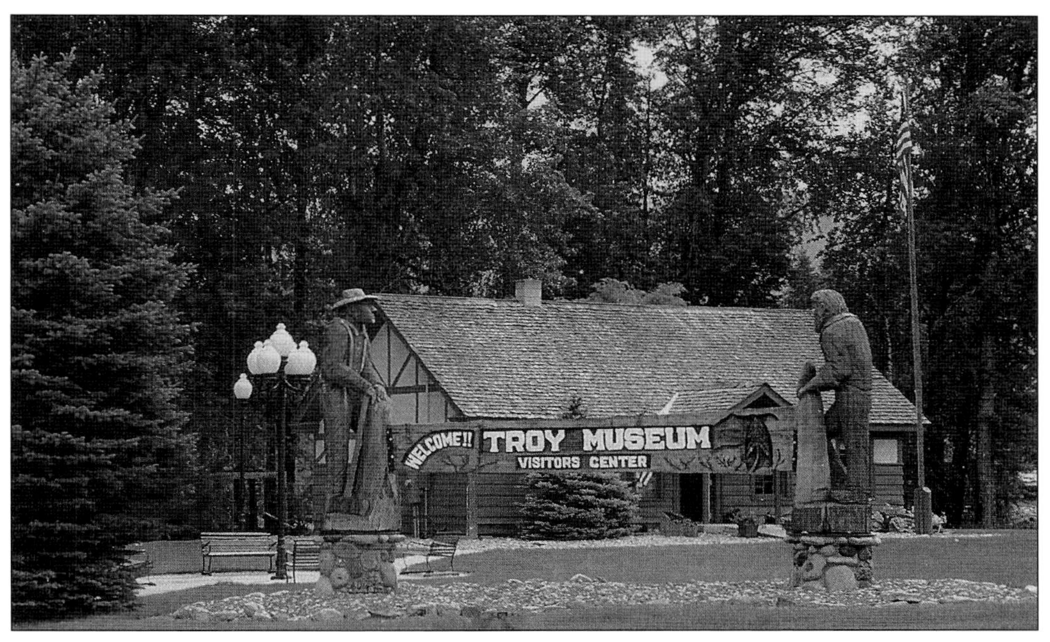

Troy Visitor's Center and Museum. Photo courtesy of Troy Museum.

LARGEST LIVING CHRISTMAS TREE

Troy is home to the world's largest living Christmas Tree. The tree is located next to the new post office at 123 East Kootenai Avenue and provides an informative sign to let all visitors know about its title. The tree is strung with Christmas lights and is lit up during the holiday season. On the first Saturday in December, Santa visits the tree for the annual lighting.

ATVs cross the single-lane Troy Bridge over the Kootenai River. Photo by Melody Condron.

DISC GOLF COURSE

The Timberbeast FOLF (frisbee golf) course is built on 10 acres directly behind the Troy Visitor's Center and Museum. Running along year-round Callahan Creek and retired rail lines, the course is used for the annual Timberbeast competition. The event is hosted by the Troy Fine Arts Council and is part of the Montana Points Series and the Inland Northwest Series. Disc golf enthusiasts from across the state come to Troy to compete, often camping in nearby Roosevelt Park.

ROOSEVELT PARK

Roosevelt City Park is located along the Kootenai River near the Troy Bridge. Visitors must cross the BNSF railroad tracks at the only crossing in downtown Troy to get to the park. Many Troy events take place at the park, including Troy's Old Fashioned 4th of July, Kootenai River Bluegrass Festival, and Troy's Annual Easter Egg Hunt. The park offers a boat launch, picnic areas, soccer fields, pavilion, two baseball fields, children's fishing pond, walking path, basketball court, playground, concession stand (for event use), bathrooms, water play area, skate park, and a yurt on the river bank for visitor rental. Many residents use the park for daily recreation, including walks, picnics, and fishing. The park is managed by the City of Troy.

Trail near Kootenai Falls across the swinging bridge. Photo by Melody Condron.

Kayaker at Kootenai Falls. Photo courtesy of For His Glory Photography.

Kootenai Falls. Photo by Melody Condron.

Shannon Lake. Photo by Melody Condron.

Swinging Bride. Photo courtesy of For His Glory Photography.

KOOTENAI FALLS & SWINGING BRIDGE

Kootenai Falls is the largest undammed falls in the state of Montana. Located between Libby and Troy on Highway 2, the Kootenai Falls Park is 135.56 acres. The area is managed by County Parks District #2 in cooperation with many other organizations.

The falls can be reached via a short (half mile) hike from a parking area located on Highway 2. Picnic areas and rest rooms are available near the parking area. The falls area has no guide rails or paved paths next to the falls, giving visitors a natural view of the falls. The amount of water coming over the falls varies depending on runoff and Libby Dam water release upstream.

Just downstream from Kootenai Falls, accessible from the same parking area and path, is the swinging bridge. Featured in the movie *The River Wild*, the swinging bridge crosses the Kootenai and connects to other hiking paths. Adventurous visitors cross the bridge to get better views of the falls.

Swinging Bridge. Photo by Melody Condron.

OLD HIGHWAY 2 TRAIL

The Old Highway 2 Trail offers hiking opportunities along the path of the old highway. Three access points to the two sections of trail can be reached from Highway 2, with another reached off of Bull Lake Road. The trail travels high above Kootenai Falls and the Kootenai River Valley, offering excellent views. Wildlife including elk, deer, and fox live along the trail. Sections of the old highway, with hand-built rock retaining walls, can be seen along the trail. Access to Shannon Lake and Grambauer Mountain Trail can also be reached from the section of Old Highway 2 Trail closes to Bull Lake Road.

View of the Kootenai River from the Old Highway 2 Trail. Photo by Melody Condron.

Events in Troy

EASTER EGG HUNT

Each year on Easter Sunday, children from all over the Troy area go to Roosevelt Park to search for treat-filled eggs. The event is a large community gathering. Event organizer Candy Clark and her team organize donations from businesses in both Troy and Libby. Eggs are filled with small treats or tickets for larger prizes. Volunteers staff the event and provide baked goods for participants and their families.

KOOTENAI RIVER BLUEGRASS FESTIVAL

The Kootenai River Bluegrass Festival is a weekend of music in Roosevelt Park. Planned by the Troy Fine Arts Council, the event features many live concerts, instrumental and vocal workshops, camping on-site in Roosevelt Park, and many evening jams with musicians. The event was in its second year in 2009 but a good showing from both families and individuals has made the event a great success. Many attendees travel to get to the event, which makes Troy a musical destination each summer.

A Year in Troy

New events in Troy, like the Kootenai River Bluegrass Festival and Timberbeast, have been met with incredible enthusiasm. Meanwhile, traditional events like Troy's Old Fashioned 4th are still going strong. Here are a few of the annual events in Troy:

March / April

Easter Egg Hunt

June

Timberbeast FOLF Tournament

July

Troy's Old Fashioned 4th of July
Kootenai River Bluegrass Festival
Arts on the Grass
Wilderness Festival

August

Mud Bogg

December

Lighting of the Largest Living Christmas Tree
12 Days of Christmas
Boy Scout Bazaar

Troy Mud Bogg. Photo by Kootenai Valley Record.

Troy's Annual Easter Egg Hunt in Roosevelt Park. Photo courtesy of Kootenai Valley Record.

TROY'S OLD FASHIONED 4TH OF JULY

Troy's Old Fashioned 4th of July is a tradition as old as Lincoln County. Even in the early 20th Century, Troy was host to children's games, live music, and celebration on July 4th. The modern celebration draws as many as 6,000 people to Troy and offers live music, car show, tug-of-war, kids games, kids carnival, food, vendors, parade, and a large fireworks display. The Troy parade runs through town on Highway 2 and side streets. Other events take place in Troy's beautiful Roosevelt Park. The event is completely volunteer run. Troy's Chamber of Commerce organizes the event.

Car show at Troy's Old Fashioned 4th of July. Photo by Melody Condron.

A field of activities: Troy's Old Fashioned 4th of July in Roosevelt Park. Photo by Melody Condron.

Old Fashioned car in the 4th of July parade. Photo courtesy of Kootenai Valley Record.

Live music in the Roosevelt Park pavilion. Photo courtesy of Kootenai Valley Record.

Participants in Troy's Old Fashioned 4th of July parade. Photo courtesy of Kootenai Valley Record.

Yaak River Valley

Spanning the area along the Yaak River from the Canadian border to the Kootenai River, the Yaak Valley is over 40 miles long and yet is remote enough that human population is limited. A narrow section of private land exists along the Yaak River, primarily surrounded by Kootenai National Forest. The area is accessible by Highway 567 from Libby and Highway 508 from Highway 2 between Troy and Idaho.

YAAK: THE LAST BEST PLACE

by LeeAnn Sanders

This remote community in the far northwest corner of Montana is considered by many of its inhabitants to be a little slice of heaven. It's an 800,000-acre parcel, carved down the middle by the Yaak River, whose valley perimeter is bordered by protective mountain peaks and ridges. It's in this seasonal wonderland the Yaak residents thrive.

The Yaak once had a reputation for being a dangerous territory of outlaws. Today, however, the Yaak is home to singles, families, and retirees who are committed to maintaining their independence and yet provide a sense of dependable community. In "downtown" Yaak you will find the core of the community, with its few visible establishments. The Yaak River Mercantile and Tavern sits across the street from the previously notorious Dirty Shame Saloon. Just down the road is the Yaak River Lodge. These are the places friends gather for food and fun as well as frequent traditional events and fundraisers.

Yaak River Mercantile and Tavern. Photo by Melody Condron.

Taking a closer look, you will also find the Yaak Rod and Gun Club, which claims 50 members and provides a place for friendly competition as well as hunter safety classes for this popular local sport. The Volunteer Fire Department, housed nearby, keeps a roster of 14 firefighters on staff and responds to a nearly 30 mile long territory up and down the valley. Just north from this core area you'll see the Tipi Art Gallery, which displays and sells local artwork. Beyond this you'll find the Yaak Elementary School, built in the 1930s. Its doors are open to students kindergarten through eighth grade and, despite its rustic appearance, it is equipped with state-of-the-art technology for a modern student body. Along with the public elementary, there is a private boarding facility a few miles east of downtown called Turning Winds School, which serves at-risk teenagers. The last public building you are likely to see would be the Community Center at the thirty-three mile mark.

Yaak Community Center. Photo by Melody Condron.

This historic building is currently used by the Yaak Community Church, which meets every Sunday and sponsors a weekly Ladies Bible Study and summertime Vacation Bible School. The Community Center is also the home of the Yaak Women's Club, which publishes a local cookbook and meets weekly for quilting and crafting. In addition, the building is used for other events such as public meetings.

A frequent question to people in the Yaak is, "How do you make a living way up there?" For those who aren't retired, the answer might be logging, teaching, construction, health-care services, trucking, sales, fire fighting, fishing or game guiding, writing, photography, ranching, gardening, milling lumber, crafts making, repair work, telecommuting, flying aircraft, taxidermy, food services, forestry service, or protecting our borders, to name more than a few. The Yaak is full of talented people who are willing to commute or keep their businesses in this valley in order to continue living there.

Once work is done, there are numerous activities to keep Yaak residents busy. During the summer camping, swimming, and fishing are popular along the river. There are numerous trails open to hikers and horseback riders. There's an annual Fourth of July celebration at the Yaak River Tavern, which includes food, games for the kids, and a fireworks finale. The Yaak Elementary School Auction and Raffle Fundraiser, too, happens each summer. Of course, it wouldn't be summer without scouring the local hills for a favorite treat: huckleberries. It's been said there are two seasons in the Yaak: winter and company. Many Yaakers stay busy in the summer hosting out of town friends and family.

Besides the visible changing color of the larch and aspen trees, you know autumn is here when you see the signs for the "Fall Free for All." The Yaak Community Church opens their doors to everyone to come in and recycle others' gently used discards. It's like going to a huge yard sale and everything is free. Fall is also the time to start practicing your throwing skills for the yearly dart league at the Tavern. When fall rolls around, Yaakers drop about everything for hunting season. The Yaak is a popular spot for locals and out of state hunters to find their game, whether it's bear, elk, deer or moose. In addition to seeing an abundance of camouflage or blaze orange, you're likely to see locals taking a late opportunity to gather firewood from the forest in an effort to stay warm through the long winter.

Despite grumbling about having to snowplow driveways, winter brings peacefulness to the Yaak Valley. Life slows down a little for most locals, who by now have their pantries and wood sheds well stocked, just in case. The school kids practice their holiday program to perform at a packed Community Center and get us in the Christmas spirit. Outside, the wildlife become more visible with the deciduous plants barren of their leaves. The larger animals take advantage of the plowed roads as an occasional break from trudging through deep snow. Adventurous Yaakers relish the winter wonderland to snowmobile on Mt. Henry or Spread Creek, sometimes meeting for a wiener roast high atop the peaks. Down below, those braving the elements might be running a trap-line or ice fishing on Vinal Lake. At the Yaak School, the kids can be seen sledding or cross country skiing at recess.

Yaak Women's Club. Photo courtesy of Yaak Women's Club.

Winter gives way to spring and the Yaak prepares for water and more water. Those along the river keep a close eye on it as it rises with spring thaw. Occasionally you'll see a canoe tied up outside someone's cabin in case a creek rises too high. Snow melts, rain falls, mud is tracked inside, spring turkeys appear, and hunters take advantage of the spring black bear hunt. Gardeners open up their green houses and begin getting their hands back in the dirt. Yaakers make sure they have plenty of mosquito repellent and the seasonal cycle repeats itself.

Yaak School. Photo by Melody Condron.

What characterizes the Yaak the most is not that it is an outdoor wonderland, but that it is filled with people who help one another. The Yaak is a long way from stores, so if someone is heading to out of town to stock up on things that aren't found locally, it's common to ask if anyone needs something picked up for them. When someone is hurt or sick and doesn't have health insurance, the community is quick to respond with fundraisers. Despite the early reputation of the Yaak, it is a generous, helpful community where many love to live, work, and play. Just ask any Yaaker. It's the last best place.

YAAK COMMUNITY CHURCH

Yaak Community Church is a non-denominational church that was started about 20 years ago by pastor Glen and his wife JoAnn Sherwood, Winnie Canavan, the Covey family, and Stenro family (all long time Yaak residents). The current board of directors include John Loney, Larry Covey, Mike Sanders, with Mary Loney as Secretary, and Jane Kelly as Treasurer.

Since it's beginning, no matter what weather the Yaak throws at them, the faithful congregation—which ranges from 7 to 50 members—has never missed a Sunday morning at the Community Center. The Community Center is located at mile marker 33, three miles north of Yaak. Services consist of singing, prayer, praise time, and sermons given by various speakers, followed by a snack and fellowship. Events sponsored by the Yaak Community Church include the Fall GiveAway, a "sale" where everything is free; Vacation Bible School in August; Easter Sunday service with free breakfast; and Ladies Bible Study most Thursdays.

YAAK WOMEN'S CLUB

The Yaak Women's Club was started in the late 1970s by Winifred (Winnie) Canavan and Zeita Romeiko. This civic organization has given generously of their time and energy through the years by quilting for fund raising and creating and selling community cookbooks. The Yaak Women's Club has been the integral instrument in the restoration and preservation of the Yaak Community Center building, built in 1925. The building is rented out for various functions, and, additionally, provides rental space for freezers for those in the Yaak still without electricity.

The first quilt made by the women of this club was for a Yaak Ambulance fundraiser. The group ha been quilting ever since for the annual Wings fund raiser and the Yaak school auction. They are often commissioned by others to make fundraising quilts for various community needs which have included gas money for the ambulance, liability insurance for the fire company, repairs for the Yaak Community Center, and other community projects, as needed. One of the Yaak Women's Club quilts is on permanent display in the St. John's Lutheran Hospital in Libby.

YAAK SCHOOL

The Yaak School was started in 1919 with the present schoolhouse being built in 1932. The logs for this building were hand hewn in 1931 by Thomas Garrison, the grandfather of current resident Martin Riedlinger. The small log school is a rare educational opportunity that continues to exist despite the closing and consolidation of many rural schools. The present schoolteacher is Jennifer Smith. She currently instructs nine students at age levels from kindergarten through eighth grade with the help of a part time teacher's aide, Debbie McNeil.

The students participate in various field trips and course work including ice fishing, snowshoeing, cross country, downhill skiing, computer usage, art and music, as well as the traditional reading, writing, and math. Students perform a Christmas play with music each year and practice public speaking skills each month with an oral report to the school board on what they are learning and doing. The school is supported by numerous community volunteers, with the present school board consisting of Pam Mayo, John Loney, and LeeAnn Sanders. Each summer an annual school fund raiser auction is held to support the school.

Dirty Shame Historic Saloon. Photo by Melody Condron.

UPPER YAAK FIRE SERVICE

The Ambulance Service got its start in the Yaak in 1986 with the help of many volunteers, including Bill and Sue Janssen, Raymond and Anna David, Warren Robb, Dick and Becky McGeary, Hugh Hollyday, and Kathy Berke. Funds from Lincoln County with the help of Larry Dozezal, commissioner, and many in the Troy and Yaak Community helped with the building costs and acquiring the ambulance. It was not until 1994-95 that another group focused on starting up a volunteer fire department, sharing the same building with the Ambulance Service. With the leadership of Martin Riedlinger and his wife JoAn, Reuben Kneller, Basil Canavan, Dick and Linda Stehlik, Kurk and Paula Breithaupt, Chuck Leidigh, and many others attending Guard School, the fledgling department became qualified as firefighters in July 1996. The current Board Members of the Upper Yaak Fire Service comprise of Basil Canavan, Chief, Sharon Sullivan, secretary-treasurer, Reuben Kneller, Ron Fagg, and Woody Chain. The totally volunteer department is made up of approximately 12 members at this time.

Yaak Wilderness Festival information booth presents wilderness issues. Photo courtesy of Kootenai Valley Record.

Yaak Falls. Photo courtesy of For His Glory Photography.

Both Ambulance and Fire Service shared the facilities with the addition of Building II as the fire department started to expand with the procurement of a water tender from Libby's VFD. In 2005, the Ambulance stopped service due to funding and lack of help.

February 14, 2008 the original building that was built burnt to the ground, completely destroying all the contents including the 1973 brush truck that the fire department started with. With the help of insurance monies, the County Road Crew and local donations, a new building is now standing in the same footprint. Annual Chili Cook-Offs are planned during National Fire Safety Month in October with dance and raffle, as well as an annual rummage sale during Memorial Day weekend.

Alan Lane Band playing at the Yaak Wilderness Festival. Photo courtesy of Kootenai Valley Record.

YAAK VALLEY FOREST COUNCIL

Yaak Valley Forest Council (YVFC) formed in 1997 because local residents were concerned with the health and management of the forest lands in the Yaak Valley. YVFC organizes efforts to advocate for and implement conservation and restoration based on the Yaak Valley's wildlife habitat for sensitive species. The group has implemented restoration projects, offers numerous community education programs, and hosts the Yaak Wilderness Festival each year. There are more than 75 local supporters and a national mailing list of over 1000. Current staff are: Robyn King, Executive Director; Randy Beacham, Community Forest Watch Coordinator; Pam Fuqua, Office Assistant; and Scott Daily, Program Development.

HISTORIC DIRTY SHAME

The Dirty Shame Saloon in Yaak, Montana is perhaps one of the most infamous institutions in the County. With a reputation for rowdiness, the saloon, bar, and restaurant is a fixture not only for the small town of Yaak, but also for the whole county. Though it has shed its dangerous past, the saloon still interests visitors as a historic fixture in the Yaak Valley. The Dirty Shame is one of the few local establishments serving food in the Yaak and offers cabins and other amenities for visitors to the area.

YAAK FALLS

Yaak Falls is a favorite local attraction for visitors and residents alike. The Falls are seven miles up Highway 508, which begins about ten miles west of Troy, Montana. Geologically, the area is quite old; many of the exposed rocks in the Falls have been dated between 800 million and 1.5 billion years old, making the site especially interesting for rockhounds. For most, however, the Falls themselves are the real draw. In the spring and early summer the Yaak Falls are particularly torrential and attract many interested in viewing the formation on the Yaak River. The area is also popular for hiking, camping, and various wintertime activities.

NORTHWEST PEAKS SCENIC AREA

Northwest Peaks Scenic Area is located in the northwest corner of the Kootenai National Forest near both the Canada and Idaho. It is reached by Forest roads extending from U.S. Highway 2 and Montana Highway 508. Part of the Selkirk Range, the areas tall peaks and deep valleys provide many primitive recreation opportunities. There are only limited trails in the area, making it a remote destination. At 7,705 and 7,583 feet, respectively, Northwest Peak and Davis Mountain are the tallest in the range. In addition to other recreation in the scenic area, the Northwest Peak Trail offers incredible views of the upper West Fork Yaak River drainage and the surrounding area.

Lake Creek Valley & Bull Lake

Many small communities exist along Highway 56 (also called Bull Lake Road), a stretch of road cut short by Highway 200 to the south and Highway 2 to the north. The valley runs along a number of waterways, with 16 miles of Lake Creek Valley terminating at Bull Lake. At 1160 acres, Bull Lake is the largest naturally formed lake in Lincoln County. It is the perfect area to enjoy watersports, boating, fishing, or camping along the shore. Bull Lake offers a public beach area along the east side, and many public and private campgrounds, both remote and closer to Highway 56.

Despite a high recreation value, Highway 56 maintains a relatively small population of residents. Most of the development is at the northern end of the valley, closest to Highway 2 and Troy. Closer groupings of houses surround Savage and Milnor Lakes. Only a few commercial enterprises exist along the road, primarily campgrounds. Little Joe's Bar and Restaurant and the Halfway House both offer food to those on the drive. Both also host various events throughout the year.

Bull Lake. Photo courtesy of Kootenai Aviation.

ROSS CREEK SCENIC AREA

The Ross Creek Scenic Area is a 100-acre ancient grove of western red cedars located four miles off of Bull Lake Road / Highway 56 in south Lincoln County. Ross Creek Cedars is considered one of the "eight must-see attractions" in Lincoln County. The grove is situated in a modified temperate rain forest climate, which has allowed many of the cedars to grow up to twelve feet in diameter and one hundred seventy-five feet tall. Some are as much as five hundred years old and others, fallen and dead, have created a lush habitat for many plants and animals on the forest floor.

The Ross Creek Scenic Area includes a self-guided nature trail loop, just less than one-mile in length, with informative signs about the history of the area and the local ecology. The loop is easy for families and wheelchair accessible. Ross Creek runs through the area and a picnic grove is available for public use. Wildlife at Ross Creek includes picas, flying squirrels, bats, and many species of birds and plants. There are no camping facilities at Ross Creek Scenic Area but Bad Medicine and Door Skeels campgrounds are located close by.

Ross Creek Cedars. Photo courtesy of For His Glory Photography.

The Future of Lincoln County

Lincoln County has much to look forward to. New growth and development can be seen around the county.

In Libby, a new St. John's Lutheran Hospital is in process, promising improved medical facilities to better serve the area into the future. Construction of the Lincoln County Credit Union's new Libby building is also underway. U Serve Tennis Club's Community Tennis Courts will become a realization in the near future, too. The ultimate sign of transition, Libby's old High School building is currently in the process of being turned into housing and office space in the downtown area. In addition, 2009 construction and renovation can be seen all along US Highway 2 and Mineral Avenue.

Lincoln County Credit Union groundbreaking of new Libby building in 2009, Photo courtesy of Kooteani Valley Record.

In Eureka, a new Stein's Market has made it appealing for area residents to show locally, rather than driving to larger Whitefish or Kalispell. A new, 22-acre business park has also recently been added to the Tobacco Valley region. A vision of creating a "business incubator" in the space will no doubt encourage business growth. Plans to improve parking and year-round road access, and to provide DSL Internet and improved power options will make the site appealing to entrepreneur and investors. Employment opportunities will follow.

In Troy, a new Athletic Center, complete with large climbing wall, was finished in 2009. The new facility will host all Troy Trojan basketball home games, and will offer recreational opportunities for the public on the climbing wall and racquetball courts. New businesses along Highway 2 have been bustling in Troy, with many storefronts, formerly empty, full with local entrepreneurship.

Logging in Lincoln County, 2008. Photo courtesy of Kootenai Valley Record.

West Kootenai Volunteer Fire Fighters are also breaking ground for a fire hall in 2009.

In 2009, Lincoln County became part of the "Top Ten Scenic Drives of the Northern Rockies." The drive, which follows Bull Lake Road to Highway 2, up Highway 37, through Eureka to Whitefish, positioned Lincoln County to receive more visitors, improving the local economy.

As far as residential growth is concerned, it is looking possible that Plum Creek plans to develop land lots in the Chain of Lakes area. If they can manage to sell additional lots without jeopardizing the recreational feel of the area, the additional residents may forge new communities in the region. In general, increased growth along Lincoln County's border with Flathead County is likely in the coming years. However, stable growth in other areas of the county imply healthy communities.

All of the communities in Lincoln County are bustling with activity from January through December. Still passionate about a heritage rich in mining, logging, and ranching, the county has nevertheless embraced new opportunities. Construction, development, and growth across the county prove that. Despite some concern over how well the area will fare with recent economic changes, employment changes, and the changing make-up of each community's population, Lincoln County will be around well past its centennial and into the next 100 years.

Libby's Old High School, currently under renovation to become office and residential space. Photo courtesy of Kootenai Valley Record.

Kootenai Falls. Photo by Melody Condron.

Community ❧ Natural Beauty ❧ Heritage
Lincoln County, Montana

Cabinet Mountains. Photo courtesy of Kootenai Aviation.

Face painting at Libby's Irish Fair. Photo courtesy of Kootenai Valley Record.

Loggers of yesteryear ride in the Logger Days parade in Libby. Photo courtesy of Kootenai Valley Record.

Old Highway 2 Trail. Photo by Melody Condron.

Fisher River Valley Battalion Chief Kirk Kraft (right), take possession of his department's new ambulance from Woodinville Deputy Chief Bud Backer and Battalion Chief Tad Wineman. Photo courtesy of Kootenai Valley Record.

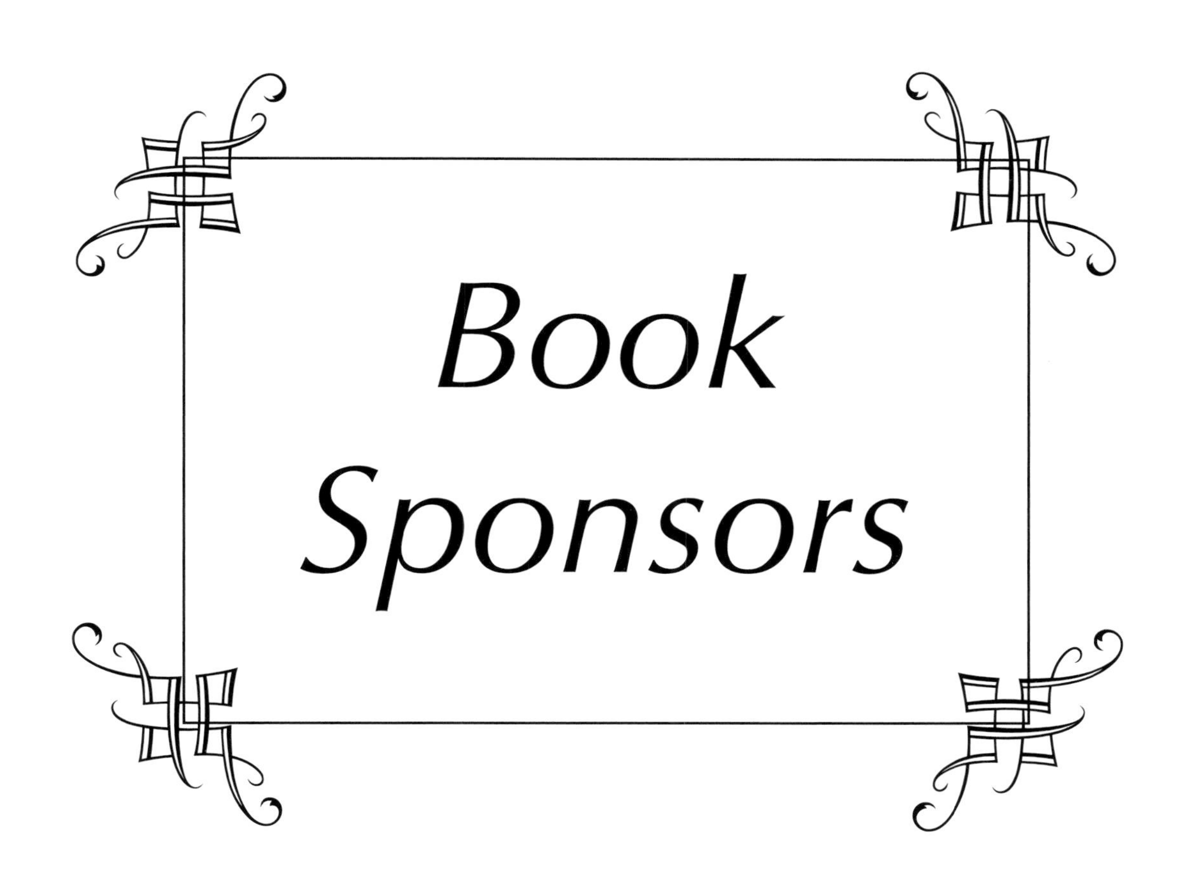
Book
Sponsors

A Legacy of Care

For more than 56 years, St. John's Lutheran Hospital has had a proud tradition of exemplary care for the residents of Lincoln County. Today the residents and visitors of South Lincoln County enjoy a full-service, technologically-advanced health care facility. They can live and play knowing that their health is in good hands.

An Anchor Employer

St. John's is the largest private employer in Lincoln County with a professional staff of 230. Employees are not only healthcare providers, but dedicated community leaders. They volunteer in our schools and churches. They coach youth sports and serve on civic boards. And they donate even more time to local ambulance and search and rescue organizations.

Always Giving Back

Proudly involved in many local health efforts:

- Annual Health Fair
- Annual Bike Safety Rodeo for Elementary Students
- Annual Back Country Wildman Triathlon Carbo Load
- Annual Festival of Trees Santa Wonderland Community Night
- Annual Breast Health Awareness Dessert
- Annual Red Cross Employee Blood Drives
- Annual "Moms and Babes" Party
- Annual Tree of Life Hospice Community Healing Ceremony
- Discounted Health Screenings
- Cancer Support Groups
- Corporate Health Screenings & Education to Local Businesses
- Diabetes Support Program
- Go Red For Women Event
- Hospice Volunteer Coordination
- Jeans Days Fundraisers for Local Not-for-profit Organizations
- Jump Rope For Heart
- Logger Days 5K/10K Run Sponsor
- Medical Scholarship Funds to Local High School Seniors Pursuing Careers in Medicine
- Middle School Anti-Smoking Week Sponsor and Presenter
- Middle School Career Days
- Monthly Health/Wellness Presentations
- Paint It Pink Free Baseline Mammography Program
- Relay for Life Sponsor & Participant
- Runnerfell Children's Race Sponsor
- School Nurse Program

St. John's also supports local Chamber of Commerce and community programs such as WINGS, Libby High School Booster Club, Rotary, Kiwanis, and Habitat for Humanity.

St John's in 1952

St. John's in 2009

St John's in 1983

St. John's planning for the future

Whitefish Credit Union Celebrates 75th Year With New Eureka Building

Eureka's downtown area took on a new look this April when Whitefish Credit Union opened a grand, new two story office building at 110 Dewey Avenue. It has been operating out of a store front office at 202 Dewey Avenue.

The Eureka office opened April 10, 2002, with JoAn Cuffe as loan officer/manager and Marilyn Parrish, who is teller and loan processor. They were later joined by Desiree Bean, and this year Karri Stenslie joined the staff. Additional employees may be added as they settle into the new office. Volunteer credit committee members for the North Lincoln County office are Margaret Brockman, Jeannie Roo, Ethel White, Tom Shay and Craig Eaton. Eaton was elected this year to the main WCU credit committee.

The new building is two stories high with a rustic finish of log corner accents, cedar shakes and rock pillars, and 4,863 sq. ft. It features a spacious lobby and attractive meeting rooms as well as a drive-up window, a vault and safety deposit boxes. General contractor was Mostly Montana Construction, a Eureka firm operated by Bob Helms, and most subcontractors were from the Tobacco Valley.

"We are proud of this new addition to Eureka's business district," Cuffe said. "We have had a goal of establishing our own building since we opened six years ago. It is part of serving our members better, and we have seen our membership in this area double since 2002." There are some 2,500 accounts and 3,600 members in the North Lincoln County.

75th Anniversary

Now the largest credit union in Montana, it will celebrate the 75th Charter Date on Aug. 29, 2009. Five railroaders, each of whom contributed $5 for total assets of $25, originated WCU during the Great Depression in 1934. Last year, in spite of turmoil in national economic circles, WCU grew to $1 billion in assets on the 74th charter anniversary, and growth has continued into the spring of 2009. By April 1 total assets were more than $1.1 Billion.

Eureka Staff from left: Karri Stenslie, Marilyn Parrish, JoAn Cuffe, Desiree Bean.

"Those original five railroad workers must feel good about the financial cooperative they started," comments President/ CEO Charles Abell. With 57,000 members, WCU has offices in Whitefish, Kalispell, Columbia Falls, Polson, Eureka and Thompson Falls.

Top Dividend

The dividend paid to members for share accounts, which are standard savings accounts where you deposit or withdraw funds at any time without penalty or fees, ranked number one in the nation on Dec. 31, 2008. That is number one for any federally insured standard savings account whether in a bank, a credit union or another financial institution. The WCU dividend is consistently the best paid in Montana and among the top 10 in the nation.

Interest on accounts is calculated daily, so dividends are paid on the average daily balance. All members are owners of WCU, and everyone gets the same percentage of return for their deposits as a true cooperative should do.

Key to this very respectable dividend is efficient operation of services and keeping money loaned out to members. In addition, all interest on loan payments stays right here in northwest Montana to help our economy grow, Abell is proud to note, because WCU never sells loans to the secondary market.

Best Place to Save, Best Place to Borrow

"We think we are the best place to save and the best place to borrow," Abell said. "There were 4,328 loans made to WCU members in 2008, and they amounted to $353,900,000." Interest on loans is the primary source of income for WCU, unlike many financial institutions which charge fees for many services.

Other services offered include payroll savings plan, automatic bill paying accounts, and debit cards which can work like a checkless checking account. The dividend rate for both bill pay and debit card accounts, at half the regular WCU regular share account rate is still more than the savings account rates at most other institutions.

Open To Lincoln County Residents

Residents of Flathead, Lake, Lincoln and Sanders counties are eligible to become a member of Whitefish Credit Union, and members are owners.

"We are easy to join. This is the kind of good deal you want to share with others. Folks in Libby and Troy and the Yaak can call us toll free at (877)862-3525," Abell said.

Credit Committee Volunteers: Tom Shay, Craig Eaton, Bob Lawson, Jeannie Roo, Margaret Brockman, Ethel White

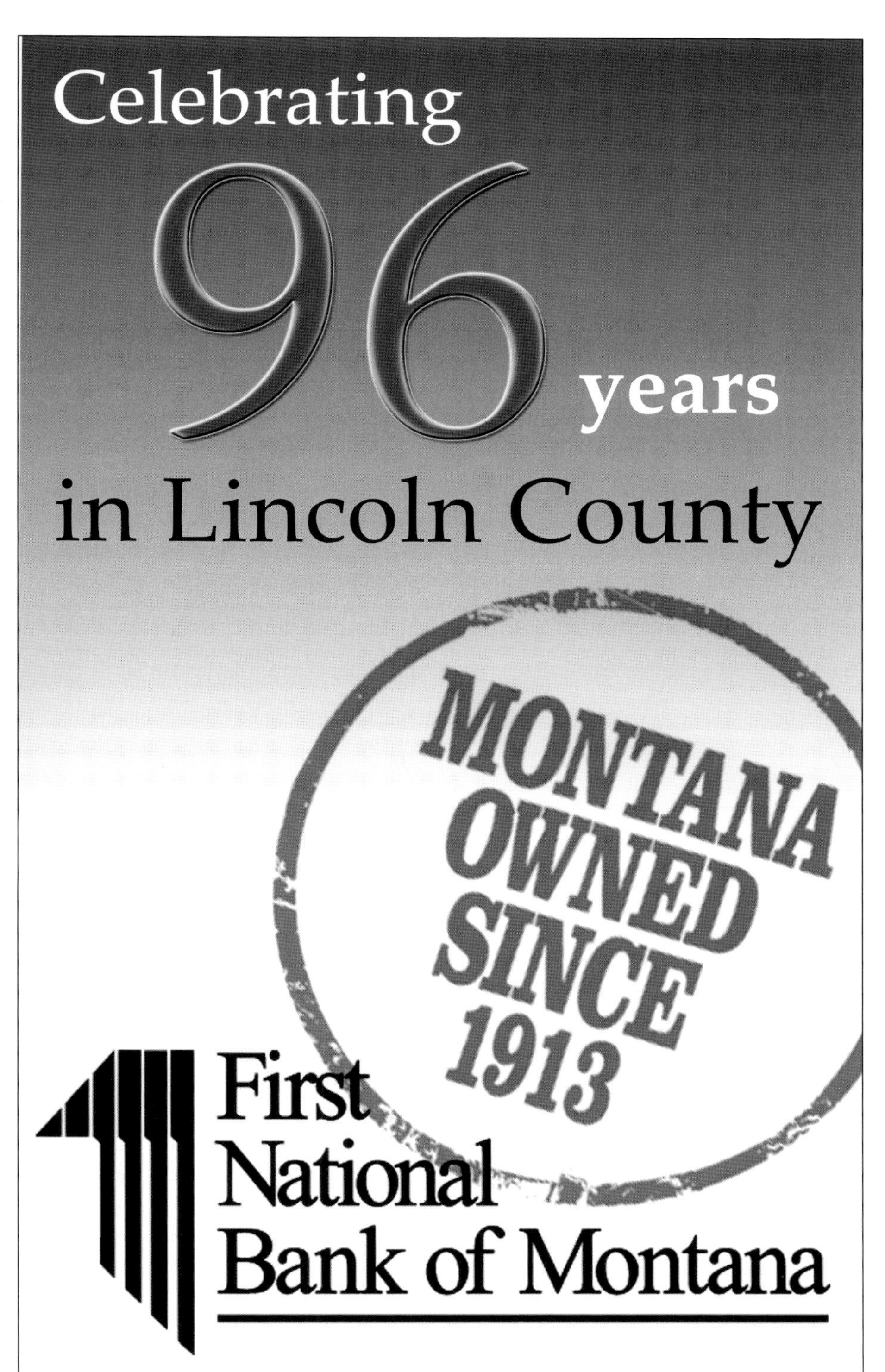

Lincoln County Public Libraries Foundation

Lincoln County Public Libraries Foundation provides fundraising support for the benefit of all three libraries in the county.

Recent projects include:

- New shelving and circulation desk at the Eureka Branch Library
- New shelving and circulation desk at the Troy Branch Library
- New carpet, shelving, and circulation desk at the Libby Library

Support your local library through the Lincoln County Public Libraries Foundation:

- All gifts are invested in the endowment unless otherwise requested.
- The easiest and most common way to give to the foundation is through a gift of cash.
- A contribution can be given as a memorial or to mark a special event.
- Contributions can also be made as a bequest in your will or a planned gift such as life insurance.

Contact the Foundation through the Lincoln County Public Libraries, Libby Library, 220 W. 6th Street, Libby, MT 59923 (406) 293-2778

Thank You ...

The following individuals made the centennial book project a possibility:

Special thanks to Lincoln County Commissioners
Marianne Roose, John Konzen & Tony Berget
for their enthusiasm & support for this project.

Volunteers:

Rich Aarstad
Esther Brandt
Jim Calvi
Joan Clough
Nathan Condron
Mike Cuffe
Sarah Daviau
Darris Flanagan
Jeff Gruber
Tyann Hermes
Roger Larson
June Maxwell
Randy McIntyre
Alana Mesenbrink
Steve Newman
Sami Pierson
Patty Rambo
Tony Rebo
Miranda Rhodes
LeeAnn Sanders
Brent Schrum
Joan Shirley
Scott Slauson
Julie Smith
Lynette Starling
Rhonda Taigaafi
Dusti Thompson
Madeline Utter
Stacy Walenter
Mark White
Judy Williams
Lynn Zimmerman
Mary Jo Zwang
For His Glory Photography
Kootenai Aviation
Kootenai Valley Record
Lincoln County Fair Board

Editing & Layout

Melody Condron
Nathan Condron
Sami Pierson
Alchemy DTP
Lincoln County Public Libraries

It is impossible to list all of the hundreds of other individuals who sent information or photos for this book. If you helped with this book in any way, please know that it was appreciated.

Project sponsors:

First National Bank of Montana

Flathead Electric

Kootenai Drug

Lincoln County

Lincoln County Credit Union

Lincoln County
Public Libraries

Lincoln County
Public Libraries Foundation

Lincoln County Title Company

St. John's Lutheran Hospital

Whitefish Credit Union

Editor's Note:

It was a wonderful experience collecting the information for this book. I learned a lot and spoke with many new people along the way. My greatest regret is that there was not enough time to track down some of the information I wanted to include and still have the book come out in our centennial year. The county is so full of history and current events that 100 pages can hardly do it justice. As such, while I feel that the book is a wonderful testament to Lincoln County on its 100 year anniversary, I would like to make a request of the reader: don't think for a minute that this is all there is!

I would like to personally thank Sami Pierson for her support on this project; my husband, Nathan, who has spent hours working with me to complete the layout and editing; and my mother, Joann Calabrese, for her support in this and all other huge projects I take on. - Melody Condron